D0846530

Colloquial
Hindi

The Colloquial Series

Series adviser: Gary King

The following languages are available in the Colloquial series:

Afrikaans
Albanian
Amharic
Arabic (Levantine)
Arabic of Egypt
Arabic of the Gulf and Saudi Arabia
Basque
Bulgarian
*Cambodian
*Cantonese
*Chinese
Croatian and Serbian
Czech
Danish
Dutch
Estonian
Finnish
French
German
Greek
Gujarati
Hindi
Hungarian
Indonesian
Italian
Japanese
Korean
Latvian
Lithuanian
Malay
Mongolian
Norwegian
Panjabi
Persian
Polish
Portuguese
Portuguese of Brazil
Romanian
*Russian
Slovak
Slovene
Somali
*Spanish
Spanish of Latin America
Swedish
*Thai
Turkish
Urdu
Ukrainian
*Vietnamese
Welsh

Accompanying cassette(s) (*and CDs) are available for all the above titles. They can be ordered through your bookseller, or send payment with order to Taylor & Francis/Routledge Ltd, ITPS, Cheriton House, North Way, Andover, Hants SP10 5BE, UK, or to Routledge Inc, 29 West 35th Street, New York NY 10001, USA.

COLLOQUIAL CD-ROMs
Multimedia Language Courses
Available in: Chinese, French, Portuguese and Spanish

Colloquial Hindi

The Complete Course for Beginners

Tej K. Bhatia
Syracuse University,
New York

London and New York

In memory of
my mother, Shrimati Krishna Wanti Bhatia,
and
my father, Shri Parma Nand Bhatia

First published 1996
by Routledge
11 New Fetter Lane, London EC4P 4EE

Simultaneously published in the USA and Canada
by Routledge
29 West 35th Street, New York, NY 10001

Reprinted 1999, 2001

Routledge is an imprint of the Taylor & Francis Group

© 1996 Tej K. Bhatia

Typeset in Times by Thomson Press (India) Ltd

Illustrations by Rebecca Moy

Printed and bound in Great Britain by Clays Ltd, St Ives PLC

All rights reserved. No part of this book may be reprinted or reproduced or utilized in any form or by any electronic, mechanical, or other means, now known or hereafter invented, including photocopying and recording, or in any information storage or retrieval system, without permission in writing from the publishers.

British Library Cataloguing in Publication Data
A catalogue record for this book is available from the British Library

Library of Congress Cataloguing in Publication Data
Bhatia, Tej K.
Colloquial Hindi: a complete language course / Tej K. Bhatia.
Includes Index.
1. Hindi language – Conversation and phrase books. 2. Hindi language – Grammar. 3. Hindi language – Vocabulary. I. Title
PK1935.B525 1996
491′.4383421 – dc20 95–14790

ISBN 0-415-11087-4 (book)
ISBN 0-415-11088-2 (cassettes)
ISBN 0-415-11089-0 (book and cassettes course)

Contents

Acknowledgements

I have contracted many debts in the process of writing this book. At the outset I am grateful to Simon Bell, the commissioning editor of this series, for his commendable patience and encouragement. My gratitude is also due to Professor William C. Ritchie for his comments and insightful suggestions. I owe special thanks to Dr Mangat R. Bhardwaj, the author of the companion volume on Panjabi. My work has benefited from his work. My heartfelt thanks are also due to Jennifer L. Smith and Vel Chesser who provided editorial assistance for this work.

I am also grateful to my teachers and colleagues Yamuna and Braj Kachru, who have taught me and influenced me since my graduate school. I am also indebted to my friends and colleagues Rajeshwari Pandharipande, Hans Hock, Meena and S.N. Sridhar, Sheela and M.K. Verma for their valuable discussions on matters of Hindi teaching and linguistics. Finally, I also owe my thanks to Dr P.R. Mehandiratta (Director, American Institute of Indian Studies, New Delhi) who supported and encouraged me to embark on my graduate studies at the University of Illinois.

My mother passed away before this book became a reality. This has left a permanent vacuum in my life. During the writing of this book I remembered how at the insistence of her children she learned to sign her name in Hindi instead of using the thumb print for signature purposes. It is still a mystery to me how and when she learned to read *Gita* in Hindi. My family migrated from the North West Frontier Province close to the Pakistan and Afghanistan border, so Hindi was her third language and according to the value system of that time she never had any formal schooling. I had thought there would still be a lot of time between us to share, and that these questions were not urgent. I was wrong. This work is particularly dedicated to her memory.

This summer my children, Ankit and Kanika, declared me not a 'normal father' who plays with them. I promise to improve my record. My wife, Shobha, kept me going with encouragement and support which enabled me to complete this work. Finally, no words can express my deepest appreciation to my brothers in India for their constant support during my entire career.

I am acutely aware that this work is not free from limitations. Therefore I would be grateful for any comments, criticisms or suggestions that perceptive scholars might have on this book. Please send them to me at the following address: Linguistic Studies Program, 312 HBC, Syracuse University, Syracuse, New York 13244-1160, U.S.A.

Introduction

A word to the learner

Welcome to *Colloquial Hindi*. Very often in social get-togethers in the West, I am asked with utmost sincerity whether or not I speak Hindu. Although I have no difficulty in understanding the real intent of the question, I find myself unwittingly in an embarrassing situation. This is particularly true if this inquiry happens to come directly from my host. You see, *Hindu* is the name of the predominant religion in India and Nepal; *Hindi* is the name of the language that is the *lingua franca* of South Asia.

About the language

Hindi is a modern Indo-Aryan language spoken in South Asian countries (India, Pakistan, Nepal) and also in other countries outside Asia (Mauritius, Trinidad, Fiji, Surinam, Guyana, South Africa and other countries). Approximately six hundred million people speak Hindi, as either a first or second language. It is ranked among the five most widely spoken languages of the world. Along with English, it is the official language of India. In addition, it is the state language of Bihar, Haryana, Himachal Pradesh, Madhya Pradesh, Uttar Pradesh and Rajasthan. Also, I should point out that Hindi is the language of Agra (the city of the Taj Mahal).

Hindi, which is a descendant of the Sanskrit language, is not strictly the name of any chief dialect of the area but is an adjective, Persian in origin, meaning Indian. Historically, it was synonymous with Hindui, Hindawi, Rexta, and Rexti. The terms Urdu and Hindustani are also employed to refer to this language. However, these labels denote a mixed speech spoken around the area of Delhi, North India, which gained currency during the twelfth and thirteenth centuries as a contact language between the Arabs, Afghans, Persian and Turks, and native residents.

Hindi is written in the Devanāgarī script which is ranked as the most scientific writing system among the existing writing systems of the world. The Devanagari script is written from left to right and is a descendant of the Brahmi script which was well established in India before 500 BC. The script is phonetic in nature and there is a fairly regular correspondence between the letters and their pronunciation. For more details see the section on Hindi writing system and pronunciation.

The literary history of Hindi goes back to the twelfth century. Some notable literary figures of Hindi are Kabir, Surdas, and Tulsidas. The two notable linguistic features of the language are as follows: (1) Hindi still retains the original Indo-European (1500 BC) distinction between aspirated and unaspirated consonants which results in a four-way contrast as shown by the following examples: ***kāl***, 'time', ***khāl***, 'skin', ***gāl***, 'cheek' and ***ghāl***, 'to put into'; (2) it has the feature of retroflexion in its consonant inventory, cf. ***Tāl***, 'to put off' and ***tāl***, 'pond'. The retroflex consonant is transcribed as the capital T. For more details see the section on Hindi writing system and pronunciation.

Hindi has an approximately three-century old, well-attested and rich grammatical tradition of its own. It is a by-product of the colonial era and was born shortly after the arrival of Europeans in India. For a detailed treatment of this topic in general and the grammatical tradition in particular, see Bhatia (1987).

About this book

This book is designed as a complete first-year language course, keeping in mind the proficiency guidelines of the American Council on the Teaching of Foreign Languages (ACTFL) and the European Community. Every attempt is made to optimize this goal by integrating the linguistic content with the culture of South Asia in general and India in particular. In fact, while teaching the language I have to answer those questions that are often asked about the culture of India.

In my professional life I have often witnessed the fact that the teaching of non-Western languages, including Hindi, is more challenging in the

West than teaching the Western languages. If you have experienced any of the following problems, this book will enable you to achieve the goals described above.

- ✓ You sweat at the mere thought of learning a foreign language.
- ✓ You think Hindi is a very difficult language to learn, so why try?
- ✓ You have some serious business, research interests or not-so-serious interests (such as travel) in India but you have been led to believe that everybody in India speaks English.
- ✓ You have learned Hindi from those tools and settings that make native speakers laugh secretly or openly at your language use.
- ✓ India is culturally and linguistically so distant from the West that one cannot help but shy away from it.

If you subscribe to one or all of the above, you are in for a surprise. First, you might discover in the process of learning the language that learning about Hindi is learning about one's own roots. European migration to India is perhaps the oldest of all migrations from Europe. For this reason, you will still find some striking similarities between Hindi and English. For example, the Hindi word for English 'name' is **nām**. The list goes on and on. The important thing to know is that Hindi belongs to the Indo-European language family and is similar to English in a number of ways. Learning to observe these similarities will make the process of learning this language full of pleasant surprises.

The book is grounded in the *current theories of language acquisition, learnability and language use.* Unlike other books (even some of the latest ones), it never loses sight of the social–psychological aspects of language use. In this book, I have not attempted to act like a protector or saviour of a language by engaging in the linguistically prescriptivist and puritan tendencies. What you will find in this book is the way the Hindi speakers use Hindi and communicate with each other in some meaningful ways. No attempt is made to translate the English word artificially into Hindi if Hindi speakers treat the English word like any other Hindi word. I was outraged when I noticed in a widely circulated course on Hindi in which the waiter asks his customers for their order, the word 'order' translated with the same verb as the English 'obey my order!' For more details see the section entitled ''English Prohibition?'' in Lesson 2.

Beware...

These prescriptivist tendencies defeat the real goal of learning a language in order to communicate with native speakers. Even some of the latest books on Hindi teaching suffer from such problems and unwittingly do a disservice to their learners because of their authors' lack of familiarity with the social–psychological dimensions of language use. I came across such instances in one of the most recent books on Hindi which teaches learners how to introduce themselves to native speakers. The sentences are grammatically correct but the author(s) fail to take into account the invisible dimension of the phenomenon of 'turn taking'. For example, it is acceptable for English speakers to introduce themselves with a string of two clauses following the word 'Hi' (e.g. 'Hi, my name is John and what is yours?). However, the Hindi speaker will pause after the Hindi equivalent of 'Hi' and wait for the listener to respond with a greeting, and only after that will the Hindi speaker perform the task of telling his name and asking about his listener's name. The failure to teach learners about 'turn taking' through naturalistic conversations makes them run the risk of being seen as 'pushy' or 'impatient' by native speakers. This book is particularly aware of such 'non-linguistic' or invisible dimensions of language use. Therefore this book never loses sight of the *cross-cultural communication* while teaching *linguistic communication.*

This book deals with the four main linguistic skills:

	receptive	*productive*
aural–oral	listening comprehension	speaking comprehension
visual	reading comprehension	writing comprehension

These skills are introduced in a manner consistent with the insights of the modern Chomskyan linguistics. The learners are exposed to rules and the discovery procedures, similar to those employed by native speakers, that enable them to generate an infinite amount of sentences in their native language. Not only this, these rules enable native speakers to generate new sentences they have never encountered before. This is the conceptual framework combined with my twenty years of classroom experience which has gone into the makeup of this book. Unlike other phrasebooks which emphasize parroting sentences without gaining insight into the linguistic system, this book emphasizes and serves as a catalytic agent in promoting linguistic creativity and optimization. This goal is achieved in a rather simple and unpretentious way while avoiding system overload.

How this book is organized

This book attempts to accommodate the two types of learners: (1) those who want to learn the language through the Hindi script called the Devanagari script; and (2) those who wish to learn the language in a relatively short period of time without the aid of the Devanagari script (or Hindi script). Such pragmatic considerations are an important feature of this book.

The book begins with Hindi script and pronunciation. The main body deals with ten conversational units which consist of the following parts: (1) dialogues with English translation; (2) vocabulary; (3) notes detailing pronunciation, grammar and usage involving the unit; and (4) exercises. The dialogues with "Tell me why?" and humour columns together with notes explicitly deal with those aspects of Indian culture about which this author has frequently been asked. The vocabulary or the new words used in the dialogues are given in the English and Devanagari script. You may wish to consult the vocabulary sections while doing exercises.

The grammar summary gives an overview of the Hindi grammatical tradition with full paradigms. This section complements the section 'Notes and grammar' given in each lesson.

The vocabulary section gives all the Hindi words used in the dialogues. The words are listed alphabetically both in Hindi and English. The basic vocabulary section classifies Hindi words into different semantic groups.

How to use this book

This book focuses on two types of tracks: (1) for those learners who want to adopt the English script path; and (2) for those who want to learn the Hindi script. Although the learning of the Hindi script is highly recommended, if you decide to choose the first track, you can bypass the lessons on the writing system. For every learner, whether on the first or the second track, the lesson on the pronunciation is a must and familiarity with the salient phonetic features of Hindi together with the notes on transcription is imperative. Examples dealing with pronunciation are also recorded on the cassettes. The exercises with the cassette icon are recorded on the cassettes, therefore they require you to listen to the recording. Due to space considerations transcripts of the listening exercises are not included in the book. The author will be delighted to provide them if you write directly to him at the address given in the Acknowledgements.

If you want to be on the Hindi script track, you will find all the dialogues and exercises in the script units starting from Unit 6. Keys are also given in the Hindi script. There is an added incentive to consult the script units. Their exercise section supplements some of the very common expressions any visitor will need in India. The expressions deal with situations such as customs and immigration, baggage handling, making reservations, sending mail, annoying and cautionary incidents, shopping, food, entertainment and renting things. The section on Hindi handwriting practice is devoted to practising handwriting in the Devanagari script.

Naturally, the vocabulary will involve memorization. The notes sections give you details of pronunciation, grammar and usage. The understanding of these notes is required and their memorization will be a catalyst in your linguistic creativity.

The reference grammar goes hand in hand with grammatical notes given at the end of each dialogue. Answers to the exercises can be found in the key to exercises, both in the Hindi and English scripts.

Icons used in this book

Some icons are used throughout this book for a number of reasons, the most important of which is to draw attention to those sections that require careful attention.

Magic Key

This icon is important for creativity and is worthy of memorization.

Sherlock Holmes

This icon enables the reader to discover those major generalizations and regularities in the language that are the primary source for creativity among the native speakers.

Remember

If you have forgotten what was covered earlier, this icon is aimed at triggering a trip through memory lane to recall the material dealt with earlier.

Caution

The material marked by this icon deserves special attention. It warns you of the activities that are hazardous to your linguistic communication.

The other icons used in the book are thematic in nature and, therefore, do not require any explanation.

Where to go from here

Obviously, I do not pretend to offer you everything that needs to be known about Hindi. Language learning can be a lifelong venture, if you set your goals very high. Obviously, your next step is to look for books dealing with the intermediate and advanced Hindi courses that are widely available. The reason I am stating this is to help remove concept, which is quite widespread in the West, about the lack of the availability of language courses at the intermediate and advanced levels in Asian and African languages. There is no shortage of material at the levels in question. The only difficulty you might face is that this material will invariably be in the Hindi script. If that poses a problem for you, there are still many ways to continue to sharpen your linguistic skills, the most important of which is Hindi films. India is the world's largest producer of films. Hindi film videos are widely accessible in the East and the West. To develop a taste for Hindi films is most important to take yourself to the advanced stages of Hindi language learning.

Best wishes.

Reference

Bhatia, Tej K. (1987) *A History of the Hindi Grammatical Tradition,* Leiden: E.J. Brill.

Hindi writing system and pronunciation

Introduction

This chapter briefly outlines the salient properties of the Devanagari script and the Hindi pronunciation. Hindi is written in a script called the Devanagari script. Even if you are not learning the script, this chapter is indispensable because you need to know the pronunciation value of the Roman/English letters used in the conversational units. Furthermore, one or two unfamiliar symbols are drawn from the International Phonetic Alphabet (IPA). The transcription scheme followed here is widely used in the teaching of Hindi and in the works of Hindi language and linguistics. As was mentioned, the best way to learn Hindi is to learn the script too. However, if it is not possible because of considerations of time, you still will need to refer to the charts on pages 9–11 until you have mastered the letters and their pronunciation value.

Listen to and repeat the pronunciation of Hindi vowels and consonants together with their minimal pairs, recorded on the cassettes accompanying this book.

The Devanāgarī script

A number of languages are written in the Devanagari script. Besides Hindi, Nepali, Marathi and Sanskrit are also written in this script. Other languages such as Punjabi, Bengali, Gujarati use a slight variation of this script. This means that roughly *half of humanity* uses either this script or its close variant which follows the same underlying system of organization.

All scripts of the Indic origin, including the Devanagari script, are the descendants of the Brahmi script which was well established some time before 500 BC in India. These scripts are considered the most scientific among the existing writing systems of the world for a number of reasons. (1) The arrangement and the classification of the letters or symbols follow a system based on physiological or phonetic principles, namely the point and the manner of the articulation. Other writing systems, including our Roman system, employ arbitrary and random criteria to arrange and categorize the letters. (2) Each letter represents only one sound. For example, in other systems the [k] sound can be rendered by the letters *k*, *q*, *c* and *ch*. This situation will not occur in the Devanagari script. Because of its scientific and phonetic nature, this script became the basis of the modern speech sciences and the International Phonetic Alphabet (IPA). The IPA is primarily the romanized version of the Devanagari script. This means there is fairly regular correspondence between the script and the pronunciation. In other words, the words are pronounced the way they are written, and that is good news for our learners.

The Devanagari script is written from left to right and from the top of the page down, like the roman script. It does not distinguish between upper-case and lower-case letters.

It is syllabic in nature, i.e. every consonant letter/symbol represents the consonant plus the inherent vowel **a**. The pronunciation of the inherent vowel is a major exception to the rule of the correspondence between script and pronunciation. These exceptions will be detailed in Script Unit 1. The other minor exceptions are indicated by the use of angular brackets < > with the words listed in the vocabulary of each Lesson.

Below you will find the Hindi vowel and consonant charts. The Devanagari script lists vowels and consonants separately because they involve distinct articulations.

Hindi vowels

Independent forms

अ	आ	इ	ई	उ	ऊ	ए	ऐ	ओ	औ	ऋ
a	ā	i	ī	u	ū	e	ɛ	o	au	ri

Dependent form: following a consonant

ø	ा	ि	ी	ु	ू	े	ै	ो	ौ	ृ
a	ā	i	ī	u	ū	e	ɛ	o	au	ri

Notes on Hindi vowels

Hindi vowels do not distinguish between the capital and non-capital form. However, they maintain independent and dependent types of contrast. The independent forms are often called 'the main' or 'full' vowels, where as the corresponding dependent forms are called 'matra' vowels and are connected to preceding consonants.

Nasalization

In the production of a nasal vowel, the vowel is pronounced through the mouth and the nose at the same time. Either the symbol ँ or, ं with the vowel is used to indicate nasalization in Hindi. Usually long vowels are nasalized in Hindi. In our transcription, the symbol tilde ~ is used to indicate vowel nasalization, as in

आँ **ā̃** ऊँ **ū̃** ऐं **ɛ̃**

The symbol ं is used to indicate vowel nasalization when any stroke of the vowel crosses the top horizontal line, as in ऐं.

Diphthongs

ऐ **ɛ** and औ **au** are pronounced as *a* + *i* and *a* + *u* in the Eastern variety of Hindi, but are pronounced as single vowels in the Standard Hindi-speaking area. They receive diphthongal pronunciation only if they are followed by *y* and *w/v*, respectively.

ऋ does not occur in Hindi. It is used in the writing of a handful of words which are borrowed by Hindi from Sanskrit.

Hindi consonants

	Voice-less Unaspi-rated	Voice-less Aspi-rated	Voiced Unaspi-rated	Voiced Aspi-rated	Nasal
k-group	क **ka**	ख **k^ha**	ग **ga**	घ **g^ha**	ङ **ŋɑ**
c-group	च **ca**	छ **c^ha**	ज **ja**	झ **j^ha**	ञ **ña**
T-group	ट **Ta**	ठ **T^ha**	ड **Da**	ढ **D^ha**	ण **Na**
t-group	त **ta**	थ **t^ha**	द **da**	ध **d^ha**	न **na**
p-group	प **pa**	फ **p^ha**	ब **ba**	भ **b^ha**	म **ma**
Others	य **ya**	र **ra**	ल **la**	व **wa/va**	श **sha**
	ष **SHa**	स **sa**	ह **ha**		
	ड़ **Ra**	ढ़ **R^ha**			

Sanskrit letters used infrequently: क्ष ksha त्र tra ज्ञ gya

Notes on the Hindi consonants

The first five groups of consonants are called stops because they are pronounced by stopping the outgoing air from the mouth. The fifth column of these five groups of consonants is called nasal because the air is released through the nose during the stopping phase in the mouth. The nasal consonants of the first two groups, i.e. ङ **ŋɑ** and ञ **ña** are never used in their syllabic form in Hindi, so you will not find them in this book. They are included due to the consideration of the traditional arrangement of the Devanagari consonant chart.

Place of articulation

All consonants arranged within each of the five groups share the same *place of articulation,* as described below:

k-group

These consonants are also called 'velar' because the back of the tongue touches the rear of the soft palate, called the velum. They are similar to the English *k* and *g*.

क	ख	ग	घ	ङ
ka	k^ha	ga	g^ha	ŋɑ

c-group

These sounds are the closest equivalent of the English sound *ch* in 'church'. The body of the tongue touches the hard palate in the articulation of these sounds.

च	छ	ज	झ	ञ
ca	c^ha	ja	j^ha	ña

T-group (the 'capital T group')

ट	ठ	ड	ढ	ण
Ta	T^ha	Da	D^ha	Na

These consonants represent the colourful features of the languages of the Indian subcontinent. They are also called 'retroflex' consonants. There is no equivalent of these sounds in English. In the articulation of these sounds, the tip of the tongue is curled back and the *underside* of the tongue touches the hard palate. The following diagram can be of further assistance in the production of these sounds:

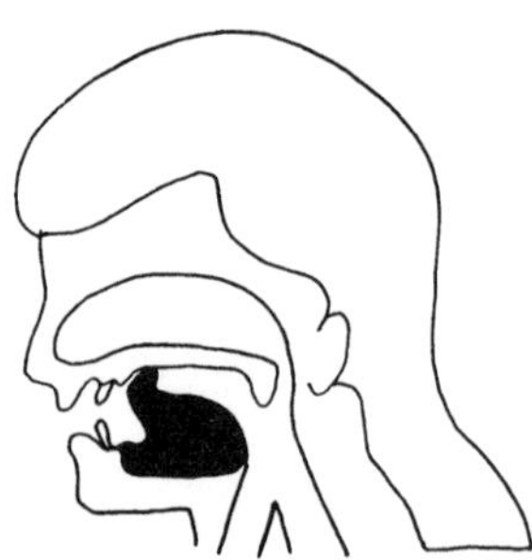

Note also that R and R^h are also pronounced with the same point of articulation.

t-group

The tip of the tongue touches the back of the teeth, and not the gum ridge behind the teeth as is the case in the pronunciation of the English **t** or **d**.

त	थ	द	ध	न
ta	t^ha	da	d^ha	na

Study the following diagrams carefully in order to distinguish the Hindi *t*-group of sounds from the English *t*-group of sounds.

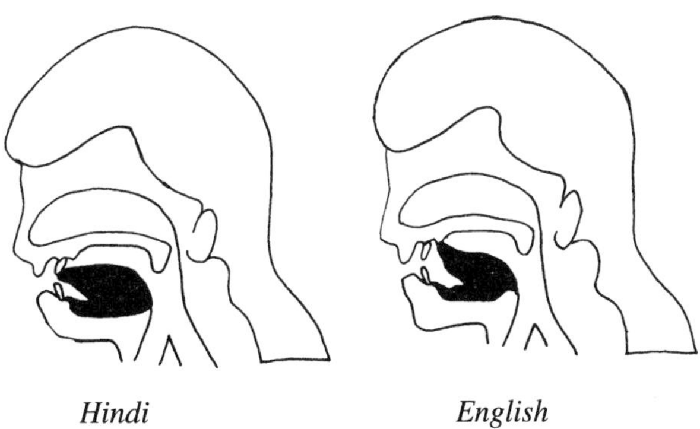

Hindi *English*

p-group

These sounds are similar to English *p* or *b* sounds. They are pronounced by means of the closure or near closure of the lips.

प	फ	ब	भ	म
pa	p^ha	ba	b^ha	ma

Manner of articulation

All columns in the five groups involve the same *manner of articulation.*

Voiceless unaspirated

क	च	ट	त	प
ka	ca	Ta	ta	pa

These sounds are like English *k* (as in *skin* but not as in *kin*), and *p* (as in *spin* but not as in *pin*). In *kin* and *pin*, the English sounds *k* and *p* are slightly aspirated, i.e. they are followed by a slight 'puff of air'. In order to pronounce the corresponding Hindi *k* and *p*, you need to reduce the stream of breath.

Voiceless aspirated

ख	छ	ठ	थ	फ
k^ha	c^ha	T^ha	t^ha	p^ha

The superscripted ^{h} means that these sounds are pronounced with a strong 'puff of air'. All you have to do is to slightly increase the air stream in the pronunciation of the English *k* and *p* sounds.

Voiced unaspirated

ग	ज	ड	द	ब
ga	ja	Da	da	ba

In the production of these sounds the vocal cords vibrate and produce a buzzing sound, like that of a bee. You should not encounter any difficulty in the production of these sounds as they are like English *g* and *b*.

Voiced aspirated (breathy voiced)

If you pronounce the voiced unaspirated consonants with a 'puff of air', you will produce voiced aspirated sounds. The superscripted ^{h} indicates the presence of the 'puff of air'. If you have difficulties with sounds, try pronouncing the voiced unaspirated consonants with an *h* (as in ho*g*-*h*og). If you pronounce the words fast enough, you will obtain the voiced aspirate g^h at the end of the first boundary between the two words.

घ	झ	ढ	ध	भ
g^ha	j^ha	D^ha	d^ha	b^ha

Nasal

ङ	ञ	ण	न	म
ŋa	ña	Na	na	ma

These sounds are similar to English nasal consonants such as English *n* and *m*. The velar and palatal nasals are similar to the nasal consonants in the English words *king* and *bunch*, respectively.

Other consonants (miscellaneous)

The following consonants listed under the group 'others' are very similar to the English sounds, therefore they do not call for detailed phonetic description. The English transcription is sufficient to give you information about their pronunciation.

य	र	ल	व	श	स	ह
ya	ra	la	wa/va	sha	sa	ha

As mentioned earlier, the following two consonants are pronounced with the curled tongue. However, the underside of the tongue is flapped quickly forward, touching the hard palate slightly, instead of making the stop articulation with the hard palate; ढ़ R^ha is the aspirated counterpart of ड़ Ra.

ड़	ढ़
Ra	R^ha

Sanskrit letters

The following four consonants are from Sanskrit. They do not exist in Hindi except in the handful of words borrowed from Sanskrit.

ष SHa क्ष ksha त्र tra ज्ञ gya

ष SHa is pronounced like श sha, and the other three letters represent consonant clusters in Hindi.

Borrowed Perso-Arabic and English sounds

By placing a dot under the following five consonant symbols, the five Perso-Arabic sounds are represented:

फ़	ज़	ख़	क़	ग़
fa	za	xa	qa	Ga

Out of the above five, the first two are used quite frequently in Hindi. The reason for this is that *fa* and *za* are also found in English. The other three consonants are usually pronounced as *k*^{h}*a*, *ka* and *ga*, respectively. Even the first two sounds *fa* and *za* can be pronounced as *p*^{h}*a* and *ja*, respectively.

It should be noted that English alveolar sounds *t* and *d* are perceived and written as *T* and *D*, respectively. So the *t* and *d* in the proper name *Todd* will be written with the letters ट and ड, respectively.

Pronunciation practice

Minimal pair practice 

Vowels

Oral vowels

vowel		*pronunciation cue (English near-equivalent)*	*Hindi words*	
अ	a	*a*bout	**kal**	yesterday/ tomorrow
आ	ā	f*a*ther	**kāl**	time, tense
इ	i	s*i*t	**din**	day
ई	ī	s*ea*t	**dīn**	poor
उ	u	b*oo*k	**kul**	total, family
ऊ	ū	b*oo*t, l*oo*t	**kūl**	shore
ए	e	l*a*te, d*a*te (without a glide)	**he**	hey
ऐ	ɛ	b*e*t	**hɛ**	is
ओ	o	b*oa*t (without a glide)	**or**	side, towards
औ	au	b*ou*ght	**aur**	and

Nasalized vowels

nasalized vowels (long)		*Hindi words*	
आं	**ā̃**	**mā̃**	mother
ईं	**ī̃**	**kahī̃**	somewhere
ऊं	**ū̃**	**hū̃**	am
एं	**ẽ**	**mẽ**	in
ऐं	**ɛ̃**	**mɛ̃**	I

ओं	**õ**	**gõd**	gum
औं	**ãũ**	**cãũk**	be alarmed, be startled

Minimal pair practice: words with oral and nasalized vowels

oral vowels				*nasalized vowels*			
आ	**ā**	**kahā**	said (m. sg.)	आँ	**ā̃**	**kahā̃**	where
ई	**ī**	**kahī**	said (f. sg.)	ईं	**ī̃**	**kahī̃**	somewhere
ऊ	**ū**	**pūc**[h]	ask	ऊँ	**ū̃**	**pū̃c**[h]	a tail
ए	**e**	**me**	the month of May	एं	**ẽ**	**mẽ**	in
ऐ	**ɛ**	**hɛ**	is	ऐं	**ɛ̃**	**hɛ̃**	are
ओ	**o**	**god**	the lap	ओं	**õ**	**gõd**	gum
औ	**au**	**cauk**	a crossing	औं	**ãũ**	**cãũk**	be alarmed, be startled

Consonants 

Listen to the recording and repeat the words.

Remember, the contrasts shown below are very important in Hindi. The failure to maintain such contrasts will result in a breakdown of communication. If you want to request food, **k**[h]**ānā**, the failure to produce aspiration will result in **kānā**. That is, you will end up asking for a one-eyed person. Similarly, if you do not distinguish between the **T**-group of consonants and the **t**-group of consonants, rather than asking for **roTī**, 'bread', you will end up reporting that the girl is crying (i.e. **rotī**.)

Minimal pair practice: words with unvoiced unaspirated stops and unvoiced aspirated stops

unvoiced unaspirated				*unvoiced aspirated*			
क	**ka**	**kāl**	time, tense	ख	**k**[h]**a**	**k**[h]**āl**	skin
च	**ca**	**cal**	walk	छ	**c**[h]**a**	**c**[h]**al**	cheat
ट	**Ta**	**Tāl**	postpone	ठ	**T**[h]**a**	**T**[h]**āl**	sit idle
त	**ta**	**tān**	tune	थ	**t**[h]**a**	**t**[h]**ān**	piece of cloth
प	**pa**	**pal**	moment	फ	**p**[h]**a**	**p**[h]**al**	fruit

Minimal pair practice: words with voiced unaspirated stops and voiced aspirated stops

voiced unaspirated				*voiced aspirated*			
ग	**ga**	**gā**	sing	घ	**g^{h}a**	**g^{h}ā**	the fourth letter of the k-series
ज	**ja**	**jal**	water	झ	**j^{h}a**	**j^{h}al**	fan
ड	**Da**	**Dāl**	a branch	ढ	**D^{h}a**	**D^{h}āl**	a shield
द	**da**	**dān**	charity	ध	**d^{h}a**	**d^{h}ān**	paddy
ब	**ba**	**bāl**	hair	भ	**b^{h}a**	**b^{h}āl**	forehead

Minimal pair practice: words with unvoiced aspirated stops and voiced aspirated stops

unvoiced aspirated				*voiced aspirated*			
ख	**k^{h}a**	**k^{h}ānā**	food	घ	**g^{h}a**	**g^{h}ānā**	Ghana, (the name of a country)
छ	**c^{h}a**	**c^{h}al**	cheat	झ	**j^{h}a**	**j^{h}al**	fan
ठ	**T^{h}a**	**T^{h}ak**	tapping sound	ढ	**D^{h}a**	**D^{h}ak**	cover
थ	**t^{h}a**	**t^{h}ān**	piece of cloth	ध	**d^{h}a**	**d^{h}ān**	paddy
फ	**p^{h}a**	**p^{h}ūl**	flower	भ	**b^{h}a**	**b^{h}ūl**	mistake

Minimal pair practice: words with the T-group (retroflex) stops and the t-group (dental) stops

T-group				*t-group*			
ट	**Ta**	**Tāl**	postpone	त	**ta**	**tāl**	pond
ठ	**T^{h}a**	**T^{h}ak**	tapping sound	थ	**t^{h}a**	**t^{h}ak**	be tired
ड	**Da**	**Dāl**	branch	द	**da**	**dāl**	lentil
ढ	**D^{h}a**	**D^{h}ak**	cover	ध	**d^{h}a**	**d^{h}ak**	palpitation, excitement

Listen to the following:

Nasal consonants

nasal consonant		*Hindi word*	
ङ	**ŋa**	**aŋg**	body, limb
ञ	**ña**	**añjū**	female name
ण	**Na**	**bāN**	arrow
ण	**na**	**nān**	bread
म	**ma**	**mān**	respect

Other consonants

Listen to the following words:

consonant		*Hindi word*	
य	**ya**	**yār**	friend
र	**ra**	**rājā**	king
ल	**la**	**lāl**	red
व	**wa/va**	**vār**	an attack
श	**sha**	**shāl**	shawl
स	**sa**	**sāl**	year
ह	**ha**	**hāl**	condition, state

Minimal pair practice: words with r, R and R^h

consonant		*Hindi word*	
र	**ra**	**par**	on, at
ड़	**Ra**	**paR**	lie, fall
ढ़	**R^{h}a**	**paR^h**	read, study

Borrowed consonants

फ़	ज़	ख़	क़	ग़
fa	**za**	**xa**	**qa**	**Ga**

As pointed out earlier these consonants were not originally present in

Hindi. Many Hindi speakers still substitute the closest corresponding Hindi consonant for them, as shown below:

फ़	**fa**	becomes	फ	**p^{h}a**
ज़	**za**	becomes	ज	**ja**
ख़	**xa**	becomes	ख	**k^{h}a**
क़	**qa**	becomes	क	**ka**
ग़	**Ga**	becomes	ग	**ga**

In other words, the dots are added to the native symbols to represent the borrowed sounds.

Now listen to the two possible pronunciations of the following words:

consonant		*word*		*consonant*		*word*
फ़	**fa**	**fīs**	tuition, fee	फ	**p^{h}a**	**p^{h}īs**
ज़	**za**	**zarā**	just, a little	ज	**ja**	**jarā**
ख़	**xa**	**xarīd**	buy	ख	**k^{h}a**	**k^{h}arīd**
क़	**qa**	**qalam**	pen	क	**ka**	**kalam**
ग़	**Ga**	**Garīb**	poor	ग	**ga**	**garīb**

Punctuation marks

With the exception of the full stop, which is represented by the sign ।, Hindi uses the same punctuation signs as English. For abbreviation purposes, a small circle ॰ is used after the first syllable. For example, प॰ stands for Pandit. Sometimes the sign ॅ is used over the vowel **ā** to represent the English sound **o**, as in John जॉन

Syllables, stress and **intonation:** see script unit 5.

Dictionary order

The dictionary order of the Devanagari script is given below, working vertically down the columns. The nasalized vowels precede the oral vowels. Conjunct forms of a consonant (non-syllabic) follow all the syllabic forms. Thus, **ā̃** precedes **ā**; whereas the non-syllabic form **k** follows **kau**.

अ	**a**	क/क़	**ka/qa**	ट	**Ta**	प	**pa**	ष	**SHa**
आ	**ā**	ख/ख़	**k^{h}a/xa**	ठ	**T^{h}a**	फ	**p^{h}a**	स	**sa**

इ	**i**	ग/ग़	**ga/Ga**	ड/ड़	**Da/Ra**	ब	**ba**	ह	**ha**
ई	**ī**	घ	**g^{h}a**	ढ/ढ़	**D^{h}a/R^{h}a**	भ	**b^{h}a**		
उ	**u**	ङ	**ŋa**	ण	**Na**	म	**ma**		
ऊ	**ū**	च	**ca**	त	**ta**	य	**ya**		
ऋ	**ri**	छ	**c^{h}a**	थ	**t^{h}a**	र	**ra**		
ए	**e**	ज/ज़	**ja/za**	द	**da**	ल	**la**		
ऐ	**ɛ**	झ	**j^{h}a**	ध	**d^{h}a**	व	**wa/va**		
ओ	**o**	ञ	**ña**	न	**na**	श	**sha**		
औ	**au**								

If you do not have the recording, either skip this section or seek the assistance of a native speaker.

अभ्यास Exercises

1

Listen to each group of three words and circle the word that is different.

	A	B	C
Example: you hear	kar	k^{h}ar	kar
Answer:		B	

(1)	A	B	C
(2)	A	B	C
(3)	A	B	C
(4)	A	B	C
(5)	A	B	C
(6)	A	B	C
(7)	A	B	C
(8)	A	B	C
(9)	A	B	C
(10)	A	B	C

2

Listen to each group of four words and circle the aspirated words.

	A	B	C	D
Example: you hear	kar	k^{h}ar	kar	g^{h}ar
Answer:		B, D		

(1)	A	B	C	D
(2)	A	B	C	D
(3)	A	B	C	D
(4)	A	B	C	D
(5)	A	B	C	D
(6)	A	B	C	D
(7)	A	B	C	D
(8)	A	B	C	D
(9)	A	B	C	D
(10)	A	B	C	D

3

Listen to a pair of words dealing with the contrast between the T-group (the retroflex) of consonants and the t-group of consonants.

A	B
Tik	**tik**

After the pair is pronounced, you will hear either 'A' or 'B'. Underline the word that you hear the third time.

Example: you hear **Tik**, then underline **<u>Tik</u>** **tik**

(1) tāk Tāk
(2) t^hak T^hak
(3) dāg Dāg
(4) d^hak D^hak
(5) par paR
(6) sar saR
(7) karī kaR^{h}ī
(8) t^hīk T^hīk

4

Listen to a pair of words which contrast in terms of vowel.

A	B
din	**dīn**

After the pair is pronounced, you will hear either 'A' or 'B'. Underline the word that you hear the third time.

Example: you hear **dīn**, then underline **din** **dīn**

1 kāl kal
2 din dīn
3 mil mīl
4 cuk cūk
5 mel mɛl
6 ser sɛr
7 bin bīn
8 bāl bal

Observation exercise

Variation in characters

अ	अ
छ	छ
झ	झ
ण	ण
ध	ध
भ	भ

Similar-looking characters

घ g^{h}a	ध d^{h}a			
ख k^{h}a	र ra	व wa/va		
ब ba	व wa/va			
भ b^{h}a	म ma			
द da	ड Da	ढ D^{h}a	ड़ Ra	ढ़ R^{h}a
थ t^{h}a	य ya			

Numerals

१	२	३	४	५	६	७	८	९	०
1	2	3	4	5	6	7	8	9	0

1 नमस्ते/नमस्कार। Greetings and social etiquette

By the end of this lesson you should be able to:

- use simple greetings
- learn expressions of social etiquette
- use expressions for leave-taking
- ask simple questions
- make simple requests
- use personal pronouns (e.g. 'I', 'we', 'you', etc.)
- use some nouns and adjectives

Dialogue

Hindu–Sikh greetings and other social etiquette

Hindi greetings vary according to the religion of the speaker, but not according to the time of the day. In some cases, the speaker may choose to greet according to the religion of his/her listener. Such a choice is socially more appealing to the listener and you can easily win the hearts of your listeners by being sensitive to their way of greetings.

Mohan goes to see Sarita in her office. They know each other but are not close friends.

MOHAN: namaste jī.
SARITA: namaste. kyā hāl <hɛ>?
MOHAN: T^{h}īk hɛ, aur āp?
SARITA: mɛ̃ b^{h}ī T^{h}īk hũ. hukam kījie.
MOHAN: hukam nahī̃, vintī hɛ.
(The conversation continues for some time.)
MOHAN: acc^{h}ā, namaste.
SARITA: namaste.

MOHAN: *Greetings.*
SARITA: *Greetings. How are you* (lit. 'What is [your] condition?')
MOHAN: *Fine. And you?*
SARITA: *I am fine too. What can I do for you* (lit. 'please order')
MOHAN: *[It is] not an order, [but] a request.*
____
____
MOHAN: *Okay. Goodbye.*
SARITA: *Goodbye.*

Vocabulary

(Note: It is a standard convention to transliterate Hindi words in lower case. The same convention is used here. Therefore the first letter of the first word is not capitalized. The only exceptions are upper case T, D, N and R which represent the retroflex sounds.)

namaste	नमस्ते	Hindu greetings and replies to the greetings; may be used by other religions too
jī	जी	honorific word (optional with greetings)
kyā	क्या	what
hāl (m.)	हाल	condition
hɛ̃	है	is
Tʰīk	ठीक	fine; okay
aur	और	and
āp	आप	you (honorific)
mɛ̃	मैं	I
bʰī	भी	also
hū̃	हूँ	am
hukam (m.)	हुकम	order
kījie	कीजिए	please do
nahī̃	नहीं	not
vintī (f.)	विनती	request

Pronunciation

In the Eastern region of the Hindi–speaking area (e.g. in the city of Banaras), the vowel **ɛ** in the words **mɛ̃** and **hɛ**, is pronounced as a diphthong, a combination of two vowels, i.e. [ai = a+i]. However, in the Western Hindi–speaking area (e.g. in Delhi), it is pronounced as a vowel [**ɛ**], as in English words such as *cat*. Since the vowel pronunciation is considered to be standard, this pronunciation is given on the cassettes. The word given in an angular bracket < > shows that its pronunciation differs from what the script suggests. This is done only when the word is introduced for the first time.

The verb form **[kījie]** can also be pronounced **[kījiye]**. The semivowel [**y**] can intervene between the last two vowels. This word can be written with the semivowel too (कीजिये).

Notes

The Hindu–Sikh greetings and their regional variants

namaste (lit. 'I bow in your respect') is the most common greeting by

Hindus and even by non-Hindus. It is expressed with the hands folded in front of the chest. It may be optionally followed by **jī** to show respect and politeness. A more formal alternative to **namaste** is **namaskār**. In the rural areas many other variants such as **rām-rām** and **jɛ rām jī kī** are found. Sikhs prefer **sat srī akāl** to **namaste**. The gesture of folding hands, however, remains the same. The Hindi greetings do not vary at different times of the day.

namaste (or **sat srī akāl** in the case of Sikhs) and its variants are used both for 'hello' and 'goodbye'.

Word-for-word translation

Where a Hindi expression differs literally from its English equivalent, we will show this difference in notes by giving a word-for-word translation. Observe the word-for-word translation of the Hindi equivalent of the English 'How are you?':

kyā	**hāl**	**hɛ?**
what	condition	is

and its reply

Thīk	**hɛ**
fine	is

Honorific pronoun

The honorific pronoun **āp** 'you', is grammatically plural, even if it refers to one person. Grammatically, it is the same as the English *you*. For example, in Standard English one will never say, *you is*.

The politeness germ

Politeness can be quite infectious. If the speaker is being very polite in his/her speech, the listener is obligated either to match or outperform the speaker. The expression

hukam	**kījie**
order	please do

Please [give me] an order = What can I do for you?

is a very formal and cultured way of asking 'What can I do for you?'. The listener appropriately uses an equally polite expression:

hukam	**nahī̃**	**vintī**	**hɛ**
order	not	request	is

It is not an order [but] a request.

Word order

Note the difference between the word order of Hindi and that of English. In Hindi, the verb (e.g., 'is', am', 'are', etc.) usually appears at the end of the sentence. The object (e.g., 'order') appears before the verb.

Dialogue

Muslim greetings and social etiquette

Muslims tend to use more Persian and Arabic words and phrases. They may refer to their language as 'Urdu' or 'Hindustani'. However, Hindi, Urdu and Hindustani are mutually intelligible (for details see Introduction).

Tahsin Siddiqui and Razia Arif run into each other in a car-park (parking lot)

TAHSIN: salām, raziā jī.
RAZIA: salām. sab xɛriyat hɛ?
TAHSIN: meharbānī hɛ, aur āp ke mizāj kɛse hɛ̃?
RAZIA: allāh kā shukra hɛ.
(The conversation continues for some time.)
TAHSIN: acc^{h}ā, xudā hāfiz.
RAZIA: xudā hāfiz.

TAHSIN: *Greetings, Razia.*
RAZIA: *Greetings. How are you* (lit. 'Is everything [pertaining to your] welfare [fine]?'
TAHSIN: *Fine.* (lit. '[It] is [your] kindness = Thank you') *And how are you*? (lit. 'how are your habits/nature?')
RAZIA: *I am fine.* (lit. 'it is the kindness/thanks of God')
TAHSIN: *Okay. Goodbye.*
RAZIA: *Goodbye.*

Vocabulary

salām	सलाम	Muslim greetings and replies to greetings
sab	सब	all
xɛriyat (f.)	ख़ैरियत	safety, welfare
meharbānī (f.)	मेहरबानी	kindness
āp ke	आप के	your
mizāj (m.)	मिज़ाज	temperament, nature
kɛse	कैसे	how
hɛ̃	हैं	are
allāh kā shukra	अल्लाह का शुक्र	fine
xudā hāfiz	खुदा हाफ़िज	goodbye

Pronunciation

xɛriyat and **xudā** are often pronounced **[kʰɛriyat]** and **[kʰudā]** respectively by non-Muslims. In other words, **x** may be pronounced **[kʰ]**.

mizāj and **hāfiz** are often pronounced **[mijāj]** and **[hāfij]** respectively by non-Muslims. In other words, **z** may be pronounced **[j]**.

Notes

The Muslim greeting and leave-taking

salām (an abbreviated form for **salām alɛkum**) is used for 'hello' by Muslims, instead of **namaste**. It is expressed by raising the right hand to the forehead. The word for 'goodbye' is **xudā hāfiz.**

Other ways of saying 'How are you?'

Another way of saying 'How are you?' is 'Is everything fine?' or 'Is all well [with you]?' The expression for this is

sab	**xɛriyat**	**hɛ**
all	welfare	is

'How are you?' (lit. 'Is everything fine [with you]?')

which is followed by an answer:

meharbānī	**hɛ**
kindness	is

[It is your] kindness i.e. because of your kindness, everything is fine with me.

Yet another interchangeable way of asking 'How are you?' is something like 'How are your habits?', as in the following sentence:

āp	**ke**	**mizāj**	**kɛse**	**hɛ̃**
you	of	habits	how	are

This question is followed by the answer 'With God's grace, everything is fine'. The Hindi expression for this is:

allāh	**kā**	**shukra**	**hɛ**
God	of	thank	is

The above exchange is considered super-polite. Such an exchange is usually used more often by Muslims. Nevertheless, Hindus and others may also use it, depending upon their regional (e.g. in the city of Lucknow) and social background (e.g. inter-ethnic dealings).

What to do when speakers of different religions meet

When speakers of different religions greet each other, it is considered polite for the person who speaks first to greet the listener according to his or her religion. Respecting others' religious feelings is the rule of politeness. Nowadays the English word 'hello' can be used to stress neutrality and modernity at the same time. However, the English word 'hello' is usually followed by the respectful and polite denoting word, **jī**.

What to do if you are not greeted with your religion's greeting

Do not feel offended; the speaker did not intend to offend you. This shows more about the socialization pattern of the speaker than his/her intention to respect your religion. It simply means the speaker does not socialize outside his/her group and is thus unaware of your religion-specific greetings.

व्याकरण Grammar

A vast majority of people learning Hindi as a foreign language find its grammar very simple. You will soon find out on your own the reasons for this perception. In this section we outline some salient features of Hindi grammar to satisfy your curiosity about Hindi already raised by the dialogues learned so far. Awareness of the grammatical points will make your learning experience more worthwhile and will allow you to make new sentences which you have not come across so far.

Word order in Hindi

The order of words in a Hindi sentence is not as rigidly fixed as is thought by prescriptive and traditional grammarians. Although *usually* (but not invariably) a Hindi sentence begins with a subject and ends with a verb, if the sentence has an object, this is sandwiched between the subject and the verb. That is why Hindi is often called an SOV language (i.e. Subject/Object/Verb language). However, Hindi speakers or writers enjoy considerable freedom in placing words to achieve stylistic effects. In the first dialogue Sarita asks:

kyā	**hāl**	**hɛ**
what	condition	is

How are you?

Usually the question word **kyā,** 'what', does not appear in the sentence in the initial position. The ordinary form of the sentence is as follows:

hāl	**kyā**	**hɛ**
condition	what	is

How are you?

The question word **kyā** 'what', is placed at the beginning of the sentence to give special emphasis to it. Also, you may have noticed the deletion of the implied element (i.e. the possessive pronoun 'your', modifying the subject noun 'condition') in the conversation. Such deletions also affect Hindi word order. For example, in the same dialogue, Mohan responds to Sarita's question in the following way:

T^{h}īk	**hɛ**
fine	is

I am fine.

The above reply by Mohan has no subject because the subject phrase is implied. The full version of the sentence is as follows:

merā	**hāl**	**T^{h}īk**	**hɛ**
my	condition	fine	is

I am fine (lit. 'My condition is fine.').

The implied subject (i.e. **merā hāl**) is rarely spelled out in the reply.

Yes–no questions

Yes–no questions involve either an affirmative or a negative answer. In spoken Hindi, yes–no questions are much simpler than in English.They are usually formed by changing *intonation*, i.e. with a rising tone of voice at the end of the sentence. You do not need to place any form of the verb before the subject as you do in English. In the second dialogue above, Razia asks

sab	**xɛriyat**	**hɛ**
all	welfare	is

Is all well? or Is everything fine?

simply by 'yes–no question intonation', i.e. raising the pitch of voice at the end of the sentence. The same sentence with a 'statement intonation' (pitch falling at the end), as in English, would mean 'All is well' = 'I am fine'.

Personal and demonstrative pronouns

The Hindi personal pronouns are

mɛ̃	मैं	I
ham	हम	we
tū	तू	you (sg.)

tum	तुम	you (pl.)
āp	आप	you (honorific)
<vo>	वह	she, he, it; that
ve	वे	they; those
<ye>	यह	this
ye	ये	these

There is *no* gender distinction in Hindi pronouns.

tū is considered to be either too intimate or too rude. We advise you not to use **tū** unless you are absolutely sure about your intimate relationship with the listener and your listener has already been using this pronoun in his/her exchanges with you. In short, you will not get much of a chance to hear and use **tū**. In the case of an emerging familiar relationship the only pronoun you will need is **tum**.

tum can be used either with one or more than one addressee. However, like the English *you*, it never takes a singular verb form.

āp is used to show respect and politeness. Most often you will use this pronoun in your exchange with your friends and strangers. Indian society is changing quickly and you should avoid stereotyping. You may have heard about the distinction between the lower and the higher caste Indians. Our advice is, use **āp** for everybody regardless of his/her caste and status. This approach is the safest form of address in the final analysis. **āp** always takes a plural verb (e.g. the Hindi equivalent of *you are* and not *you is*) regardless of the number of addressees.

<vo> is written as **vah**, but is pronounced as **vo** *most widely.*

vo, 'that', and **ve**, 'those', (called 'remote demonstrative' pronouns) are also used to refer to person(s) or object(s) far from the speaker.

<ye>, 'this, these' (called 'proximate demonstrative' pronouns), can be used to refer to both singular and plural person(s) or object(s) close to the speaker. The only difference is the singular form **<ye>**, which is written differently. It is written as *yah.*

Number and gender (plural formation of unmarked nouns)

Hindi nouns (like Spanish, Italian and French) are marked for both number and gender. There are two numbers (singular and plural) and two genders (masculine and feminine). Adjectives and verbs *agree* with nouns in number and gender.

The following box will provide you with Magic Key 1 to open a treasure chest of different noun and verb forms. Just let your imagination capture the suffixes boxed, and then you will begin to make new forms of nouns, adjectives and verbs. The only limit is the one set by your imagination!

	Singular	*Plural*	
Masculine	-ā	-e	
Feminine	-ī	-iā̃	(nouns)
		-ī	(adjectives; verbs)

Here are some examples of nouns and adjectives. Verbs will be exemplified in the next lesson. You will find slight changes in the feminine plural forms of verbs which are discussed in chapter 5.

masculine					
singular			*plural*		
beTā	बेटा	son	**beTe**	बेटे	sons
baccā	बच्चा	child	**bacce**	बच्चे	children
burā	बुरा	bad	**bure**	बुरे	bad

feminine					
singular			*plural*		
beTī	बेटी	daughter	**beTiā̃**	बेटियाँ	daughters
baccī	बच्ची	child	**bacciā̃**	बच्चियाँ	children
burī	बुरी	bad	**burī**	बुरी	bad

Masculine nouns ending in **-ā** and feminine nouns ending in **-ī** are called *unmarked nouns* in Hindi grammars. Similarly the adjectives that end **-ā** are called *unmarked adjectives.*

Nouns have gender too. In fact, most of the boxed suffixes draw their cues from the gender and number markings of nouns. However, there are no absolutes, as is the case in the real world. The logical gender holds only in the case of animate nouns. Male human beings receive masculine gender, whereas females receive feminine gender. However, inanimate and abstract nouns can either be masculine or feminine. **senā**, 'army', which (in India) does not admit women is feminine; in addition, **dāRī**, 'beard', is also feminine. Some animate nouns (species of animals, birds, insects, etc.) are either masculine or feminine. For example, **macc^{h}ar**, 'mosquito', **k^{h}aTmal**, 'bug', **cītā**, 'leopard', and **ullū**, 'owl', are masculine in gender and nouns such as **ciRī**, 'bird', **makk^{h}ī**, 'fly' and **macc^{h}ī**, 'fish', are feminine. However, do not worry about the absolute gender in the case of inanimate and abstract nouns. The following are some rules of thumb for you to navigate by in the unpredictable waters of gender.

Look at the following representative list of Hindi words and see if you can guess the gender rules.

masculine			*feminine*		
laRkā	लड़का	boy	**laRkī**	लड़की	girl
g^{h}oRā	घोड़ा	horse	**g^{h}oRī**	घोड़ी	mare
kamrā	कमरा	room	**kursī**	कुरसी	chair
darvāzā	दरवाज़ा	door	**k^{h}iRkī**	खिड़की	window
landan	लन्दन	London	**dillī**	दिल्ली	Delhi
g^{h}ar	घर	house	**kitāb**	क़िताब	book
hāth	हाथ	hand	**nazar**	नज़र	vision
namak	नमक	salt	**mirca**	मिर्च	pepper
ādmī	आदमी	man	**aurat**	औरत	woman
c^{h}ātā	छाता	umbrella	**mātā**	माता	mother

Most Hindi nouns ending in **-ā** are masculine and those ending in **-ī** are feminine. There are exceptions though: **ādmī,** 'man', ends in **-ī** and is masculine and **mātā,** 'mother', ends in **-ā** and is feminine. But you have probably guessed that the *semantic criterion* takes precedence over the sound-based criterion. After all, how could the word for *mother* be other than feminine in gender? and the word *man* be other than masculine? These two criteria-semantic and sound-based conditions can solve the mystery of Hindi gender in nearly every case.

Agreement: adjectives and possessive adjectives

You have already come across one very productive adjective, **acc^{h}ā**, 'good/ fine', which ends in **-ā**. It is a majority (unmarked) adjective. By substituting the suffixes given in the box, we can produce other forms. For example:

acc^{h}ā laRkā	अच्छा लड़का	**acc^{h}e laRke**	अच्छे लड़के
good boy		good boys	
acc^{h}ī laRkī	अच्छी लड़की	**acc^{h}ī laRkiyā̃**	अच्छी लड़कियाँ
good girl		good girls	

The question word **kεsā,** 'how', also behaves like an adjective ending in **-ā**.

kεsā laRkā	कैसा लड़का	**kεse laRke**	कैसे लड़के
what kind of boy		what kind of boys	
kεsī laRkī	कैसी लड़की	**kεsī laRkiyā̃**	कैसी लड़कियाँ
what kind of girl		what kind of girls	

The Hindi equivalents of the English possessive pronouns (*my*, *our* etc.) are:

merā	मेरा	my
hamārā	हमारा	our
terā	तेरा	your (sg., most intimate/non-honorific)
tumhārā	तुम्हारा	your (pl., familiar)
āp kā	आप का	your (pl., honorific)
us kā	उस का	his/her (remote)
un kā	उन का	their (remote)
is kā	इस का	his/her (proximate)
in kā	इन का	their (proximate)

Hindi possessive pronouns listed above follow the pattern of adjectives ending in **-ā**.

merā laRkā	मेरा लड़का	**mere laRke**	मेरे लड़के
my boy		my boys	
merī laRkī	मेरी लड़की	**merī laRkiyā̃**	मेरी लड़कियाँ
my girl		my girls	

From the above examples, it is clear that adjectives ending in **-ā** agree with the nouns that follow them. Therefore they behave like 'majority' adjectives.

In English, it is the gender of the *possessor* in the third person singular pronouns (i.e. '*his* girl', '*her* girl') that is marked on the possessive adjectives. Such a distinction is not made in Hindi. Notice, however, that because possessive adjectives agree with the nouns that follow them, the form of a possessive adjective can change in accordance with the gender and the number of the *possessed* noun. Thus the following phrases are ambiguous in Hindi:

us kā laRkā	उसका लड़का	**us ke laRke**	उसके लड़के
his/her boy		his/her boys	
us kī laRkī	उसकी लड़की	**us kī laRkiyā̃**	उसकी लड़कियाँ
his/her girl		his/her girls	

us kā laRkā means both 'his boy' and 'her boy'. Since **laRkā,** 'boy', is masculine, the possessive adjective **us kā,** 'his/her', takes the masculine form, regardless of whether the boy in question belongs to a man or a woman. Similarly, **us kī laRkī** can mean both 'his girl' or 'her girl'. It is the feminine gender of the word **laRkī,** 'girl', that assigns gender to the possessive pronoun.

अभ्यास Exercises

1

How would you reply to someone who said this to you?

(a) namaste.
(b) kyā hāl hɛ?
(c) salām.
(d) mizāj kɛse hɛ̃?
(e) acc^{h}ā, namaste.
(f) sat srī akāl jī.
(g) sab xɛriyat hɛ?
(h) namaste jī.
(i) hukam kījie.

2

Match the replies in Column B with the greetings or questions in Column A:

	A	B
(a)	namaste.	T^{h}īk hɛ.
(b)	kyā hāl hɛ?	allāh kā shukra hɛ.
(c)	āp ke mizāj kɛse hɛ̃?	namaste.
(d)	xudā hāfiz.	xudā hāfiz.
(e)	sab xɛriyat hɛ?	salām.
(f)	salām.	meharbānī hɛ.

3

Fill in the gaps in the two conversations given below:

Conversation I

A: salām.
B: ————
B: sab xɛriyat hɛ?
A: ———— hɛ, aur āp ke ———— kɛse hɛ̃?
B: allāh kā ———— ————.

Conversation II

A: ————.
B: sat srī akāl jī.
B: kyā ———— hɛ?
A: ———— hɛ, aur ————?
B: mɛ̃ bhī ———— ————.
A: acc^{h}ā, ———— ———— ————.
B: sat srī akāl.

4

Answer the following questions.

(a)

Question: kyā hāl hɛ?

Answer:
Question: aur āp?
Answer:

(b)

Question: āp kɛse hɛ̃?
Answer:

5

Give short sentences corresponding to the long sentences in the left-hand column.

	long sentences	*short sentences*
(a)	**aur āp kɛse hɛ̃?**	________
(b)	**mɛ̃ b^{h}ī Thīk hū̃.**	________
(c)	**āp kī meharbānī hɛ.**	________
(d)	**āp ke mizāj kɛse hɛ̃?**	________

6

If you have the recording, listen to the dialogue and identify the religion of the speakers on the basis of their use of greetings and goodbyes:

A: male voice B: female voice

Vocabulary

kitāb (f.)	किताब	book
ke liye	के लिये	for
koī	कोई	some
bāt (f.)	बात	matter

2 आप कहाँ के/की हैं? Where are you from?

By the end of this lesson you should be able to:

- introduce yourself and others
- say and ask what you and others do
- say and ask where you and others work
- learn self-disclosure techniques about you and your family
- ask someone's address
- refer to inseparable possessions
- use very common adjectives
- form plurals
- form simple present tense

English prohibition?

Hindi speakers are not snobbish in their linguistic attitudes. They treat English as one of their languages; therefore, many English words have been nativized into Hindi and have their own Hindi pronunciation. The realization that the English words are not alien to Hindi speakers will give you a thrill, like running into a long-lost friend. Moreover, there are a number of modern terms in contexts such as jobs and titles which cannot be adequately translated into Hindi from the viewpoint of their social meaning. Wait a minute! Do not be quick to value judge Hindi or Indians. The lack of a word does not mean that the language is not rich enough. It simply means Hindi responds to new contexts and new needs by borrowing from English or from some other languages rather than inventing new words. In this way, Hindi is like English.

In the following dialogues, no attempt is made to translate an English word/expression artificially into Hindi, if the English word has become a natural part of the Hindi language. The original English words in the text are italicized. Their native pronunciation is also given.

Dialogue

Small-talk

A young stockbroker, Mukesh Bhargava, wants to meet a distinguished looking gentleman standing alone in a corner gazing at the wall. On learning from a friend that his name is Dr. Anup Patel, Mr. Bhargava approaches him. Having exchanged greetings, Mukesh Bhargava undertakes the task of introducing himself.

MUKESH: kahiye, āpkā nām DākTar anūp patel hɛ na?
ANUP: jī hā̃, merā nām anūp patel hɛ.
(extending his hand to shake hands)
MUKESH: merā nām mukesh hɛ.
ANUP: mil ke baRī xushī huī. āp kā pūrā nām kyā hɛ?
MUKESH: mukesh b^hārgava hɛ.
ANUP: āp kyā karte hɛ̃?

MUKESH:	mɛ̃ sTāk brokar [*stockbroker*] hū̃. āp mɛDikal DākTar [*medical doctor*] hɛ̃?
ANUP:	jī nahī̃, mɛ̃ mɛDikal DākTar nahī̃ hū̃. dūsrā DākTar hū̃.

MUKESH:	*Excuse me, you are Dr. Anup Patel, aren't you?*
ANUP:	*Yes, my name is Anup Patel.*
MUKESH:	*My name is Mukesh.*
ANUP:	*Pleased to meet [you].* (lit. having met [you] big happiness happened) *What is your full name?*
MUKESH:	*My name is Mukesh Bhargava.*
ANUP:	*What [work] do you do?*
MUKESH:	*I am a stockbroker. Are you a medical doctor?*
ANUP:	*No, I am not a medical doctor. [I] am the other [kind of] doctor.* (i.e. I am a Ph.D)

Vocabulary

kahnā (+ne)	कहना	to say
kahiye	कहिये	Excuse me!
nām (m.)	नाम	name
na?	न	isn't it?
hā̃	हाँ	yes
mil ke baRī xushī huī.	मिल के बड़ी ख़ुशी हुई	pleased to meet you
pūrā (m.; adj.)	पूरा	full
karnā (+ne)	करना	to do
dūsrā (m. adj.)	दूसरा	second, other

Notes

Attention getters

The Hindi literal equivalent of the English expression 'Excuse me!' is **'māf kījiye'**. However, the Hindi expression actually means 'I apologize' or 'I beg your pardon'. Therefore, it is not suited in those contexts observed in the above dialogue where the real intent of 'Excuse me' is to get attention. Although some educated English-speaking Indians tend to translate

directly from English, it is not the natural tendency of the native speakers. The expression 'Excuse me' is best paraphrased by the native Hindi speakers either as 'please say' (**kahiye**) or 'please listen' (**suniye**). Actually this is true of many other languages, such as Spanish.

*Do not use '**māf kījiye**' if you do not intend to apologize. Such an inappropriate choice could make a learner the easy target of unwanted jokes.*

Social linguistic rituals

Every language employs some expressions that are often fixed and invariable. For instance, in greeting someone, one might use the expression 'Hi, there'; but if one examines this expression, it is rather a strange one since there is no subject, no verb and no chance of changing the expression even slightly, for example, to 'Hi, here'. In some respects, Hindi expressions such as 'Pleased to see you' belong to this category. For the time being, you should memorize them without going further into their composition. Also, learn their appropriate usage.They are usually used in introductions. However, if a waiter is introducing himself, one does not need to use this expression in response.

The mystery of what the correct subject of 'Pleased to see you' is will become clear later when the concept of **ko** subjects (called 'dative subjects'or 'experiencer subjects') is introduced. For the time being, use the expression as if it were a subject-less sentence.

Word-for-word translation

The Hindi expression of 'I am pleased to meet you' is

mil	**ke**	**baRī**	**xushī**	**huī**
met	having	big	happiness	happened

In the above expression, the object 'you' is implied. However, for emphasis the object can be inserted into the above expression:

āp	**se**	**mil**	**ke**	**baRī**	**xushī**	**huī**
you	with	met	having	big	happiness	happened

Notice the Hindi equivalent of the English 'I am pleased to meet you' is 'I am pleased to meet with you'.

Word order of the question word 'what'

Observe the place of the question word **kyā** 'what', in the following sentences:

āp kā	**pūrā**	**nām**	**kyā**	**hɛ**
your	full	name	what	is

What is your full name?

āp	**kyā**	**kām**	**karte**	**hɛ̃**
you	what	work	do	are

What do you do? = What is your job?

When one compares these sentences with the socially ritualistic expression **kyā hāl hɛ**, one might be tempted to conclude that 'anything goes' regarding the placement of **kyā** in a sentence. The following sentences strengthen this belief further, because one can say the above two sentences in the following way:

āp kā	**kyā**	**pūrā**	**nām**	**hɛ**
your	what	full	name	is

What is your full name?

āp	**kām**	**kyā**	**karte**	**hɛ̃?**
you	work	what	do	are

What do you do? = What is your job?

The placement of **kyā** at the beginning or at the end of the sentences, or between the two verbal elements, will lead to some problems. Such placements will change the meanings of the sentences, and may even sound abrupt and impolite. Therefore, the rule of thumb is to keep the question word closer to the word that is the subject of the inquiry. Usually, **kyā** is placed before the noun or the verb it modifies. If the noun phrase is modified, as the noun **nām** is modified in the following sentence by two modifiers – 'your' and 'full' – rather than breaking the bond between the the noun and the modifier as in,

āp kā **kyā** **pūrā** **nām** **hɛ?**

the question word is placed after the noun:

āp kā pūrā nām kyā hɛ?

In the following sentence, the noun **kām** is, however, not modified further; thus, it is better to say

āp kyā kām karte hɛ̃?

i.e, literally, 'What work do you do?' instead of the following sentence. The following sentence has some negative connotations, as in the English sentence: 'Tell me, what do you do anyway?':

āp kām kyā karte hɛ̃?

Dialogue

Where are you from?

Indian train travel can be nostalgic. Two female college students on their way to Banaras from Delhi engage in a dialogue that is typical of Indian travellers, whether from the urban or rural areas. After exchanging names, Kanika Bhatia and Sunita Divan start inquiring about each other's family background.

KANIKA: āp kahā̃ kī hɛ̃?
SUNITA: mɛ̃ dillī kī hū̃. aur āp?
KANIKA: mɛ̃ banāras mẽ rɛhtī hū̃.
SUNITA: āp ke kitne bʰāī-bɛhɛnẽ hɛ̃?
KANIKA: ham cār bʰāī aur do bɛhɛnẽ hɛ̃.
SUNITA: merā ek bʰāī aur ek bɛhɛn hɛ̃.

KANIKA: *Where are you from?*
(lit. of where [= of what place] are you?)
SUNITA: I *am from Delhi* (lit. I am of Delhi). *And you?*
KANIKA: *I live in Banaras.*
SUNITA: *How many brothers and sisters do you have?*
(lit. how many your brothers and sisters are?)
KANIKA: *We are four brothers and two sisters.*
SUNITA: *I have one brother and a sister.*

Vocabulary

kahā̃	कहाँ	where?
mẽ	में	in
dillī (f.)	दिल्ली	Delhi (the capital city)
kī (f.)	की	of
banāras	बनारस	Banaras (one of the oldest cities of India)
<rɛhnā>	रहना	to live
kitnā (m.)	कितना	how much?
kitne	कितने	how many?
b^{h}**āī** (m.)	भाई	brother/brothers
<bɛhɛn> (f.)	बहन	sister
cār	चार	four
do	दो	two
ek	एक	one

Pronunciation

The word for 'sister' is written **bahan** (बहन), but is pronounced **bɛhɛn**. You must have noticed by now that the sound **h** in the middle (when sandwiched between the vowel **a** and the final position) alters the pronunciation of the preceding vowel. Go back to Lesson 1 and check the pronunciation of the third-person singular pronouns, in case you have forgotten their pronunciation. Similarly, the verb 'to live' is written **rah** (रह) but is pronounced **rɛh**.

Notes

Word-for-word translation: 'Where are you from?'

The Hindi equivalent of the English 'Where are you from?' is

āp	**kahā̃**	**kī**	**hɛ̃**
you	where	of	are

The response to the English question in Hindi is

mɛ̃	**dillī**	**kī**	**hū̃**
I	Delhi	of	am

As we saw in the last chapter, like other possessive pronouns, **kī** agrees with the number and the gender of its possessor. In the above two sentences the subject pronoun is the possessor. Since the subjects are feminine, the feminine form **kī** is selected. It is not difficult to guess what would happen if the subjects were masculine. If these sentences are uttered by males, the sentences are

āp	**kahā̃**	**ke**	**hɛ̃**
you	where	of	are

mɛ̃	**dillī**	**kā**	**hū̃**
I	Delhi	of	am

Remember the honorific pronoun **āp** always takes the plural form.

Don't be surprised if you hear someone using **se**, 'from' instead of **kā**, **ke** or **kī**.

āp	**kahā̃**	**se**	**hɛ̃**
you	where	from	are

mɛ̃	**dillī**	**se**	**hū̃**
I	Delhi	from	am

Usually, an educated Hindi–English bilingual would construct such sentences. The important thing is to know that **se** is invariable whereas **kā** is variable. You will learn about the invariable elements such as **se** later under the section on invariable postposition.

Also, notice the placement of the English 'from' in the Hindi sentence.

Postpositions

The Hindi equivalents of English 'in Banaras' and 'from Delhi' are

banāras	**mẽ**	**dillī**	**se**
Banaras	in	Delhi	from

Notice the English preposition is placed after the noun of the prepositional phrase. In other words, the word order of the prepositional phrase is reversed in Hindi. Since the prepositional elements always follow the noun they modify, they are called *post*positions in Hindi grammar.

Question words: 'where' and 'how many/much'

From the Hindi sentence 'Where are you from?' it should be obvious that the Hindi word for 'where' is **kahā̃**. Like the English question word, Hindi **kahā̃** does not change its shape. Also, it is not placed at the beginning of the sentence. Its usual place is before the verb. However, this word is rather mobile within a sentence.

The Hindi equivalent of 'how many/much' is **kitnā**. This question word agrees with its following noun in number and gender.

kitnā	**kām**	how much work
kitne	**b^hāī**	how many brothers
kitnī	**bɛhɛnẽ**	how many sisters

This question word is like a 'majority' possessive adjective.

Dialogue

Where are you from?

During the train journey, Kanika and Sunita become friends; they are ready to exchange addresses.

SUNITA:	ye merā patā hɛ.
KANIKA:	ye patā bahut baRā hɛ.
SUNITA:	hā̃, baRā shɛhɛr, baRā patā.
KANIKA:	lekin, c^hoTā shɛhɛr, choTā patā.
	(both laugh)
SUNITA:	acc^hā, p^hir milẽge.
KANIKA:	milẽge.

SUNITA:	*This is my address.*
KANIKA:	*This address is very big.* (i.e. long).
SUNITA:	*Yes: big city, big address.*
KANIKA:	*But small city, small address.*
	(*both laugh*)
SUNITA:	*Okay, [we] will meet again.*
KANIKA:	*[We] will meet.*

Vocabulary

patā (m.)	पता	address
bahut	बहुत	very
baRā (m.; adj.)	बड़ा	big
<shɛhɛr> (m.)	शहर	city
lekin	लेकिन	but
c^{h}oTā (m.; adj.)	छोटा	small
p^{h}ir	फिर	again, then
acc^{h}ā (m.; adj.)	अच्छा	good, okay
milnā (-ne)	मिलना	to meet
milẽge	मिलेंगे	will meet

Pronunciation

Like the word **bahan**, the word for 'city' is written **shahar** but is pronounced **shɛhɛr**. However, the pronunciation of **bahut** does not change because **h** does not have the vowel **a** on both sides.

Notes

Word-for-word translation

ye	**patā**	**bahut**	**baRā**	**hɛ**
this	address	very	big	is

Notice that the sentence ends with a verb and not with an adjective, as is the case with 'This address is very long'.

Subject omission

The Hindi expression for 'we will meet again' is

p^{h}ir	**milege**
again	will meet

The subject ‘we’ is implied. It is rarely spelled out. Such subjectless expressions are considered ungrammatical in many languages, including English; however, they are quite normal in Hindi. Other languages, such as Chinese, follow the tendency to drop subjects. Subject/pronoun dropping languages are called ‘pro-drop’ languages.

व्याकरण Grammar

Tag question

A tag question is usually ‘tagged’ to a statement. The Hindi equivalent of ‘You are Dr. Anup Patel, aren’t you?’ is very simple – just add **na** at the end of the statement. It will take care of both the positive tags (e.g. is it? will you?, do you? etc.) and the negative ones (e.g. isn’t it?, won't you?, don’t you? etc.) which are attached to a statement in English. The only difference is that the English speakers will pause at the point where a comma is placed in the English sentence, whereas the Hindi speakers will not pause at this point. Therefore, no comma is placed between the statement and the tag. However, both in English and Hindi the tag question will receive a rising intonation.

Verb ‘to be’

This section will guarantee smooth sailing into the land of different tenses. Once you master the forms given below, your adventure into different tenses becomes more rewarding and worthwhile.

There is a striking resemblance between English and Hindi ‘to be’ verbs. Just as English will not say ‘you am’, ‘I is’, 'he am' or 'they is', the same is true of Hindi. Depending on the person and number of the subject, different forms are used. The Hindi counterparts of the English ‘to be’ verb are given below in Magic Key 2.

Magic Key 2

	singular	*plural*	*honorific*
first person	**hū̃** (I) am	**hɛ̃** (we) are	–
second person	**hɛ** (you sg.) are	**ho** (you pl.) are	**hɛ̃** (you honorific) are
third person	**hɛ** (he/she/it) is	**hɛ̃** (they) are	–

Surely you have found some differences between Hindi and English. It is possible to say in Hindi 'You is', provided the Hindi singular you, **tū**, is selected. Of course, the second person honorific pronoun **(āp)** always takes a plural form. As we mentioned in the first lesson, be careful when you need to use Hindi second person pronouns. The chances are you will rarely get to use the pronoun **tū** and, thus, the singular second-person 'to be' form.

Present habitual actions = simple present tense

The Hindi sentences

āp	**kyā**	**karte**	**hɛ̃?**	
you	what	do	are	
mɛ̃	**banāras**	**mẽ**	**rɛhtī**	**hū̃**
I	Banaras	in	live	am

are equivalent to the English 'what do you do?' and 'I live in Banaras', which refer to habitual or regularly repeated acts. Look at the verb form/phrase, and you will readily observe that there are two main parts of the Hindi verb form. The first one, usually called the 'Main Verb', is composed of three elements:

kar	+ **t**	+ **e**
stem 'to do'	+ aspect marker	+ gender-number marker (m. pl.)
rɛh	+ **t**	+ **ī**
stem 'to live'	+ aspect marker	+ gender-number marker (f. sg.)

The first element of the first part is the verb stem. The second element is the aspect marker. The aspect marker simply shows whether the act is completed or ongoing. At this point it is important to understand the difference between tense and aspect. As mentioned just now, aspect is concerned about the ongoing, repeated or completed state of the action whereas tense (present, past or future) renders time information, i.e. as to what point in time the action took place. The third element of the main verb is the same masculine plural ending from Magic Key 1 discussed in the previous chapter.

The second part of the verb is called the 'auxiliary verb'. In the two sentences, the auxiliary verb is the same 'to be' verb form discussed above in Magic Key 2.

This verb form is referred to with various technical names. The most widely used forms are the following three: present imperfect tense, present habitual tense and simple present tense. We will call it the *simple present tense.* The full paradigm is given in the Grammatical Summary section of the book.

Verb 'to have'

The Hindi expression for 'how many brothers and sisters do you have?' is

āp ke	**kitne**	**b^hāī-bɛhɛnẽ**	**hɛ̃?**
your	how many	brothers-sisters	are

Note that the Hindi sentence contains neither an equivalent of the English verb 'to have' nor the subject 'you'. In Hindi, the subject takes a possessive form and the verb 'to have' becomes the verb 'to be'. As we proceed further, it will become clear that many languages of the world do not have the exact equivalent of English 'have'. Such a Hindi construction is used to express inseparable or non-transferable possessions (such as body parts, relationships, or dearly held possessions such as a job, house or shop). Transferable possession will be dealt with later on.

Number and gender (plural formation of marked/ 'nerd' nouns)

Now do some detective work and discover Magic Key 3 for the following nouns.

masculine

	singular			*plural*	
b^{h}āī	भाई	brother	**b^{h}āī**	भाई	brothers
g^{h}ar	घर	house	**g^{h}ar**	घर	houses
hāt^h	हाथ	hand	**hāt^h**	हाथ	hands
mard	मर्द	man	**mard**	मर्द	men
ādmī	आदमी	man	**ādmī**	आदमी	men

feminine

	singular			*plural*	
bɛhɛn	बहन	sister	**bɛhɛnẽ**	बहनें	sisters
kitāb	किताब	book	**kitābẽ**	किताबें	books
aurat	औरत	woman	**auratẽ**	औरतें	women
mātā	माता	mother	**mātāẽ**	माताएं	mothers

If you think that the masculine nouns that do not end in **ā** remain unchanged and the feminine nouns that do not end in **ī** take **ẽ** to form plurals, you are right. The masculine nouns that depart from the normal trend, i.e. those that do *not* end in **ā** and the feminine nouns that do *not* end in **ī**, are called 'marked' nouns. We affectionately call them 'nerd' nouns for recall purposes.

Here is your Magic Key 3.

	singular	*plural*
masculine *feminine*	non-**ā** non-**ī**	**ø** (zero=unchanged) **ẽ**

अभ्यास **Exercises**

1

The packman has swallowed either some parts of the word or whole word. Supply the missing part where you see the ◎ sign:

mɛ̃ dillī ◎ hū̃ me ◎ cār b^{h}āī ◎. merā choT ◎ b^{h}āī *Chicago* mẽ kām kar ◎ hɛ. mer ◎ do baR ◎ b^{h}āī *England* mɛ̃ rɛht ◎ ◎. merā nām amar ◎. mɛ̃ *school* jā ◎ hū̃. mer ◎ do bɛhɛn ◎ b^{h}ī ◎. mer ◎ pitā jī b^{h}ī kām kart ◎ hɛ̃. āp ◎ rɛhte hɛ̃? āp ◎ kit ◎ b^{h}āī-bɛhɛnẽ hɛ̃. āp ◎ mātā jī kyā ◎ kar ◎ hɛ̃.

2

Pair the words on the right with those on the left:

acc^{h}ā	c^{h}oTā
baRā	laRkī
bɛhɛn	aurat
laRkā	burā
ādmī	nahī̃
hā̃	b^{h}āī

3

The software system of our computer has imposed some weird system on the following Hindi phrases. Your job is to correct them:

se	banāras
mẽ	shɛhɛr
das	bɛhɛn
cār	b^{h}āīyā̃
do	ādmīyā̃
kitnā	b^{h}āīyā̃
pīlā	sāRī

4

Unscramble the following words/phrases and fill the unscrambled expressions in the blank spaces on the right:

hiyeka	______		
shīxu	______		
bīRa xuīsh hīu	______	______	______
rūpā mnā	______	______	
dūrās	______		
kinte b^{h}īā	______	______	
mẽlieg	______		

5

In this puzzle there are four Hindi words from our dialogues. Find the words and circle them. They can be found horizontally and vertically. Note that long vowels are repeated, for example, ī = ii.

```
a d g a b a d z x s u n i y e z y x u f g
l l k j a z x c v b n m a s p q w e r t y
z x c v R a d g a r t y f g h a s g h j o
r t y f i b g t x u s h i i z q t s k x p
c v b n i w s x e d v r a t g h t a h z c
q a z w c w s v f r y h n m h u i k a u c
```

6

If you have the cassette recording, listen to it, and then play the role of Meenu Bharati. You can record your response orally.

Setting: A crowded shop

Vocabulary

māfī: (f.) apology
b^hīR (f.) crowd

Now play the role of Meenu Bharati and record your response.

ABHILASHA: (bumps into Meenu) māf kījiye.
MEENU: ________. bahut bhīR hɛ.
ABHILASHA: sac.
MEENU: ________.
ABHILASHA: aur merā nām Abhilasha Pande hɛ.
MEENU: ________.
ABHILASHA: āp dillī kī hɛ̃ na?
MEENU: ________.

3 आप को क्या चाहिये ? What would you like?

By the end of this lesson you should be able to:

- tell someone what you wish to get
- describe locations
- use some skills of negotiation
- make reservations
- describe possession (transferable)
- understand verb agreement with subjects and objects
- express physical states (fever, headache)

Dialogue

Buying a saree

Meghan Ashley and Anita Sharma go to a saree shop in Jaipur. Anita visits the shop quite regularly. After greeting each other, Anita tells the shopkeeper, Rajendra Singh, that Meghan is visiting from London and wants a saree.

ANITA: zarā naye *fashion* kī sāRī dik^{h}āiye.
RAJENDRA: kaun sī sāRī cāhiye? reshmī yā sūtī?
ANITA: reshmī.
RAJENDRA: ye dek^{h}iye. āj-kal is kā bahut rivāj hɛ.
dek^{h}iye, *silk* kitnā acc^{h}ā hɛ!
(*Rajendra shows a number of sarees. Anita asks Meghan about her choice.*)
ANITA: Meghan, āp ko kaun sī sāRī pasand hɛ?
MEGHAN: ye pīlī.
(*turning to Rajendra to ask the price*)
ANITA: is kā dām kyā hɛ?
RAJENDRA: bārā sau rupaye.
ANITA: T^{h}īk batāiye, ye bāhar se āyī hɛ̃.
RAJENDRA: āj-kal itnā dām hɛ...acc^{h}ā gyāra sau.
ANITA: acc^{h}ā T^{h}īk hɛ.

ANITA: *Please show me a saree that is in fashion.*
(lit. please show me a little bit of a new fashion saree)
RAJENDRA: *What kind of saree [do you] want? Silk[en] or cotton?*
ANITA: *Silk[en].*
RAJENDRA: *Look at this. Nowadays it is very much in fashion*
(lit. nowadays it's very much custom is)
See how good the silk is!
(lit. how much good the silk is!)
(*Rajendra shows a number of sarees. Anita asks Meghan about her choice.*)
ANITA: *Meghan, which saree do you want?*
MEGHAN: *[I] want this yellow [one].*
ANITA: *What is its price?*

(*turning to Rajendra to ask the price*)

RAJENDRA: *Twelve hundred rupees.*

ANITA: *Please tell [me] the right [price]; she is the visitor.* (lit. she came from outside)

RAJENDRA: *This is the price nowadays...okay, eleven hundred [rupees].*

ANITA: *Okay, [that] is fine.*

Vocabulary

zarā	ज़रा	little, somewhat
nayā (m.)	नया	new
naye	नये	new
sāRī (f.)	साड़ी	saree
dik^{h}ānā	दिखाना	to show
dik^{h}āiye	दिखाइये	please show
kaun sā (m.; adj.)	कौन सा	which one
kaun sī	कौन सी	which one
cāhiye	चाहिये	desire, want
resham (m.)	रेशम	silk
<reshmī>	रेशमी	silken
yā	या	or
sūt (m.)	सूत	cotton
sūtī	सूती	cotton (adj.)
dek^{h}nā (+nū̃)	देखना	to see
dek^{h}iye	देखिये	please see
āj-kal	आज-कल	nowadays
rivāj (m.)	रिवाज़	custom
āp ko	आप को	to you
pasand (f.)	पसन्द	choice, liking
pīlā (m.; adj.)	पीला	yellow
pīlī	पीली	yellow
dām (m.)	दाम	price
<bārā>	बारह	twelve
sau	सौ	hundred
rupaye (m.)	रुपये	Rupees (Indian currency)

batāiye	बताइये	please tell
bāhar	बाहर	outside
āyī	आयी	came
itnā	इतना	this much
<gyārā>	ग्यारह	eleven

Pronunciation

The numerals eleven and twelve are written **gyārah** and **bārah**, but are pronounced **gyārā** and **bārā**, in Standard Hindi. In the other varieties of Hindi, they are pronounced **gyārɛ** and **bārɛ,** respectively.

The Hindi word for 'silken' is written as **reshamī** but the vowel **a** is dropped. Therefore, it is pronounced **reshmī**. For the time being, satisfy yourself with this observation. The rule of dropping **a** is given in Script Unit 4.

Notes

Rules of negotiation

The rules of bargaining or negotiating can be very complex indeed, and are beyond the scope of this book. However, one strategy deserves special mention. Towards the end of the conversation, the subject of visitors is brought up. Since Indian culture shows a great deal of sensitivity towards foreign visitors, it is a signal to request a discount.

The politeness germ

As we showed in the last lesson, Hindi is a very rich language as far as politeness is concerned.

When **zarā** 'little, somewhat' is used at the beginning of a request, its main function is politeness. It is almost like the English 'I do not want to impose on you but....' By adding **zarā**, Hindi speakers convey the meaning, 'I want to put as little burden as possible on you by my request'. **zarā** remains invariable.

cāhnā, 'want' vs. *cāhiye*, 'desire/want'

As the English expression 'what do you want?' would be considered less polite than 'what would you like to have?', similarly in Hindi

āp	**kaun sī**	**sāRī**	**cāhtī**	**hẽ**
you	what kind of	saree	want	are

would be considered less polite than

āp	**ko**	**kaun sī**	**sāRī**	**cāhiye**
you	to	what kind of	saree	desire

(lit. what kind of saree is desirable to you?)

In the first sentence the subject **āp** indicates a *deliberate* subject, whereas in the second sentence the subject **āp ko** is an *experiencer* one. Sometimes the politeness is achieved in Hindi by means of experiencer subjects. In other words, the verb **cāhiye** is the relatively polite counterpart of English 'to want' (and Hindi **cāhnā** 'to want') because it always selects an experiencer subject. Experiencer subjects render polite reading in some contexts. Hereafter the Hindi verb **cāhiye** will be glossed as 'want' because 'desire' is not its best translation.

For more information, see the discussion of the experiencer subject in the next lesson.

Word-for-word translation

The Hindi equivalent of the English 'It is very much in fashion' is

is kā	**bahut**	**rivāj**	**hɛ**
its	very	custom	is

Similarly, the English expression 'This [she] is a visitor' is realized in Hindi as

ye	**bāhar**	**se**	**āyī**	**hẽ**
these (honorific)	outside	from	came	are

In other words, the Hindi expression is literally 'She has come from outside'. The past tense will be dealt with later on; for the time being memorize this sentence and learn to make number and gender changes in **āyī** (**āyā** for masculine singular subjects, **āye** for masculine plural, and **āyī̃** for feminine plural) and person and number changes in the 'to be' form.

Polite commands

The Hindi equivalent of English 'please show' and 'please see' are:

dik^{h}ā-iye	**dek^{h}-iye**
show-imperative (polite)	see-imperative (polite)

The other examples of polite commands you have encountered earlier are:

kah-iye	**sun-iye**
say-imperative (polite)	listen-imperative (polite)

In short, **iye** is added to a verbal stem to form polite commands. It is called 'polite imperative' in grammatical literature.

No word for 'please'

There is really no *exact* equivalent of the English word 'please'. The most important way of expressing polite requests is by means of a polite verb form, i.e. by adding **-iye** to a verb stem. If one looks for word-for-word Hindi equivalents of 'please', there are two: **kripyā** or **mehar bānī kar ke**; even then the verbal form with **-iye** has to be retained. **kripyā** and **meharbānī kar ke** mean 'kindly' in Hindi.

Context

Note the use of the change in meaning of Hindi **kaun sā**, 'which one', in the following two contexts: when a saree has yet to be shown by the shopkeeper

kaun sī	**sāRī**	**cāhiye?**
what kind of	saree	want

'What kind of saree do [you] want?'

and in the context of choosing a saree from a set of sarees which are shown to the customer

āp	**ko**	**kaun**	**sī**	**sāRī**	**pasand**	**hɛ?**
you	to	which	one	saree	choice/liking	is

'Which saree do (you) like?'

Subject omission

kaun sī	**sāRī**	**cāhiye?**
what kind of	saree	want

'What kind of saree do [you] want?'

Dialogue

Booking a flight

John Smith goes to the airline booking office to make a flight booking for Jaipur (the Pink City). He talks to the agent.

JOHN:	jaipur kī ek TikaT (*ticket*) cāhiye.
AGENT:	kaun se din ke liye?
JOHN:	kal ke liye.
AGENT:	kampuTar (*computer*) par dek^{h}tā hū̃, hɛ̃ yā nahī̃.
JOHN:	subā kī flāiT (*flight*) cāhiye.
AGENT:	TikaT (*ticket*) hɛ.
JOHN:	to dījiye. *flight* kab caltī hɛ?
AGENT:	subā das baje.
JOHN:	mere pās *cash* nahī̃ hɛ.
AGENT:	to krɛDiT kārDa (*credit card*) dījiye.

JOHN:	*[I] want one ticket for Jaipur.*
AGENT:	*For which day?*
JOHN:	*For tomorrow.*
AGENT:	*[I] must look at the computer [to see] whether or not* [I have it]. (*lit. [it] is or not*)

JOHN:	*[I] need a morning flight.*
AGENT:	*[I] have a ticket.*
JOHN:	*Then [please] give [it to me]. When does the flight leave?*
AGENT:	*10 o' clock.*
JOHN:	*I do not have cash.*
AGENT:	*Then use a credit card.* (*lit. give a credit card*)

Vocabulary

din (m.)	दिन	day
ke liye	के लिये	for
kal	कल	yesterday, tomorrow
par	पर	on, at
dek^{h}nā (+ne)	देखना	to see
<subā>	सुबह	morning
to	तो	then
denā (+ne)	देना	to give
dījiye	दीजिये	please give
kab	कब	when (question word)
calnā (-ne)	चलना	to leave, to walk
das	दस	ten
baje	बजे	o'clock
pās	पास	near, possession (have)

Pronunciation

The word for morning is written **subah**, but is pronounced **subā**.

In the borrowed words from English such as *computer* and *ticket*, the English *t* is pronounced with the retroflex **T** (see section on Hindi pronunciation and writing system for the pronunciation of Hindi sounds).

Notes

Word-for-word translation

jaipur	**kī**	**TikaT**
Jaipur	of (f.)	ticket (f.)

'A ticket for Jaipur' (lit. Jaipur's ticket)

The English borrowed words such as *ticket* and *computer* are assimilated into Hindi and, consequently, are assigned feminine and masculine gender, respectively.

The equivalent Hindi expression for 'morning flight' is

subā	**kī**	**flāiT**
morning	of	flight

Guess the gender of *flight* in Hindi. Of course, it is feminine (clue: the feminine form **kī**).

Short form of tab, 'then'

The short form of **tab**, 'then', is **to**, as in

to	**dījiye**
then	please give

Compound and oblique (peer pressure) postpositions

Observe the structure of the English preposition in Hindi:

(noun)	postposition	postposition
kal	**ke**	**liye**
tomorrow	of	for

As we proceed further we will introduce the concept of the 'oblique' case in Hindi, which I affectionately call the 'peer pressure' case. Languages do show the effects of peer pressure! You will notice, as we go on, that the compound postpositions will either begin with **ke** or **kī**, but never with **kā**. The reason is that **kā** and **kī** have to be followed by another postposition in the compound postposition, and the succeeding postposition influences the preceding postposition. In the above expression **liye** changes **kā** to **ke**. That is, the postposition ending **ā** becomes **e**.

The oblique effect does not last to the preceding postposition but to the phrase as a whole.

kaun sā	**din**
which	day (m.)

Note that the **sā** part of the question word 'which' agrees in number and gender with the following noun, i.e. **din**, 'day', which is masculine singular. Now, if we expand this phrase by adding the Hindi compound postposition **ke liye**:

kaun se	**din**	**ke**	**liye**
which	day (m.)	of	for

Now the peer pressure of **liye** not only extends to **ke** but all the way to **se**. The way **kā** gives in to the peer pressure of **liye** is similar to the way **sā** gives in to **se**. As a matter of fact, even the noun **din** is affected too. The only difference concerns the marked noun (or nerd nouns: remember this distinction from the last chapter), where the effect does not occur. However, if we replace the marked noun with an unmarked noun **laRkā**, 'boy', you will see a clear change.

kaun se	**laRke**	**ke**	**liye**
which	boy	of	for

For which boy

Although under the peer pressure **laRkā** 'boy', changes to **laRke**, its meaning does not change. It still keeps its singular identity. Remember, normal people give in to peer pressure superficially!

Separable or transferable possessions

In the last lesson we dealt with non-transferable and inseparable possession, i.e. expressions such as 'I have four brothers'. Let us turn our attention to separable possession, as in

mere	**pās**	***cash***	**nahī̃**	**hɛ**
my	near	cash	not	is

I do not have cash.

Similarly, in Hindi the expression 'you have a ticket' will be

āp ke	**pās**	**TikaT**	**hɛ**
your	near	ticket	is

You have a ticket

In other words, in the case of separable possession the subject receives **ke pās** compound postposition and, subsequently, the following changes take place. Note that **ke** makes the subject oblique masculine possessive.

mɛ̃	+	**ke pās**	==>	**mere pās**	I have
āp	+	**ke pās**	==>	**āp ke pās**	You have

Dialogue

A visit to the doctor

Kushwant Singh is suffering from the cold weather. He has a fever and a headache. He goes to his doctor, Charan Chaturvedi. After exchanging greetings, Kushwant tells Charan the purpose of his visit

KUSHWANT:	DākTar sāhib, muj^h ko kuc^h buxār hɛ.
CHARAN:	kab se hɛ?
KUSHWANT:	kal rāt se.
CHARAN:	sir-dard b^{h}ī hɛ?
KUSHWANT:	jī hā̃.
	(putting the thermometer into Kushwant's mouth)
CHARAN:	*thermometer* lagāiye.
	(after taking the thermometer from Kushwant's mouth)
CHARAN:	t^{h}oRā buxār hɛ...ye davāī din mẽ do bār lījiye... jaldī T^{h}īk ho jāẽge.

KUSHWANT:	*Doctor, sir, I have some fever.*
CHARAN:	*Since when [it is]?*

KUSHWANT:	*Since last night.*
CHARAN:	*[Do you have] a headache too?*
KUSHWANT:	*Yes.*
	(putting the thermometer in to Kushwant's mouth)
CHARAN:	*[You] have a little fever... please take this medicine twice a day. (lit. please take this medicine two times in a day) [You] will soon be fine.*

Vocabulary

DākTar	डाक्टर	Doctor
<sāhib>	साहिब	sir
muj^h ko	मुझ को	to me
kuc^h	कुछ	some
buxār (m.)	बुख़ार	fever
kab	कब	when
kal	कल	yesterday/tomorrow
rāt (f.)	रात	night
sir (m.)	सिर	head
dard (m.)	दर्द	pain
lagānā (+ne)	लगाना	to fix, to put into, to stick
lagāiye	लगाइये	please fix, put into, stick
thoRā (m. adj.)	थोड़ा	little
davāī (f.)	दवाई	medicine
do	दो	two
bār (f.)	बार	time, turn
lenā (+ne)	लेना	to take
lījiye	लीजिये	please take
jaldī	जल्दी	soon, quickly
ho jāẽge	हो जाएंगे	will become

Pronunciation

The word **sāhib** has other variants: **sāhab** and, more colloquially **sāb**.

Notes

'sahib'

The original meaning of the Hindi word **sāhib** is 'master', or 'lord'. This word is relatively more formal than the English 'sir'. In highly formal addresses, **sāhib** can be substituted for the Hindi **jī**. Usually it is used with last names and titles (e.g. **jaj** ('judge'); **sāhib**). The other two variants are **sāhab** and **sāb**.

'Since'

The Hindi equivalent of 'since' is the postposition **se**, 'from', e.g.

kab	**se**	**kal**	**rāt**	**se**
when	from	yesterday	night	from
Since when		Since last night		

'Tell me why' column

savāl: hindustānī auratẽ bindī kyõ lagātī hɛ̃?

question: Why do Indian women put a dot [on their foreheads]?

Circle the correct response:

(a) **siŋgār**	[for] make up
(b) **shādī-shudā hɛ**	[to show she] is married
(c) **donõ**	[for] both [reasons]

javāb: (c) **dono**
Answer: (c) both

Vocabulary

b^{h}ārat (m.)	भारत	India
hindustān (m.)	हिन्दुस्तान	India

b^{h}āratīya	भारतीय	Indian
hindustānī	हिन्दुस्तानी	Indian
bindī (f.)	बिन्दी	dot
kyõ	क्यों	why
savāl (m.)	सवाल	question
javāb (m.)	जवाब	answer
singār (m.)	सिंगार	make up
shādī-shudā	शादीशुदा	married
donõ	दोनों	both

Dialogue

Humour column

Two thieves are being interrogated in a Delhi police station. The inspector is interrogating the thieves and his assistant is taking notes

INSPECTOR: tumhārā nām?
THIEF: Banerjī.
(*now turning to the other*)
INSPECTOR: tumhārā nām?
THIEF: Chatterjī.
(*inspector talking to both thieves*)
INSPECTOR: corī karte ho aur nām ke sāt^{h} 'jī' lagāte ho.
(*turning to his assistant*)
INSPECTOR: in kā nām lik^{h}iye, Baner aur Chatter.

INSPECTOR: *Your name?*
THIEF: *Banerjii.*
(*Now turning to the other*)
INSPECTOR: *Your name?*
THIEF: *Chatterjii.*
(*Inspector talking to both thieves*)
INSPECTOR: *[You] steal and use jī with your name.*
(turning to his assistant)
Write their names, Baner and Chatter.

Note (cultural)

Most of the last names in the state of Bengal end with **-jī**. However, this **jī** is not an honorific as in Hindi.

Vocabulary

corī karnā (+ne)	चोरी करना	to steal
likʰnā (+ne)	लिखना	to write
likʰiye	लिखिये	please write
ke sāth	के साथ	with
lagānā (+ne)	लगाना	to attach, to fix

व्याकरण Grammar

cāhiye and verb agreement

The verb **cāhiye** is a frozen verb. It agrees neither with a subject nor with an object in Standard Hindi.

Simple present tense: subject–verb agreement

As pointed out earlier, the verb agrees with the subject in person, number and gender. The first part of the verb (called the 'main verb') agrees in number and gender and the second part of the verb (called the 'auxiliary verb') agrees in person and number with the subject.

flight	**kab**	**caltī**	**hɛ?**
flight (f.)	when	move/walk	is

When does the flight leave?
(lit. When does the flight walk/move?)

Object–verb agreement (postposition syndrome)

āp	**ko**	**sāRī**	**pasand**	**hɛ?**
you	to	saree (f.)	choice/liking	is

Do you like the saree?

Notice that, unlike in English, the Hindi verb does not agree with the subject. Instead, it agrees with the object. The rule of thumb is whenever the subject is followed by any postposition, the verb does not agree with it. Recall the 'have' construction:

mere	**cār**	**b^{h}āī**	**hẽ**
my	four	brothers(m. pl.)	are

I have four brothers.

In the above sentence, the verb form is not **hū̃**, indicating that the verb does not agree with the subject. The verb agrees with **b^{h}āī** 'brothers', and takes the plural ending.

mere	**pās**	**sāRiā̃**	**hẽ**
my	near	sarees	are

I have sarees.

Similarly, the verb agrees with **sāRiā̃** which is plural.

How about the expression 'I have some fever'?

muj^{h}	**ko**	**kuc^{h}**	**buxār**	**hɛ**
me	to	some	fever	is

I have some fever.

Once again the verb does not agree with the subject because it is followed by the postposition **ko**. Instead, it agrees with 'fever'.

In fact, if both the subject and the object are followed by a postposition, the verb never agrees with either. In such a case, it stays masculine singular (called 'default agreement').

When does the subject take a postposition?

Hindi verbs such as **pasand honā**, 'to like', and **cāhiye,** 'to want', select the **ko** postposition with their subject. You will have to remember which verb takes which postposition with the subject. For example, you will have to remember that the English verb 'to have' takes three different postpositions in the Hindi subject:

subject postposition	*possession*
ke pās	separable, transferable
kā, ke, kī	inseparable
ko	physical states (such as fever, headache)

अभ्यास Exercises

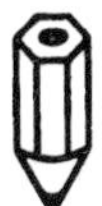

1

Translate the following sentences into Hindi according to the model: (Remember Hindi does not have articles. Therefore articles 'a', 'an' and 'the' cannot be translated into Hindi.)

Model

āp	**ko**	**kitāb cāhiye.**	You want a book
muj^{h}	**ko**	**kitāb cāhiye.**	I want a book

(a) I want a ticket for Jaipur.
(b) Do you want medicine?
(c) I want two houses.
(d) I want a car in my garage. (garage: use the English word)
(e) you want this beautiful saree. (beautiful: **sundar**)

2

Fill in the blanks by making an appropriate choice from the following Hindi subjects:

merā, mere, merī, mere pās, muj^{h} ko

(a) ———— ek bɛhɛn hɛ.
(b) ———— do b^{h}āī hɛ̃.
(c) ———— ek *computer* hɛ.
(d) ———— hāl T^{h}īk hɛ.
(e) ———— sir-dard hɛ.
(f) ———— kām cāhiye.
(g) ———— laRkā g^{h}ar letā hɛ.

3

Match the parts of the sentences given on the right with parts on the left to make a complete sentence:

muj^h ko	g^{h}ar mẽ kitne ādmī hɛ̃?
mere pās	kyā hɛ?
āp ke	buxār hɛ.
merā	āp ke liye hɛ.
ye *flight*	shɛhɛr bahut sundar hɛ.
is kā dām	rupiye hɛ̃.

4

Listen to what the waiter is saying on the recording and answer each question in Hindi. Your part of the answer is given below in English. After the beep you are given some time during which you should reply. After your reply, listen to the recorded correct version. To distinguish you from the waiter, your voice is represented by a female voice.
Use the glossary to familiarize yourself with food items.

WAITER:	
YOU:	(appropriate greeting)
WAITER:	
YOU:	*I am fine.*
WAITER:	
YOU:	*No, what is the special for lunch?*
WAITER:	
YOU:	*The vegetarian special is fine. What is it?*
WAITER:	
YOU:	*I need my daal a little spicy. (No need to translate 'my' here.)*
WAITER:	T^{h}īk hɛ.

4 आप के शौक क्या हैं? What are your hobbies?

By the end of this lesson you should be able to:

- talk about your and others' hobbies and interests
- talk about your and others' likes and dislikes
- manage some more expressions of health and ailments
- learn expressions with 'generally'
- form derived adjectives
- note asymmetry between English and Hindi expressions

Dialogue

What are your hobbies?

Professor James Jones, an internationally acclaimed expert on international advertising, is being profiled in an ethnic Indian newspaper from California. After talking about his research, the interviewer, Y. Malik, wants to report Professor Jones' interests to his readers

MALIK:	kyā āp b^{h}ārat jāte hɛ̃?
JONES:	jī hā̃, kaī bār.
MALIK:	āp ko hindustānī k^{h}ānā pasand hɛ?
JONES:	jī hā̃, tandūrī cikan *(tandoori chicken),* dosā *(dosa)...* vɛse samosā b^{h}ī bahut pasand hɛ.
MALIK:	āp ke shauk kyā kyā hɛ̃?
JONES:	muj^{h} ko tɛrne kā shauk hɛ, is ke alāvā b^{h}āratīya sangīt kā b^{h}ī shauk hɛ.
MALIK:	gāne kā b^{h}ī?
JONES:	zarūr, mere gāne se mere bacce hɛD fon (*head phone*) lagāte hɛ̃.
MALIK:	vāh! vāh!

MALIK:	*Do you visit India [quite frequently]?*
JONES:	*Yes, quite often* (lit. several times)
MALIK:	*Do you like Indian food?*
JONES:	*Yes, tandoori chicken, dosa...* *in addition [I] like samosa very much.*
MALIK:	*What are your hobbies?*
JONES:	*I am fond of swimming; besides this, [I] am fond of Indian music.*
MALIK:	*[Fond] of singing too?*
JONES:	*Of course; my children put on headphones [because of] my singing.* (lit. [my] children put on headphones from my singing.)
MALIK:	*Excellent!* (i.e. what an excellent sense of humour)

Vocabulary

jānā (**-ne**)	जाना	to go
kaī	कई	several
k^{h}ānā (m.); v. (**+ne**)	खाना	food (n.), to eat (v.)
vɛse	वैसे	otherwise, in addition
shauk (m.)	शौक	hobby, fondness, interest
tɛrnā (**-ne**)	तैरना	to swim
sangīt (m.)	संगीत	music
ke <alāvā>	के अलावा	besides, in addition to
gānā (m.), v. (**+ne**)	गाना	song (n.); to sing (v.)
zarūr	जरूर	of course, certainly
par	पर	on, at
vāh	वाह	ah! excellent! bravo!

Pronunciation

alāvā is also pronounced **ilāvā**.

Notes

The experiencer subject

The Hindi equivalent of the English 'I am fond of swimming' is:

muj^h	**ko**	**tɛrne**	**kā**	**shauk**	**hɛ**
me	to	swimming	of	fondness	is

In English 'I' is the subject of the sentence. However, in Hindi the equivalent of English 'I' is **muj^h ko** 'to me'. Such a distinction is very important in South Asian languages. The nominative subjects (e.g. 'I') denote volitional/deliberate subjects, as in the English 'I met him'. The experiencer (**ko**) subjects are non-volitional/non-deliberate, as in the English 'I ran into him'. In other words, expressions such as the following are expressed in a slightly different fashion:

English	*Hindi*
I am fond of swimming	The fondness of swimming is to me.
You want a ticket	The desire of a ticket is to you.
I have some fever.	Some fever is to me.
She likes this book.	The choice of this book is (i.e.experienced by) to her.

The experiencer subjects receive the **ko** position in Hindi. Recall the postposition syndrome of Hindi verbs which refuse to agree with any element that contains a postposition. Therefore, the 'to be' verb in Hindi does not agree with the experiential subject. For agreement purposes, **shauk**, 'fondness', becomes the element of agreement.

There are two other terms for experiential subjects – dative subjects and the **ko** subjects. We will call them experiential subjects in this book.

Verbal nouns (infinitive verbs)

Now observe the status of the word 'swimming' in the English sentence 'I am fond of swimming'.

The word 'swimming' functions like a noun in the above sentence. As a matter of fact, one can replace it with a noun, e.g. 'I am fond of chocolate'. The only difference is that 'chocolate' is a noun to begin with and 'swimming' is derived from the verb 'swim' by adding '-ing' to it. Such derived nouns are called verbal nouns or gerunds. We will call them verbal nouns throughout this book.

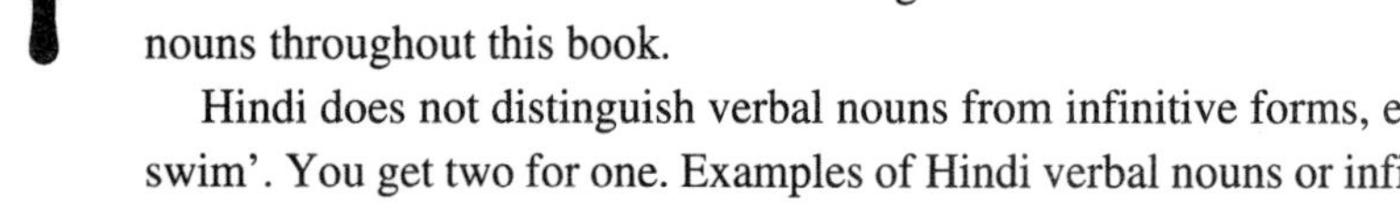

Hindi does not distinguish verbal nouns from infinitive forms, e.g. 'to swim'. You get two for one. Examples of Hindi verbal nouns or infinitive forms are given below:

verb stems		*verbal nouns/infinitive verbs*	
kar	do	**kar*nā***	to do/doing
ā	come	**ā*nā***	to come/coming
jā	go	**jā*nā***	to go/going
dek^h	see	**dek^h*nā***	to see/seeing
batā	tell	**batā*nā***	to tell/telling
tɛr	swim	**tɛr*nā***	to swim/swimming
k^{h}ā	eat	**k^{h}ā*nā***	to eat/eating

gā	sing	**gā*nā***	to sing/singing
lik^h	write	**lik^h*nā***	to write/writing

You must have discovered by now that the only counterpart of the English infinitive 'to' (as in 'to leave') and the verbal noun marker '-ing' (as in 'leaving') in Hindi is **-nā**. It is like English '-ing' in the sense that it follows a verbal stem rather than the English infinitive marker 'to', which precedes a verbal stem rather than follows it.

Oblique verbal nouns

Remember the peer-pressure influence of postposition on the words in a phrase? See the section on 'compound and oblique postposition' in case you have forgotten it.

Now consider the Hindi counterpart of the English 'of swimming' as in 'I am fond of swimming':

tɛrne	**kā**
swimming	of

Under the peer pressure from the postposition **kā**, the Hindi verbal noun **tɛrnā** 'swimming', undergoes a change exactly like the noun **laRkā**. Thus, it becomes **tɛrn*e***. Study the following sentences carefully. Do you see the same change?

muj^h	**ko**	**gāne**	**kā**	**shauk**	**hɛ**
me	to	singing	of	fondness	is

I am fond of singing.

muj^h	**ko**	**k^{h}āne**	**kā**	**shauk**	**hɛ**
me	to	eating	of	fondness	is

I am fond of eating.

āp	**ko**	***movie***	**dek^{h}ne**	**kā**	**shauk**	**hɛ**
you	to	film	seeing	of	fondness	is

You are fond of watching movies.

āp	**ko**	**k^{h}āne**	**kā**	**shauk**	**hɛ**
you	to	eating	of	fondness	is

You are fond of eating.

Yes–no questions with kyā

In Lesson 1, we saw how to change a statement into a yes–no question with merely a change in the intonation. One can also place **kyā** in front of a statement and form a yes–no question out of it. (Yes, it is the same word **kyā** that means 'what'!) Even if **kyā** is placed at the beginning of a sentence, the rising question intonation is imperative. Since it is difficult to show intonation in writing, **kyā** is more prevalent in written Hindi, and its omission is common in speech.

The statement

āp	**b^{h}ārat**	**jāte**	**hɛ̃**
you	India	go	are

You go to India.

becomes a yes–no question with the mere addition of **kyā** to the front of it:

kyā	**āp**	**b^{h}ārat**	**jāte**	**hɛ̃?**
[Q]	you	India	go	are

Do you go to India?

You do not need any verb forms at the beginning of a yes–no question in Hindi.

Reduplication of question words

The repetition of a question word is quite common in Hindi. In many languages of South East Asia repetition indicates plurality. Almost the same is true in Hindi.

āp ke	**shauk**	**kyā**	**kyā**	**hɛ̃?**
your	interests/hobbies	what	what	are

What are your interests/hobbies?

In English one cannot repeat the question word 'what' even if one knows that the person in question has many interests. However, the repetition of **kyā** has a 'listing' function, and thus asks the person to give a list of interests which are more than one according to the speaker's viewpoint.

Similarly, if someone asks in Hindi

āp	**kahā̃**	**kahā̃**	**jāte**	**hɛ̃?**
you	where	where	go	are

What places do you go to?

the speaker has reason to believe that the listener goes to more than one place.

Dialogue

Indian films

India is the largest producer of films in the world. More movies are produced by the Bombay film industry than by Hollywood. It is no wonder, therefore, that Hindi films dictate social conversation and are an excellent mode of expressing agreement–disagreement, liking–disliking and social and political thoughts. In this dialogue, the topic of discussion is Hindi films. The participants are Akbar Ali and Suhas Ranjan. Suhas saw a movie called **kʰalnāyak** *(villain), and he is ready to express his delight over it.*

SUHAS: *kʰalnāyak* merī man-pasand *film* hɛ.
AKBAR: vo kɛse?
SUHAS: gāne bahut accʰe hɛ̃, kahānī aur *acting* bʰī shāndār hɛ.
AKBAR: Hindi *filmẽ* to mujʰ ko bilkul pasand nahī̃. sirf *formula.*
SUHAS: lekin ye *formula* film nahī̃, is kā andāz aur hɛ.
AKBAR: sab Hindi *filmẽ* ek sī hotī hɛ̃, laRkā laRkī se miltā hɛ, donõ mẽ pyār hotā hɛ, pʰir kʰalnāyak ātā hɛ...
(Suhas interrupts)
SUHAS: aur donõ kī shādī hotī hɛ̃. jī nahī̃, ye ɛsī *film* nahī̃.
AKBAR: to pashcim kī nakal hogī.
SUHAS: to āp ke xayāl se sirf pashcimī *filmẽ* accʰī hotī hɛ̃?
AKBAR: mɛ̃ ye nahī̃ kɛhtā, purānī hindī *filme* accʰī hotī hɛ̃.
(Ajit Singh listens patiently to this discussion, and then intervenes :)
AJIT: *film* kī bāt par mahābʰārat kyõ?

SUHAS:	*Khalnaayak is my favourite movie.*
AKBAR:	*How come?*
SUHAS:	*[The] songs are very good; [the] plot and acting are great too.*
AKBAR:	*I dislike Hindi films – [They are] only formula [films].*
SUHAS:	*But this [one is] not a formula film. Its style is different.*
AKBAR:	*All Hindi films are alike – a boy meets a girl, both fall in love,* (lit. love happens in both) *then a villain comes...* *(Suhas interrupts)*
SUHAS:	*And both get married. No, this is not such a film.*
AKBAR:	*Then it must be an imitation of the West.*
SUHAS:	*[Do] you think only the Western films are [generally] good*? (lit. in your opinion only the Western films are *[*generally*]* good)
AKBAR:	*I do not say this; the old Hindi films are good.* *(Ajit Singh listens patiently to this discussion, then intervenes:)*
AJIT:	*Why [wage a] fierce battle over the topic of films?* (implying that the topic of films is not worthy of such a serious discussion)

Vocabulary

k^{h}alnāyak (m.)	खलनायक	villain
man-pasand (m.)	मनपसन्द	favourite
vo kɛse	वह कैसे	how come?
kahānī (f.)	कहानी	story
shāndār	शानदार	splendid, great
nāpasand	नापसन्द	dislike
aur	और	and, more, other, else
andāz (m.)	अन्दाज़	style
ek-sā	एक-सा	alike
pyār (m.)	प्यार	love
shādī (f.)	शादी	marriage
honā (-ne)	होना	to be
hotī hɛ	होती है	generally happens, generally takes place (sg.)
hotī hɛ̃	होती हैं	generally happen, generally take place (pl.)

hogī	होगी	will be
ɛsā	ऐसा	such
pashcim (m.)	पश्चिम	west
pashcimī	पश्चिमी	western
nakal (f.)	नकल	copy, fake, imitation
<xayāĩ> (m.)	ख़याल	opinion, viũw
sirā̃	सिर्फ़	onĩy
<kɛhnā> (+**nū̃**)	कहना	to say
purānā (m.)	पुराना	oĩĩ (inanimate)
bāt (f.)	बात	matter, conversation, topic
mahā	महा	great
mahābʰārat	महाभारत	one of the two greatest epics from Sanskrit; fierce battle (non-literal context)
kyõ	क्यों	why

Pronunciation

The Hindi word for 'opinion' can be pronounced and written in two ways: **xayāl** (ख़याल) and **xyāl** (ख़्याल). The latter form is more frequent among the educated; we will use this form here.

The verb is pronounced **kɛh** but is written **kah** (कह).

Notes

'Filmẽ'

The English word 'film' is assimilated into Hindi. It is no longer treated as a foreign word in the language; therefore, it has gender. From the plural ending **ẽ**, you can predict its gender. It is, of course, feminine. (It is treated as a feminine of the nerd category, i.e. marked.)

Negative marker: nahī̃, na

The short version of **nahī̃** 'not', is **nā**. It is written as **na** (न) but in pronunciation the vowel **a** becomes long, i.e. **ā**.

With polite orders **nā** is used instead of **nahī̃**. It is also used with subjunctives. Do not worry about subjunctives for now. However, observe the use of **nā** with polite orders ('polite imperatives').

nā	**dījiye**
not	please give

Please do not give.

It is also used with the word ***nā*pasand**, 'dislike'. However, with nouns it is not as productive as with polite commands. For example, you cannot make the word 'dissatisfaction' using **nā** with the Hindi equivalent of 'satisfaction'.

aur **as an adjective or adverb**

is kā	**andāz**	**aur**	**hɛ**
its	style	***different***	is

The conjunction 'and' in Hindi expresses a range of meanings when used either as a predicate as in the above sentence or as an adjective, as below:

aur	**cāy**	**dījiye**
more	tea	please give

Give me [some] more tea.

aur	**sāRī**	**dikʰāiye**
other	Saree	please show

Show [me some] other Saree.

aur is equivalent to the English words 'different', 'more', 'else'. Observe another frequent expression with **aur**:

aur	**kucʰ**	**cāhiye?**
else	some	want

Do you want something else?

Note the word–order difference.

ek-sā: **'same', 'alike'**

sab	**Hindi**	***filmẽ***	**ek**	**sī**	**hotī**	**hɛ̃**
all	Hindi	films	one	-ish	generic BE	are

Generally all Hindi films are alike.

The -**sā** is like the English '-ish' (e.g. boyish). Therefore the Hindi sentence is literally in English 'generally all Hindi films are one-ish'.

Generic 'be'

The sentence given above gives the generic meaning. There is no separate word exactly equivalent to the English 'generally' in the sentence. It is the verb **hotī** that contributes to this meaning. Compare this sentence with the following:

sab	**Hindi**	***filmẽ***	**ek**	**sī**	**hɛ̃**
all	Hindi	films	one	-ish	are

All Hindi films are alike.

which expresses the universal truth, i.e. without exception, Hindi films are alike.

Notice the slight difference in the two conjugations of **honā** 'to be':

generic							*non-generic*
ho	+	**t**	+	**ī**		**hɛ̃**	**hɛ̃**
be	+	aspect	+	number, gender		are	are

It is the generic conjugation that contains the English word 'generally' in Hindi. The verb agrees with the subject. Now observe the two other examples of the Generic BE in Hindi:

donõ	**mẽ**	**pyār**	**hotā**	**hɛ**
both	in	love (m.)	generic Be	is

Generally, love blossoms [lit.happens] between the two.

donõ	**kī**	**shādī**	**hotī**	**hɛ**
both	of	marriage (f.)	generic Be	is

Generally, their marriage [lit. the marriage of both] takes place.

hotā agrees with **pyār**, 'love', which is masculine singular in Hindi, whereas **hotī** agrees with **shādī** 'marriage'. Similarly, **hɛ** agrees with its respective subjects.

Direct object – ko or se

The English expression ‘boy meets girl’ in Hindi is

laRkā	**laRkī**	**se**	**miltā**	**hɛ**
boy	girl	with	meet	is

The boy meets the girl.

laRkā	**laRkī**	**ko**	**dek^{h}tā**	**hɛ**
boy	girl	object	see	is

The boy sees the girl.

Notice the English animate object ‘girl’ is followed by a postposition, either **se** or **ko**. Usually, the most frequent object postposition is **ko**. Only some verbs such as ‘meet’ and the verbs of communication (e.g. ask, say, speak, even love!!) are exceptions – they take **se** instead of **ko**.

Remember that only animate objects take **ko**. The inanimate objects do not take any object marker.

laRkā	**g^{h}ar**	**dek^{h}tā**	**hɛ**
boy	house	see	is

The boy sees the house.

The object **g^{h}ar**, ‘house’, is not marked with **ko** because it is an inanimate noun. More details are given in the Grammar section.

Word-for-word translation

pashcim	**kī**	**nakal**	**hogī**
west	of	copy	be-will

[The film] will be an imitation of the West.

The verb formation is as follows:

ho	+	**g**	+	**ī**
be	+	future tense	+	number gender

'Tell me why' column

savāl:	**kyā hindustānī log kɛhte hɛ̃:** 'I love you'.	
Question:	Do Indians say: 'I love you'?	
javāb/*answer:*	(a) **ā̃khõ se, lekin shabdõ se nahī̃.**	By eyes, but not in words.
	(b) **sirf shabdõ se.**	Only by words.

Circle the correct answer:

Tʰīk javāb: (a)
Correct answer: (a)

savāl:	**hindustānī shabdõ se kabʰī kɛhte hɛ̃:** 'I love you'.	
question:	Do Indians ever say: 'I love you'?	
javāb/*answer:*	(a) **kabʰī nahī̃**	Never
	(b) **kabʰī kabʰī**	Sometimes

Circle the correct answer:

Tʰīk javāb: (b)
Correct answer: (b)

savāl:	**hindustānī shabdõ se kɛse kɛhte hɛ̃:** 'I love you'.
question:	How do Indians say in words: 'I love you?'

Circle the correct answer:

javāb/*answer:*	(a) **mɛ̃ tum se pyār kartā hū̃.**	I love you.
	(b) **mujʰ ko tum se pyār hɛ.**	Love with you is to me.

Tʰīk javāb: (b)
Correct answer: (b)

Vocabulary

log (m.)	लोग	people
ãk^h (f.)	आँख	eye
ãk^{h}õ (f. oblique)	आँखों	eyes
se	से	from, with, by
shabda (m)	शब्द	word
shabdõ (m. oblique)	शब्दों	words
sirf	सिर्फ़	only
kab^{h}ī	कभी	ever
kab^{h}ī nahĩ	कभी नहीं	never
kab^{h}ī kab^{h}ī	कभी-कभी	sometimes

Note

'I love you' prohibition

The name for 'Cupid' is **kāma dev** ('the God Kāma'). **kāma dev** carried bows and arrows exactly the same way as 'Cupid' in the West. Did you notice the similarity between the two words – 'Cupid' and **kāma**? Although **kāma** has delighted Indians since approximately 3000 BC, Indians do not like to express 'I love you' exactly the same way as one does in English. Some expressions are better captured non-verbally than verbally. Such is the preference of Indians. If one has to say 'I love you' in words, it is better to express it by means of experiential subject construction rather than by the non-experiential deliberate subject. The following expression is almost vulgar:

mẽ	**tum**	**se**	**pyār**	**kartā**	**hū̃**
I	you	with	love	do	am

Therefore, the expression 'I love you' is best expressed in the following words:

muj^h	**ko**	**tum**	**se**	**pyār**	**hɛ**
me	to	you	with	love	is

However, nowadays among the educated and the younger generation the English expression 'I love you' is becoming quite popular.

Reduplication and pluralization

The reduplication of the adverb **kab^{h}ī,** 'ever', gives the plural meaning 'sometimes'.

Oblique plural nouns

Remember the peer influence. Notice the influence of a postposition on plural nouns.

	masculine		*feminine*	
singular	**shabda**	word	**ā̃k^{h}**	eye
plural	**shabda**	words	**ā̃k^{h}ẽ**	eyes

The plural nouns yield to the pressure of the postposition and take the ending **õ**.

shabdõ	**se**	by words
ā̃khõ	**se**	by eyes

Dialogue

What do you eat for breakfast?

Rakesh Seth visits his doctor and complains about his stomach problems. Apparently, he suffers from gas. The doctor begins by inquiring about his food habits

DOCTOR:	Rakesh jī, nāshte mẽ āp kyā k^{h}āte hɛ̃?
RAKESH:	das samose.
DOCTOR:	aur, kyā pīte hɛ̃?
RAKESH:	muj^{h}e cāy bahut acc^{h}ī lagtī hɛ. savere bahut cāy pītā hū̃.
Doctor:	āp ko sharīr kī bimārī nahī̃. dimāg kī bimārī hɛ. is liye āp *psychiatrist* ke pās jāiye.

DOCTOR:	*Rakesh jii, what do you eat for breakfast?* (lit. what do you eat in breakfast?)

RAKESH: *Ten samosas.*

DOCTOR: *And, what [do you] drink?*

RAKESH: *I like tea very much. [In the] morning [I] drink a lot of tea.* (lit. to me a lot of tea feels good)

DOCTOR: *You do not have [any] physical illness. [You] have a mental illness.*
Therefore, you [should] go to the psychiatrist.

Vocabulary

nāshtā (m.)	नाश्ता	breakfast
pīnā (+ne)	पीना	to drink
cāy (f.)	चाय	tea
muj^{h}e, muj^{h}ko	मुझे-मुझ को	(to) me
lagnā (+ko)	लगना	to seem, to be applied
acc^{h}ā lagnā (+ko)	अच्छा लगना	to like
saverā (m.)	सवेरा	morning
sharīr (m.)	शरीर	body
bimārī (f.)	बिमारी	illness
dimāg (m.)	दिमाग़	brain
isliye	इसलिये	therefore, so, thus, because of this

Notes

acc^{h}ā lagnā, 'to like'

You have already learned expressions such as

muj^{h}	**ko**	**cāy**	**pasand**	**hɛ.**
to	me	tea	liking	is

Another common way of saying the same expression is

muj^{h}	**ko**	**cāy**	**acc^{h}ī**	**lagtī**	**hɛ**
me	to	tea (f)	good	feel	is

I like tea. (lit. tea feels good to me)

'Ghost' postposition

The Hindi equivalent of 'breakfast' and 'morning' are **nāshtā** and **saverā**, respectively.

If we attach the postposition **mẽ**, 'in', to these nouns, the peer pressure of the postposition makes the nouns oblique.

unmarked nouns masculine	*oblique singular (unmarked nouns)*		
nāsht*ā*	**nāsht*e***	**mẽ**	for (in) breakfast
saver*ā*	**saver*e***	**mẽ**	in the morning

However, the English time expression 'in the morning' in Hindi is **savere**. Although the effect of the Hindi postposition is quite apparent, the postposition **mẽ** is dropped. The oblique form indicates its presence. Therefore, we call it the 'ghost' postposition.

Word-formation: derived adjectives

Do some detective work and see how English adjectives such as 'silken' are formed in Hindi:

nouns		*adjectives*	
resham	silk	**reshamī**	silken
sūt	cotton (crop)	**sūtī**	cotton (as in cotton clothes)
nakal	copy	**nakalī**	fake
asal	fact	**asalī**	real, genuine
hindustān	India	**hindustānī**	Indian
banāras	Banaras	**banārasī**	from Banaras (lit. Banarasian)

If you think that the addition of **ī** at the end of the word makes it an adjective, you are right. Notice that all nouns (and place names) end in a consonant. You cannot derive an adjective by adding **ī** to the nouns ending in a vowel. For example, the expressions 'from Delhi' or 'from Agra' cannot be reduced to one-word adjectives by the addition of **ī**. Only the postposition **se** can rescue the expressions.

Now, observe how the words such as 'physical', and 'mental' are formed in Hindi:

sharīr	**kī**	**bimārī**		**dimāg**	**kī**	**bimārī**
body	of	illness (f.)		brain	of	illness (f.)
Physical/bodily illness				Mental illness		

The possessive construction is used instead. Is it possible to reduce **sharīr kī** and **dimāg kī** to the **ī** types of adjectives? Yes, of course!

sharīrī	**bimārī**		**dimāgī**	**bimārī**
Physical/bodily illness			Mental illness	

Always remember, though, that word-formation can be quite tricky sometimes in human languages.

Go to the doctor

You have observed that English 'to' is usually **ko** in Hindi. However, the English expression 'go to the psychiatrist' is

Psychiatrist	**ke**	**pās**	**jāiye**
Psychiatrist	of	near	please go

In other words, the English expression is phrased as 'Please go near the psychiatrist'. The compound postposition **ke pās** is used instead of **ko**. Similarly, the Hindi sentence of 'Please go to the doctor' will be

dākTar	**ke**	**pās**	**jāiye**
Doctor	of	near	please go

Contractive e pronoun forms

muj^{h}e is the short form of **muj^h ko.**

अभ्यास Exercises

1

Choose any word from the following six columns and form at least seven sentences. You may choose a word from the columns as many times as you like.

muj^{h} ko	paR^{h}nā	kā	shauk	hɛ
āp	gāne	ke	pasand	hɛ̃
	kyā			
	tɛrne			
	k^{h}āne			
	kyā-kyā			

2

Read the following statements and then answer the question about each statement. Your answer should be in Hindi.

(a) statement : John is fond of dancing and singing. (Hint: dancing = nācnā)
question: gāne ke alāvā John ko kyā pasand hɛ?
answer:

(b) statement: Judy loves to write stories and poems. (hint: poem: kavitā (f.))
question: Judy ko kyā kyā shauk hɛ̃?
answer:

(c) Statement: Ramesh's likes and dislikes are given below:

likes	*dislikes*
to eat Samosa	to eat chicken
vegetarian food	non-vegetarian
stories	poems
Indian music	country music

question: Ramesh ko kyā kyā nāpasand hɛ/hɛ̃?
answer:

question: Ramesh ko kyā kyā pasand hɛ/hɛ̃?
answer:

3

There are two possible interpretations of the following sentences. Uncover their ambiguity by translating them into English.

(a) John ko k^{h}ānā pasand hɛ.
(b) John ko gānā pasand hɛ.

4

Write two things children do not like about their parents.

5

How many ways can you find to say 'I like swimming' in Hindi?

6

If you have the recording, circle the items the speaker's daughter likes:

(a) cats
(b) dogs
(c) spicy foods
(d) cricket (game)
(e) b^{h}aratnātyam
(f) rock music

5 छुट्टियों में क्या करेंगे?
What would you do during the break?

By the end of this lesson you should be able to:

- talk about your own and others' plans
- compare people and objects
- develop paraphrasing skills
- use desiratives
- use future tense
- use capabilitatives
- use progressive tense forms

Dialogue

I want to go to India

Suman Kumar is planning to spend his Christmas vacation in India. He knows that December and January are excellent months to visit India. Summers are hot, and they are followed by monsoons. So he goes to an ethnic travel agent in Toronto to make his travel plans

TRAVEL AGENT: kyā sevā kar saktī hū̃?
SUMAN: hindustān ke liye TikaT [*ticket*] cāhiye.
TRAVEL AGENT: sirf apne liye?
SUMAN: parivār ke liye.
TRAVEL AGENT: kitne log hɛ̃?
SUMAN: cār–do baRe aur do bacce.
TRAVEL AGENT: baccõ kī umar bārā se kam hɛ?
SUMAN: laRkī kī umar bārā hɛ aur laRke kī che.
TRAVEL AGENT: kab jānā cāhte hɛ̃?
SUMAN: *Christmas* mẽ.
TRAVEL AGENT: *peak season* hɛ, TikaT [*ticket*] mɛhɛ̃gī hogī.
SUMAN: koī bāt nahī̃.

TRAVEL AGENT: *What can I do [for you]* (lit. what service can I do)?
SUMAN: *I need a ticket for India.*
TRAVEL AGENT: *Only for yourself?*
SUMAN: *For the family.*
TRAVEL AGENT: *How many people are* [*there in the family*]*?*
SUMAN: *Four – two adults and two children.*
TRAVEL AGENT: *Is the age of the children less than twelve?*
SUMAN: *The girl is twelve and the boy (is) six* (lit. the age of the girl is twelve and [the age] of the boy [is] six).
TRAVEL AGENT: *When do [you] want to go?*
SUMAN: *During Christmas.*
TRAVEL AGENT: *[It is the] peak season. The ticket will be expensive.*
SUMAN: *It does not matter* (lit. none matter).

Vocabulary

sevā (f.)	सेवा	service
saknā	सकना	can, be able to
apnā	अपना	one's own
parivār (m.)	परिवार	family
<umar> (f.)	उमर	age
se	से	than, from, by
kam	कम	less
cāhnā	चाहना	to want
mẽ	में	in, during
<mɛhẽgā> (m., adj.)	महँगा	expensive
koī	कोई	some, any, someone, anyone

Pronunciation

The word for 'age' is pronounced and written in two ways: **umar** (उमर) and **umra** (उम्र).

The Hindi word **mẽhẽgā** is written as **mahãgā** (महँगा).

Notes

saknā **'can'**

The expression 'What can I do [for you]' is expressed as

mɛ̃	**kyā**	**sevā**	**kar**	**saktī**	**hū̃?**
I (f., sg.)	what	service	do	can	am

Notice the placement of **saknā** 'can/to be able to', which is like any other verb in Hindi. It is conjugated in different tenses.

Consider one more example:

mɛ̃	**bol**	**saktā**	**hū̃.**
I (m., sg.)	talk	can	am

I can talk.

The form **saktā hū̃** agrees with the subject and the real verb **bol,** 'talk' precedes **saktā hū̃**.

apnā 'one's own'

apnā is a possessive pronoun which means 'one's own'. The English possessive pronouns can either be translated as regular possessives or with the **apnā** form. Observe the distinction Hindi makes in this regard.

merā	**nām**	**John**	**hɛ**
my	name	John	is

My name is John.

and

mɛ̃	**apnā**	**nām**	**lik^{h}tā**	**hū̃.**
I	own	name	write	am

I write my name.

In other words, the English phrase 'my' can be said in two ways in Hindi: **merā** or **apnā**. The possessive pronoun does not show any relationship to the subject of the sentence, whereas **apnā** shows this relationship. In the second sentence, the possessed thing, **merā nām,** belongs to the subject of the sentence; therefore **merā** changes to **apnā**. In the first sentence, however, the subject, **nām**, is part of the possessed element. The rule-of-thumb is if in a simple clause you come across the following situation *in the same clause*, the possessive pronoun becomes **apnā**.

subject	*possessive*	*possessive changes to*
mɛ̃	**merā**	**apnā**
ham	**hamārā**	**apnā**
tū	**terā**	**apnā**
tum	**tumhārā**	**apnā**
āp	**āp kā**	**apnā**
vo	**us kā**	**apnā** (**vo...us kā** must refer to the same person)
ve	**un kā**	**apnā** (**ve...un kā** must have the same referent)

Prediction

In Hindi **mɛ̃** ... **merā** type of combinations cannot be found in a simple sentence. In the third person, **vo** ... **us kā (ve...un kā)** combination cannot occur if the possessed thing and the possessor subject refer to the same person.

vo	**apnā**	**kām**	**kartā**	**hɛ**
he	own	job	do	is

He [John] does his [John's] work.

However, if in the English sentence,'he' refers to John and 'his' refers to Bill, then **apnā** will not be used. When the subject possessor and the possessed thing are not identical, possessive pronouns will occur.

vo	**us kā**	**kām**	**kartā**	**hɛ**
he	his	job	do	is

He [John] does his [Bill's] work.

apnā is masculine singular in form. Its two other number gender variants are: **apne** (m., pl.) and **apnī** (f.). In the dialogue:

sirf	**apne**	**liye?**
only	own	for

the subject **āp** is implied. Because of the following postposition, **apnā** becomes oblique.

Comparative/superlative se, 'than'

While learning Hindi, you do not need to memorize the different forms such as 'good, better, best'. Only the **se** postposition is used with the standard of comparison.

baccõ	**kī**	**umar**	**bārā**	**se**	**kam**	**hɛ**
children	of	age (f.)	twelve	than	less	is

The children's age is less than twelve.

The **se** is used after the standard/object of comparison, which is 'twelve'. Also, the adjective follows the postposition. Similarly,

John	**rām**	**se**	**acc^{h}ā**	**hɛ**
John	Ram	than	good	is

John is better than Ram.

Thus, the word of the comparative phrase 'better than Ram' is just reversed in Hindi, i.e. Ram than good.

The superlative degree is expressed by choosing **sab**, 'all' as the object of comparison. The English sentence 'John is best' will be expressed as 'John is good than all,' as in

John	**sab**	**se**	**acc^{h}ā**	**hɛ**
John	all	than	good	is

John is the best.

Again notice the Hindi word order – all than good.

The adjective can be further modified by words indicating degree, such as **zyādā,** 'more':

John	**rām**	**se**	**zyādā**	**acc^{h}ā**	**hɛ**
John	Ram	than	more	good	is

John is much better than Ram.

cāhnā, **'to want'**

Notice the word order of the English sentence 'you want to go'.

āp	**jānā**	**cāhte**	**hɛ̃**
you	to go	want	are

You want to go.

The infinitive form 'to go' precedes the verb **cāhnā,** 'to want'. The verb **cāhnā** receives tense conjugation. Study one more example:

vo	**nācnā**	**cāhtī**	**hɛ**
she	to dance	want	is

She wants to dance.

Dialogue

Thinking about India

On the same day Suman Kumar runs into his colleague Al Nasiri. They start talking about the Christmas break. Al catches him off-guard, lost in his own world. He draws Suman's attention by saying

Al:	b^{h}aī, kis duniyā mẽ ho? kyā soc rahe ho?
Suman:	hindustān ke bāre mẽ soc rahā thā.
Al:	kyõ, sab T^{h}īk hɛ na?
Suman:	hā̃, *Christmas break* mẽ hindustān jā rahe hɛ̃.
Al:	akele yā parivār ke sāt^{h}?
Suman:	bībī bacce yānī ki pūrī Trāib *(tribe)* ke sāt^{h}.
Al:	hā̃ b^{h}āī, nahī̃ to bībī talāk ke liye kahegī. kahā̃ jāoge?
Suman:	dillī, āgrā aur jaipur.
Al:	āgrā kɛse jāoge?
Suman:	havāī jahāz se.
Al:	havāī jahāz se jānā bekār hɛ.
Suman:	kyõ?
Al:	havāī jahāz se gāRī mẽ kam samaya lagtā hɛ.

Al:	*Well, in what world are you? What are you thinking?*
Suman:	*I was thinking about India.*
Al:	*Why, everything is all right, isn't it?*
Suman:	*Yes [everything is fine]; [we] are going to India during the Christmas break.*
Al:	*Alone or with the family?*
Suman:	*Wife, children, that is, with the whole tribe.*
Al:	*Yes, brother; otherwise, [your] wife will ask for a divorce. Where will [you] go?*
Suman:	*Delhi, Agra and Jaipur.*
Al:	*How will [you] go to Agra?*
Suman:	*By plane.*
Al:	*[It is] useless to go to Agra by plane.*
Suman:	*Why?*
Al:	*[It] takes less time [to go to Agra] in the train than by plane.*

Vocabulary

bʰaī	भई	hey, well (excl.)
kis	किस	which
duniyā (f.)	दुनिया	world
socnā (-ne)	सोचना	to think
ke bāre mẽ	के बारे में	about, concerning
tʰā	था	was
sab	सब	all
akelā (m., adj.)	अकेला	alone
parivār (m.)	परिवार	family
ke sātʰ	के साथ	with, together
bībī (f.)	बीबी	wife
yānī	यानी	that is, in other words
nahī̃ to	नहीं तो	otherwise
talāk (m.)	तलाक	divorce
havā (f.)	हवा	air, wind
jahāz (m.)	जहाज़	a ship, vessel, plane
bekār	बेकार	useless
gāRī (f.)	गाड़ी	train, vehicle, cart
samaya (m.)	समय	time
lagnā (-ne)	लगना	to take, to cost

Notes

bʰaī, 'Hey' vs. bʰāī, 'Brother'

The short vs. long vowel can make a considerable difference in meaning. The case in point is the contrast between **bʰ*a*ī** and **bʰ*ā*ī**. The former is used as an exclamatory marker to express surprise, happiness, etc. The latter (**bʰ*ā*ī**) is a kinship term, and you will recall that it means 'brother'. However, in the Hindi-speaking community, it can be used as an address for a friend, stranger, shopkeeper, both for young and old. Sometimes in very informal circumstances, it can be used even for females who are familiar to the speaker. Our advice is not to use it for females. In non-relationship situations, its main function is as an attention-getter while establishing a social relationship by using a kinship word for a person who is not related to the speaker. Therefore, it carries some sense of affection. The attention-getters such as **suniye** and **kahiye** are neutral in terms of social relationship.

The feminine counterpart of **b^h^āī** is **bɛhɛn**. The honorific particle **jī** is used with **bɛhɛn** more frequently than with **b^h^āī**. Believe it or not, women are very much respected and cared about (sometimes more than men) in very large segments of the South Asia Society! Of course, South Asia is not a perfect society.

kyā 'what', kaun, 'who', and kis, 'what, who'

kis is the oblique singular counterpart of both **kyā**, 'what' and **kaun**, 'who'. (Remember the 'peer pressure' phenomenon.)

kyā duniyā	what world
kis duniyā mẽ	in what world

For details see the grammar section.

Compound postpositions

You have come across postpositions of one and two elements. Here is the compound postposition consisting of three elements. Remember you will not find any compound postposition with **kā**.

ke bāre mẽ	about, concerning (lit. with regard to)

Observe the usage of this postposition:

hindustān ke bāre mẽ	about India
kahānī ke bāre mẽ	about the story
laRkõ ke bāre mẽ	about the boys (**laRkõ** = boys, oblique plural)

Past tense: 'to be' verb

The Hindi forms for English 'was' and 'were' are the following four:

	masculine		*feminine*	
singular	**t^{h}ā** था	was	**t^{h}ī** थी	was
plural	**t^{h}e** थे	were	**t^{h}1** थी	were

As in English, these forms agree with their subject. The only difference is that in Hindi they agree in gender as well as number.

Progressives

So far you have observed that Hindi verbs either consists of one unit (e.g. polite commands) or two units (the simple present). Now you have an opportunity to familiarize yourself with a verb that has three units.

mẽ	**hindustān**	**ke bāre mẽ**	***soc***	***rahā***	***t^{h}ā***
I	India	about	think	-ing	was

I was thinking about India.

The Hindi equivalent of English ‘was thinking’ is ***soc rahā t^{h}ā***. The Hindi verb is broken into three units: ‘verb stem’ (**soc**), ‘ing’ (**rahā**), ‘was’ (**t^{h}ā**). The only difference between Hindi and English is that in Hindi ‘-ing’ is a separate word and the auxiliary ‘was’ ends the verbal string. Sentences such as the above are called either ‘past progressive’ or ‘past continuous’. We will call them *past progressive.*

Like an adjective ending in **-ā**, **rahā** has three variants: **rahā** (masculine singular), **rahe** (masculine plural) and **rahī** (feminine).

In order to form the *present progressive* as in English the auxiliary ‘was’ is replaced by present forms such as ‘am’, ‘is’, ‘are’. The same is true in Hindi. Just substitute the present ‘to be’ forms and you will get the present progressive verb form. For instance:

mẽ	**hindustān**	**ke bāre mẽ**	**soc**	**rahā**	**hū̃**
I	India	about	think	ing	am

I am thinking about India.

Future

The English future tense consists of two verbal units, whereas it is only one unit in Hindi. You came across an example of a Hindi future tense in Lesson 3:

ham	**p^{h}ir**	**milẽge**
we	again	meet-will

We will meet again.

tum	**kahā̃**	**jāoge?**
you	where	go-will

Where will you go?

The Hindi verb forms can be broken up in the following manner:

mil	+	**ẽ**	+	**g**	+	**e**
stem	+ person (**āp**)		+ future 'will'		+ number-gender (m. pl.)	

jā	+	**o**	+	**g**	+	**e**
stem	+ person (**tum**)		+ future 'will'		+ number-gender (m. pl.)	

jā	+	**ū̃**	+	**g**	+	**ī**
stem	+ person (**mɛ̃**)		+ future 'will'		+ number-gender (f. sg./pl.)	

The ghost postposition ko, 'to', with locations

āp	***Christmas break***	**mẽ**	**hindustān**	**jā**	**rahe**	**hɛ̃**
you	Christmas break	in	India	go	ing	are

You are going to India during the Christmas break.

Although the postposition **ko** is dropped in Hindi, this is the ghost postposition we referred to in the earlier chapter. Recall the discussion of the phrase 'in the morning', **savere**. If we place, say, **apnā** 'own' before 'India', the ghost postposition will change it to its oblique form – **apne**.

Dialogue

The train to Agra

Al Nasiri and Suman Kumar continue to discuss the best ways of getting to Agra. Finally, Al convinces Suman to take a train.

AL:	āgrā ke liye sab se acc^{h}ī gāRī Taj Express hɛ.
SUMAN:	Taj Express kahā̃ se caltī hɛ?
AL:	nayī dillī se, savere sāt baje.
SUMAN:	aur āne ke liye?
AL:	vahī gāRī shām ko vāpas ātī hɛ.
SUMAN:	lekin ham log rāt ko tāj mɛhɛl dek^{h}nā cāhte hɛ̃.
AL:	hā̃, tāj rāt ko aur b^{h}ī sundar lagtā hɛ.
SUMAN:	to ek rāt āgrā rukẽge, agle din dillī lauTẽge.
AL:	cā̃ndnī rāt, tāj mɛhɛl aur bībī sāt^{h}... mazā kījiye.

AL:	*The best train for Agra is the Taj Express.*
SUMAN:	*Where does the Taj Express leave from?*
AL:	*From New Delhi, [at] seven o'clock in the morning.*
SUMAN:	*And to come [back]?*
AL:	*The same train comes back [to New Delhi] in the evening.*
SUMAN:	*But we people want to see Taj Mahal at night.*
AL:	*Yes, Taj looks even more beautiful at night.*
SUMAN:	*Then, we will stay [for a] night [in] Agra; the next day [we] will return to Delhi.*
AL:	*The moonlit night, Taj Mahal and with (your) wife...[you] enjoy [both].*

Vocabulary

nayā (m., adj.)	नया	new
sāt baje	सात बजे	seven o'clock (see English–Hindi glossary for more details on time, fractions etc.)
ānā (**-ne**)	आना	to come
vah <vo>	वह	that, he, she
vahī (**vah+hī**)	वही	same, that very
shām (f.)	शाम	evening
vāpas	वापस	back
vāpas ānā (**-nū̃**)	वापस आना	to come back
rāt (f.)	रात	night
tāj (m.)	ताज	crown
mɛhɛl (m.)	महल	palace
tāj mɛhɛl	ताज महल	the Taj Mahal

aur bʰī	और भी	even more
lagnā (+ko)	लगना	to seem, to appear
ruknā (-ne)	रुकना	to stop
aglā (m., adj.)	अगला	next
din (m.)	दिन	day
lauTnā (-ne)	लौटना	to return, to come back
cā̃d (m.)	चाँद	moon
cā̃dnī	चाँदनी	moonlit
mazā karnā (+ne)	मज़ा करना	to enjoy

Pronunciation

mɛhɛl is written as **mahal**.

Notes

Time expressions

savere	in the morning
dopɛhɛr ko	at noon
shām ko	in the evening
rāt ko	at night

With the exception of **savere**, the **ko** postposition is uniformly used with other time adverbs. **savere** has the ghost postposition **ko**. (See also p. 317.)

Emphatic particle hī – 'only, right, very'

The particle of exclusion is **hī**, 'only'. The English word 'same' is equivalent to 'that very' in Hindi. It can be used with nouns, pronouns and adverbs. It is usually used as a separate word except with those pronouns and adverbs ending in **-h**. It undergoes contraction with **-h** ending pronouns and adverbs (assuming the final vowel is dropped in adverbs).

pronoun			*particle*		*emphatic pronoun*	
vah	he/she/ that	+	**hī**	=	**vahī**	that very, same
yah	this	+	**hī**	=	**yahī**	this very

adverbs			*particle*		*emphatic adverb*	
vahā̃	there	+	**hī**	=	**vahī̃**	right there
yahā̃	here	+	**hī**	=	**yahī̃**	right here

Irregular commands

Remember that polite commands are formed by adding **-iye** to a stem. The following four stems are irregular because the stem undergoes a change with **-iye**:

stem		*irregular stem*	*polite command*	
kar	do	**kīj**	**kīj-iye**	please do
de	give	**dīj**	**dīj-iye**	please give
le	take	**līj**	**līj-iye**	please take
pī	drink	**pīj**	**pīj-iye**	please drink

Reading practice

An ancient folk tale : *'To build castles in the air'*

This is a folk story of a poor Brahmin from the ancient times. He was a miser and used to save flour which he got from his clients in a ceramic pitcher. He used to guard the pitcher jealously and keep it next to his bed. One day he begins to day-dream.

(1) ek din desh mẽ akāl paRegā.
(2) mɛ̃ āTā becū̃gā.
(3) aur kuc^{h} jānvar xarīdū̃gā.
(4) to mɛ̃ amīr banū̃gā.
(5) ek din merī shādī hogī.
(6) p^{h}ir merā baccā hogā.
(7) ab mɛ̃ ārām se kitābẽ paR^{h}ū̃gā.
(8) baccā mere pās āyegā.

(At this point he continues to dream that he will ask his wife to take away the child. Because she is busy she won't be able to hear him; he will therefore kick her. Thinking this, he actually kicks out and hits the pitcher with his leg. The pitcher falls down and breaks. With this, the castle he built in the air vanishes.)

(1) *One day [there] will be a famine in the country.*
(2) *I will sell the flour.*
(3) *And will buy some animals.*
(4) *Then I will become rich.*
(5) *One day my marriage will occur.* (lit. my marriage will take place)
(6) *Then I will have a child.* (lit. my child will happen)
(7) *Now, I will read books comfortably.*
(8) *The child will come to me.* (lit. come near me)

Vocabulary

desh (m.)	देश	country
akāl paRnā	अकाल पड़ना	famine to occur
āTā (m.)	आटा	flour
becnā (+ne)	बेचना	to sell
kuc^h	कुछ	some
jānvar (m.)	जानवर	animal
xarīdnā (+ne)	ख़रीदना	to buy
amīr	अमीर	rich
bannā (-ne)	बनना	to become
ārām (m.)	आराम	comfort
paR^{h}nā (+/-ne)	पढ़ना	to study, to read

अभ्यास Exercises

You land at the New Delhi airport and, on arrival at immigration, the officer asks you the following questions in Hindi. First, translate the questions into English in the space given next to the question, then, answer the questions in Hindi.

OFFICER:	āp kā nām?	________
YOU:		
OFFICER:	āp b^hārat mẽ kitne din rahẽge?	________
YOU:		
OFFICER:	kahā̃-kahā̃ jāẽge?	________
YOU:		
OFFICER:	hindustān mẽ patā kyā hɛ?	________
YOU:		
OFFICER:	vāpas kab jāẽge?	________
YOU:		
OFFICER:	koī *illegal* sāmān hɛ?	________
YOU:		

2

There are a few incorrect verbs in the following passage. Pick them out and replace them with the right verbs.

mɛ̃ āp ke liye kyā karnā saktā hɛ? ham āgrā jā cāhtā hɛ. āgrā kitnī dūr hɛ̃? bahut dūr nahī̃, lekin āp kab jā rahā hɛ? ham kal jāegā. gāRī subah dillī se calte hɛ. āp gāRī se jā cāhtā hɛ̃?

3

The sentences in the following letter are in the wrong order. Rearrange them in the correct order.

Priya Rakesh:
tumhārā milā xat. paR^h kar xushī huī. tum rahe kab ā ho? kal mɛ̃ *Chicago* hū̃ jā rahā. *Chicago* bahut shɛhɛr hɛ baRā. mɛ̃ *Chicago* se hawāī jahāz (*aeroplane*) jāū̃gā. lekin mɛ̃ jānā cāhtā hawāī jahāz se nahī̃ hū̃. gāRī muj^he pasand hɛ se zyāda hawāī jahāz. bākī sab hɛ T^hīk.

tumhāra dost,

Rājīv.

4

Here are the answers. What were the questions?
(Wherever needed, the object of the inquiry is underlined.)

Q:
A: mɛ̃ <u>*Chicago*</u> jā rahī hū̃.

Q:
A: mɛ̃ yahā̃ <u>*sāt din*</u> rahū̃gā.

Q:
A: mɛ̃ <u>*apnā*</u> kām kar rahā hū̃.

Q:
A: jī hā̃, <u>*cāy*</u> bahut pasand hɛ.

Q:
A: mere <u>*cār bʰāī*</u> hɛ̃.

5

If you won a million dollars, what would you do? Use the following words or phrases.

king	become crazy
queen	buy diamonds for my wife/girlfriend
buy a yacht, Rolls Royce	return to the job
travel around the world	with happiness

6

This fast-talking robot is programmed for the 'me' generation. Could you change his speech to the 'we' generation. Note the gender of Robot is masculine in Hindi.

mɛ̃ *robot* hū̃. mɛ̃ *California* se hū̃. mɛ̃ hindī bol saktā hū̃. mɛ̃ hindī samajʰ bʰī saktā hū̃. mɛ̃ hindī gāne gā saktā hū̃. merī *memory* bahut baRī hɛ. mɛ̃ har savāl pūcʰ saktā hū̃ aur har javāb de saktā hū̃. yānī har kām kar saktā hū̃. mɛ̃ hameshā kām kar saktā hū̃. mɛ̃ kabʰī nahī̃ tʰaktā hū̃. mere pās har savāl kā javāb hɛ. lekin masāledār kʰānā nahī̃ kʰā saktā.

7

Listen to Mr Smith's comments about a forthcoming visit to North America and then answer the following questions in Hindi:

(a) Mr. Smith *America* kab jāẽge?
(b) ve kaun sī *airline* se *New York* jāẽge?
(c) kyā ve apne parivār ke sāth *New York* pahũcẽge?
(d) ve *Disney World* kyõ jānā cāhte hɛ̃?
(e) ve *Disney World* mẽ kitnẽ din rahẽge?

6 कल क्या किया ? What did you do yesterday?

By the end of this lesson you should be able to:

- talk about past events/actions
- use time adverbials with full clauses
- talk about topics dealing with 'lost and found'
- learn to express sequential actions
- learn more about paraphrasing devices
- employ some more very frequent expressions

Dialogue

Someone has picked my pocket

Aditi Chatterji is coming to America for graduate studies. She lands at Kennedy Airport. As she is cleared from customs and is ready to take her flight to Chicago, she gets the horrifying feeling that her passport and traveller's cheques have been stolen. She calls her family in Calcutta. She gets in touch with her father, Suman Chatterji, who is anxiously waiting for news of her arrival in the USA.

SUMAN:	hɛllo.
ADITI:	hɛllo, DɛD, mɛ̃ Aditi bol rahī hū̃.
SUMAN:	kahā̃ se bol rahī ho?
ADITI:	New York se.
SUMAN:	kyõ, $ab^{h}ī$ Chicago nahī̃ pahū̃cī?
ADITI:	nahī̃.
SUMAN:	kyā bāt hɛ? pareshān lag rahī ho. sab $T^{h}īk$-$T^{h}āk$ hɛ na?
ADITI:	mɛ̃ to $T^{h}ik$ hū̃, lekin merā *passport*, mere pɛse aur Trɛvlarz (*traveller's*) *cheques* gum ho gaye.
SUMAN:	kyā!
ADITI:	kisī ne merī jeb kāTī – ɛsā lagtā hɛ.
SUMAN:	sac!
ADITI:	hā̃.

ADITI:	*Hello, Dad, this is Aditi calling.* (lit. I am Aditi speaking)
SUMAN:	*Where are you calling from?*
ADITI:	*From New York.*
SUMAN:	*Hey, you have not reached Chicago yet?* (lit. why, you did not reach Chicago yet?)
ADITI:	*No.*
SUMAN:	*What is the matter?* [*You*] *seem to be upset. Everything is fine, isn't it?*
ADITI:	*As regards me, I am fine, but my passport, money and traveller's cheques are lost.*
SUMAN:	*What !* (lit. What! I do not believe it!)
ADITI:	*Someone picked my pocket – it appears.*

SUMAN:	*Is that right!* (lit. Truth!)
ADITI:	*Yes.*

Vocabulary

hɛllo	हैलो	Hello
abʰī	अभी	right now
pahũcnā (-ne)	पहुँचना	to reach, arrive
bāt (f)	बात	matter
kyā bāt hɛ?	क्या बात है?	What is the matter?
pareshān (adj.)	परेशान	troubled
sab	सब	all
Tʰīk-Tʰāk	ठीक-ठाक	fine, hale and hearty
to (particle)	तो	then, as regards
gumnā (-ne)	गुमना	to be lost
gaye (m., pl.)	गये	went
kyā!	क्या!	What! I do not believe it!
kisī	किसी	someone
ne	ने	agent marker in the past tense
jeb (f.)	जेब	pocket
kāTnā (+ne)	काटना	to cut
jeb kāTnā	जेब काटना	to pick pocket
ɛsā	ऐसा	such, it
sac!	सच	Truth! It can't be true!

Notes

The perfective form (the simple past)

We introduced the simple past tense forms of the verb 'to be'. Now, observe the Hindi equivalent of the English, 'Didn't [you] reach Chicago?':

(tum)	**abʰī**	**Chicago**	**nahī̃**	**pahũcī̃?**
you	right now	Chicago	not	reached (f.pl.)

Although the Hindi verb **pahũcĩ** is translated as 'reached', it has no intrinsic tense reference as words such as **hɛ**, 'is', and **thā**, 'was'. It simply shows that the action or situation is completed. The act may be completed in present, past or future tense. Usually, adverbs such as 'yesterday' and 'tomorrow' and the verbal form of the 'to be' verb provide the tense information.

Now recall the suffixes given in Magic Key 1 and do some detective work regarding the feminine forms.

verb stem	*perfective form*	
pahũc reach	**pahũcā**	masculine singular
	pahũce	masculine plural
	pahũcī	feminine singular
	pahũcĩ	feminine plural

Yes, feminine plural forms for the first time compete with masculine forms and have a distinct plural identity. The Hindi pronoun **tum** always takes the plural form.

Now observe another perfective form from the above dialogue:

kisī	**ne**	**merī**	**jeb**	**kāTī**
someone	agent	my	pocket (f.)	cut (f. sg.)

Someone picked my pocket. (lit. someone cut my pocket)

You will notice two things different from the previous sentence: (1) the use of the postposition **ne**, and (2) the verb agreement. The postposition **ne** occurs with those subjects that have transitive verbs in the perfective form. Notice that verbs such as 'come', 'go', and 'reach' are intransitive, whereas verbs such as 'cut', 'write', 'do', and 'buy' are transitive. The Hindi word for English 'someone' is **koī**. Because of the postposition **ne**, the subject pronoun **koī** becomes **kisī**. In other words, the peer pressure makes it oblique. Also, recall that the verb does not agree with those subjects followed by a postposition. Therefore, the verb does not agree with the subject; instead, it agrees with the object **jeb**, 'pocket', which is feminine singular in Hindi. For details about the perfective forms see the grammar section.

Because the perfectives mark a situation or action as *completed*, they are usually associated with the past tense.

'Went' – an exception in verb form

The English verb 'to go' is an exception in the past tense form – 'went' rather than 'goed'. Similarly, it is also irregular in Hindi in the perfective form. Here are the Hindi equivalents of the English verb form 'went':

verb stem	*perfective form*	
jā go	**gayā**	went (masculine singular)
	gaye	went (masculine plural)
	gayī	went (feminine singular)
	gayl	went (feminine plural)

Because Hindi and English belong to the same language family, what is remarkable is that the English 'g' of the verb stem 'go' shows up in the Hindi irregular form and then it takes the Hindi perfective suffixes. The sound 'y' intervenes in the two vowels which is quite common, occurring in many languages.

The other three important verbs that are irregular in the past tense are the following: **lenā** 'to take', **denā** 'to give', and **pīnā** 'to drink'.

stem	*masculine singular*	*masculine plural*	*feminine singular*	*feminine plural*
le take	**liyā**	**liye**	**lī**	**lī̃**
de give	**diyā**	**diye**	**dī**	**dī̃**
pī drink	**piyā**	**piye**	**pī**	**pī̃**

Word-for-word translation

mere	**pɛse**	**aur**	***traveller's***	***cheques***	**gum**	**gaye**
my	money	and	traveller's	cheques	lost	went

My money and traveller's cheques [are] lost.

Notice the clustering of the two verbs **gum**, 'be lost', and **gaye,** 'went', (m.pl.). This clustering of the real verbs is a special property of Hindi and other South Asian languages. They are called 'compound verbs'. We will deal with such a class of verbs later on in this book. For the time being, observe such verb clustering and memorize the sentence given above.

Echo words

You have already come across the word **T^{h}īk**, 'fine, correct'. In the phrase **T^{h}īk-T^{h}āk**, the second word, **T^{h}āk**, does not have any meaning of its own. It just echoes the first word by making a slight vowel change in it. The meaning added by the echo word is 'etc.', 'and all that', or 'other related things/properties'. Therefore, **T^{h}īk-T^{h}āk** means 'fine, etc'. Very often the first consonant sound is changed in the Hindi echo words, e.g. ***k*****ām *v*****ām**. 'work etc.', ***n*****ām *v*****ām**, 'name etc.'. The most preferred consonant change is by means of **v**.

Dialogue

My passport is lost

Aditi Chatterjii continues to talk with her father, Suman Chatterjii, about the incident. She informs her father that she filed a report at the airport and that American Express will issue her new traveller's cheques, but not without her passport. So she needs some money by telegram and in the meanwhile she needs to go to the Indian Consulate office in New York. At the Consulate, she talks with an officer.

ADITI: merā pāsporT *(passport)* gum gayā hɛ. nayā pāsporT *(passport)* cāhiye.

OFFICER: kab gumā?

ADITI: āj, karīb pā̃c g^{h}anTe pɛhɛle.

OFFICER: āp ko mālūm hɛ ki kahā̃ gumā?

ADITI: jī hā̃, *Kennedy* havāī aDDe mẽ.

OFFICER: kɛse?

ADITI: jab *Immigration* se bāhar āyī, to mere pās t^{h}ā. p^{h}ir, Chicago kī *flight* ke liye dūsre Tarmīnal (*terminal*) gayī, tab b^{h}ī t^{h}ā. jab kāunTar (*counter*) par pahũcī, to dek^{h}ā, *passport, ticket*, pɛse, aur *traveller's cheques purse* mẽ nahī̃ t^{h}e.

OFFICER:	*police* ko riporT (*report*) kī?
ADITI:	jī hā̃, ye dek^{h}iye.
OFFICER:	acc^{h}ā ye *form* b^{h}ariye, ek-do mahīne mẽ nayā *passport* āp ko milegā.
ADITI:	is se jaldī nahī̃ mil saktā?
OFFICER:	jī nahī̃, pɛhɛle *report* hindustān jayẽgī aur *clearance* ke bād hī *passport* mil saktā hɛ.
ADITI:	shukriyā.
OFFICER:	koī bāt nahī̃.

ADITI:	*My passport is lost. [I] need a new passport.*
OFFICER:	*When was [it] lost?*
ADITI:	*About five hours ago today.*
OFFICER:	*Do you know where [it] was lost?*
ADITI:	*At Kennedy Airport.*
OFFICER:	*How?*
ADITI:	*When I came out of Immigration, I had [it].* (lit. then *[it]* was near me.) *Then [I] went to the other terminal [to catch] the flight for Chicago; even then I had [it].* *When I reached the counter, then [I] noticed the passport, ticket, money and the traveller's cheques were not in [my handbag].*
OFFICER:	*[Did you] report [this] to the police?*
ADITI:	*Yes, look at this (referring to the police report).*
OFFICER:	*OK. Fill out this form. In one or two months you will get a new passport.*
ADITI:	*Can't [I] get [it] earlier than that? (lit: can't [I] get it before than this)?*
OFFICER:	*No, first the report will go to India and only after the clearance, [you] can get [it].*
ADITI:	*Thanks.*
OFFICER:	*You are welcome (or do not mention).* (lit. [it] is no matter.)

Vocabulary

nayā (m., adj.)	नया	new
karīb	करीब	about, approximately
g^{h}anTā (m.)	घंटा	hour
pɛhɛlā (m., adj.)	पहला	first
pɛhɛle	पहले	(at) first, ago, previously
mālūm honā (+ko)	मालूम होना	to know, to be known
havāī aDDā (m.)	हवाई अड्डा	airport
jab (relative pronoun)	जब	when
bāhar	बाहर	out, outside
ānā (-ne)	आना	to come
āyī (f., sg.)	आयी	came
dūsrā (m., adj.)	दूसरा	second, other, another
to	तो	then
dek^{h}nā (+ne)	देखना	to see, to look at, to notice
dek^{h}iye	देखिये	please see, look at, notice
b^{h}arnā (+ne)	भरना	to fill
b^{h}ariye	भरिये	please fill, please fill out
ek-do	एक-दो	one or two
mahīnā	महीना	month
milnā (-ne, +ko)	मिलना	to meet, to get, to be available
milegā (m., sg.)	मिलेगा	will get
jaldī	जल्दी	quickly
(**ke**) **bād**	के बाद	after, later
shukriyā	शुक्रिया	thanks

Pronunciation

dūsre is written **dūsare**. The vowel **a** is dropped in the colloquial pronunciation.

Notes

malūm honā **vs.** jānnā **'to know'**

Consider a word-for-word translation of the Hindi equivalent of the English expression 'do you know...?' in our dialogue.

āp	**ko**	**mālūm**	**hɛ ...?**
you	to	known	is

Do you know...?

The Hindi sentence is similar to English 'Is it known to you...?'. The only difference is that in Hindi **āp ko** is still the subject. Remember the discussion of dative subjects in Lesson 3; Hindi verbs distinguish between the non-volitional and volitional verbs. The verb **mālūm honā** points to the type of knowing or knowledge that is non-volitional or unintentional in nature. The verb **jānnā** also can be translated as 'to know', but the difference is that **jānnā** refers to an act of knowing that is volitional, and some effort or research has gone into that knowledge. As pointed out earlier, the volitional verbs do not take dative **ko** marking with their subjects. Observe the following volitional counterpart of **mālūm honā**.

āp	**jāntī**	**hɛ̃...?**
you (f.)	know	are

Do you know...?

Notice that the verb agrees with the subject **āp**, which is feminine in our dialogue. In the former sentence **āp ko** is the subject and the verb does not agree with it. We will detail the question of agreement again in this chapter. In the former sentence the verb agrees with the object **ye**, 'this', which is masculine singular, and that is why the verb takes the singular form **hɛ**.

Similarly, you have already come across two different usages of the verb **milnā** 'to meet', and **milnā** 'to get, to obtain'.

ham	**milẽge**
we	meet-will

We will meet.

The understood subject in the Hindi expression of English 'you will get the passport' is supplied below:

āp	**ko**	***passport***	**milegā**
you	to	passport	get-will

You will get the passport.

The English verbs such as 'to get' or 'to obtain' are treated as unintentional acts in Hindi and many other South Asian languages. That explains why the

Hindi subject is followed by the postposition **ko**. Can you predict the element which the verb **milegā** agrees with? No more suspense; it agrees with the object *passport,* which is masculine singular in Hindi.

The ने ne construction

If we fill in the understood subjects in the following two expressions witnessed in the above dialogue

to	**dek^{h}ā**
then	saw

and

police	**ko**	***report***	**kī?**
police	to	report	did

the complete sentences will be

to	**mɛ̃**	**ne**	**dek^{h}ā**
then	I	agent	saw

Then I saw.

and

āp	**ne**	**police**	**ko**	***report***	**kī?**
you	agent	police	to	report (f.)	did (f. sg.)

Did you report to the police?

The **ne** postposition is attached to the subject. Without the postposition the sentences will be ungrammatical. However, observe the following sentences:

jab	**mɛ̃**	***immigration***	**se**	**bāhar**	**āyī.**
when	I (f. sg.)	Immigration	from	out	came (f. sg.)

When I came out of Immigration.

and

mɛ̃	**dūsre**	***terminal***	**gaī.**
I (f. sg.)	other	terminal	went (f. sg.)

I went to the other terminal.

The above two sentences do not require the **ne** postposition. But why not? The difference is that verbs such as 'come' and 'go' are intransitive verbs. The **ne** postposition is restricted to the transitive verbs in the Perfective form. Verbs such as 'to see' and 'to report' are transitive and are used in the perfective form; therefore, the postposition **ne** is required with the subject. Such a construction is called 'the ergative' construction in linguistic literature. Many languages of the world such as Basque and some Australian Aboriginal languages have this property.

The pronominal forms with the ने **ne** postposition are as follows:

nominative pronouns		*the* **ne** *pronouns*		
mɛ̃	मैं	**mɛ̃ ne**	मैं ने	I
ham	हम	**ham ne**	हम ने	we
tū	तू	**tū ne**	तू ने	you (singular)
tum	तुम	**tum ne**	तुम ने	you (plural)
āp	आप	**āp ne**	आप ने	you (honorific)
vo	वह	**us ne**	उस ने	she, he, it; that
ve	वे	**unhõne**	उन्होंने	they; those
ye	यह	**is ne**	इस ने	this
ye	ये	**inhõne**	इन्होंने	these

Notice that the third person pronouns show the peer group pressure as a result of **ne**. If you are learning the script, it is written as one word with the third person plural pronouns.

The **ne** forms of the question pronoun are: **kis ne** किस ने 'who' (singular) and **kinhõne** किन्होंने 'who' (plural).

Complex verbs

As in English, in Hindi a noun can be turned into a verb. The only difference is that the noun has to be anchored in verbs such as **karnā** 'to do' and **honā** 'to be'. This is a very productive process which allows Hindi to take nouns from languages such as Sanskrit and Persian and turn them into verbs. English has not been spared either. So you can take English nouns such as the following and turn them into verbs:

English noun	*Hindi verb*	*complex verb*
report	**karnā**, 'to do'	report **karnā**, 'to report'
telephone	**karnā**	telephone **karnā**, 'to telephone'
pay	**karnā**	pay **karnā**, 'to pay'
complain	**karnā**	complain **karnā**, 'to complain'

As a matter of fact, even English adjectives and verbs can be used to generate Hindi complex verbs:

English adjective/verb	*Hindi verb*	*complex verb*
better	**honā**	better **honā**, 'to recover'
choose	**karnā**	choose **karnā**, 'to choose'

This construction can be extremely useful in those situations where one fails to recall the Hindi verb. For example, if you fail to recall the Hindi verb **paR^{h}nā** 'to read/study', do not give up that idea easily; you can custom-make the verb **study karnā** from the English word study. We will nickname Hindi anchor verbs such as **karnā** and **honā** as 'transformers'.

The omission of 'to'

We pointed out earlier the English preposition in expressions such as 'I went to the other terminal'. In Hindi no postposition is used with the target; therefore, it will not be appropriate to substitute Hindi **ko** for English 'to'.

Approximation by compounding

ek-do	**mahīne**	**mẽ**
one-two	month	in

In one or two months.

Dialogue

Visiting an astrologer

John Kearney has visited India several times, and he loves Indian philosophy. The concept of reincarnation fascinates him, and therefore he *never* misses any chance to visit an astrologer or a fortune-teller. An international fair is being held in London. John visits the Indian pavilion and there he finds an astrologer and palmist. He shows the palmist his hand in order to learn about his past. The palmist looks at his hand and makes some general remarks about him, and finally asks about the purpose of John's visit

JOHN:	mɛ̃ apne bʰūt ke bāre mẽ jānnā cāhtā hū̃.
PALMIST:	apane farishte ke bāre mẽ pūcʰiye, bʰūt ke bāre mẽ kyõ?
JOHN:	mū̃rā matlab hɛ ki picʰle janma ke bāre mẽ.
PALMIST:	patre ke binā mushkil hɛ.
JOHN:	to mere bacpan ke bāre mẽ batāiye.
PALMIST:	ye lāinẽ batātī hɛ̃ ki āp kā bacpan bahut accʰā tʰā...sundar parivār...baRā gʰar...ye Tʰīk hɛ?
JOHN:	jī hā̃, ...lekin...
PALMIST:	lekin picʰle pā̃c sāl accʰe nahī̃ tʰe.
JOHN:	pitā jī ke marne ke baad parivār par bahut mushkilẽ āyī̃.
PALMIST:	ye baRe afsos kī bāt hɛ.

JOHN:	*I want to know about my past/ghost.**
PALMIST:	*Please ask about your angels; why ask about [your] ghost?*
JOHN:	*I mean about my last birth.* (lit. my meaning is that [I want to ask] about my last birth)
PALMIST:	*It is difficult [to tell] without the astrological chart.*
JOHN:	*Then, tell me about my childhood.*
PALMIST:	*These lines [on your hand] tell me that your childhood was very good...beautiful family...a big house...is this right?*
JOHN:	*Yes,...but...*
PALMIST:	*But your last five years were not good.*
JOHN:	*After the death of my father, [our] family faced a lot of difficulties.* (lit. very many difficulties came on the family)
PALMIST:	*I am sorry [to hear] this.* (lit. this is the matter of great sorrow)

(*The word **bʰūt** is ambiguous. The palmist interprets it as ghost just for fun.)

Vocabulary

b^{h}ūt (m.)	भूत	ghost, past
farishtā (m.)	फ़रिश्ता	angel
pūc^{h}nā (+/-ne)	पूछना	to ask
pūchiye	पूछिये	please ask
matlab (m.)	मतलब	meaning
janma (m.)	जन्म	birth
patrā (m.)	पत्रा	astrological chart
(**ke**) **binā**	के बिना	without
mushkil (f.)	मुश्किल	difficult, difficulty
bacpan (m.)	बचपन	childhood
batānā (**+ne**)	बताना	to tell
batāiye	बताइये	please tell
sāl (m.)	साल	year
marnā (-ne)	मरना	to die
ānā (**-ne**)	आना	to come
afsos (m.)	अफ़सोस	sorrow

Notes

Very frequent expressions: word-for-word translation

Consider how the following three very frequent English expressions are phrased in Hindi.

English	*Hindi*				
I mean	**merā**	**matlab**	**hɛ**		
	my	meaning	is		
I am glad to hear this	**ye**	**xushī**	**kī**	**bāt**	**hɛ.**
	this	happiness	of	matter (f.)	is
	This is a matter of happiness.				
I am sorry to hear this	**ye**	**afsos**	**kī**	**bāt**	**hɛ**
	this	sorrow	of	matter (f.)	is
	This is a matter of sorrow.				

lāinẽ 'lines'

āp	**kī**	**lāinẽ**	**batātī**	**hɛ̃**
you	of	lines	tell	are

Your lines tell.

Notice the English word 'line' takes the feminine gender in Hindi.

अभ्यास Exercises

1

Rearrange the following words to make correct sentences in Hindi:

mere dost, ve t^he acc^{h}e kitne din! mɛ̃ socā ne ve rahẽge din hameshā. ve bacpan din ke t^he. mɛ̃ t^hā hameshā k^heltā aur nāctā t^hā. har sundar cīz t^hī. har thā din nayā aur har rāt andāz kā t^hā. din ab ve nahī̃ rahe.

2

Circle the correct form of the subject and the verb in the following sentences:
(hint: the gender of the English word 'report' is feminine):

(a) (mɛ̃ ne/mɛ̃) vahā̃ (gaye/gayī).
(b) (vo/us ne) muj^h ko (batāyā/batāye).
(c) (ham/ham ne) g^har (āyā/āye).
(d) (tum/tum ne) g^har der se (pahũce/pahũcā).
(e) (ve/ve ne/unhõne) *police* ko *report* (kī/kiyā/kiye).
(f) (āp/āp ko/āp ne) ye kitāb kab (milā/mile/milī).

3

Activity: asking about your family history

First talk about your family history, making use of the cues to make questions. Use the same method to ask your friends or partners questions about their family.

Examples **parivār**, 'family' / **kahā̃ se / ā** 'come'
āp kā parivār kahā̃ se āyā?

mātā-pitā, 'mother-father'/ **janma**, 'birth'/ **ho** 'be, happen'
āp ke mātā-pitā kā janma kahā̃ huā?
(Hint: use the English word for 'arranged marriage'.)
The verb 'to be married' = marriage to take place/ happen.
younger / older = small / big.

(a) parents / where / born
(b) parents / when / born
(c) rich or poor
(d) marriage / when / happen
(e) how old
(f) arranged marriage / love marriage
(g) mother younger than your father.

4

Make questions from the following statements; the object of an inquiry is indicated by the underlined words in the statements:

Examples: shādī ke bād mere mātā-pitā England gaye?
shādī ke bād mere mātā-pitā kahā̃ gaye?
merā parivār das sāl pɛhɛle yahā̃ āyā.
āp kā parivār kitne sāl pɛhɛle yahā̃ āyā?

(a) kal John kā janma din t^{h}ā.
(b) John ke parivār ne ek *party* kī.
(c) vo party shām ko huī.
(d) John ko *party* ke bāre mẽ mālūm nahī̃ t^{h}ā?
(e) ye surprise *party* t^{h}ī.
(f) kal John kā janma din t^{h}ā.

5

purānā zamānā 'old days'

Indians, like most of us, have nostalgic feelings about the past. The past is good and glorious. But the present... If you have the recording, listen to the passage. After the beep, answer each statement either by saying **sac** (true) or **j^{h}ūT^h** (false).

Circle True (**sac**) or false **(j^{h}ūT^h)** statements:

(a) āj-kal log love *marrige* karte hɛ̃. **s** (true) **j^h** (false)
(b) purāne zamāne mẽ ādmī g^{h}ar

	mẽ kām karte t^{h}e.	s (true)	j^{h} (false)
(c)	āj-kal sirf ādmī *TV* dek^{h}te hɛ̃.	s (true)	j^{h} (false)
(d)	āj-kal sirf ādmī k^{h}ānā banāte hɛ̃.	s (true)	j^{h} (False)
(e)	purāne zamāne mẽ parivār acc^{h}ā t^{h}ā.	s (true)	j^{h} (false)
(f)	purāne zamāne mẽ *TV* nahī̃ t^{h}ā.	s (true)	j^{h} (false)
(g)	aur āj-kal samaya nahī̃ hɛ.	s (true)	j^{h} (false)

Now write sentence corrections of the false statements.

7 क्या आप हिन्दी बोल सकते हैं? Can you speak Hindi?

By the end of this lesson you should be able to:

- talk about your skills
- give advice
- use obligatives
- observe compound verbs
- use emphatic and persuasive forms

Dialogue

You can speak Hindi!

Vijay Mishra lives in Vancouver, Canada, and he takes a bus from the University of British Columbia to downtown Vancouver. The bus is not crowded. He puts the money into the slot of the fare box. The bus driver, who is a white, blue-eyed Canadian, utters something and Vijay understands it as 'downtown eh', and he replies, 'yes', and sits down. As he settles down, he thinks that what he heard was not English but Hindi. A bit puzzled, he does not want to rule out that what he actually heard was the Hindi language. In fact, the driver had asked, 'downtown ***jānā hɛ****'. So Vijay asks:*

VIJAY:	māf kī̃jiye, āp ne kyā kahā?
DRIVER:	mɛ̃ ne pūc^hā ki *downtown* jānā hɛ.
VIJAY:	are! āp to bahut acc^hī hindī bol sakte hɛ̃.
DRIVER:	hā̃, t^hoRī t^hoRī hindī bol letā hū̃.
VIJAY:	hindī āp ne kahā̃ sīk^hī?
DRIVER:	dusrī *World War* ke samaya mẽ *British Army* mẽ sɛnik t^hā. us samaya hindustān mẽ sīk^hī.
VIJAY:	ab^hī b^hī acc^hī hindī ātī hɛ.
DRIVER:	kāfī samaya se yoga aur *meditation* sīk^h rahā hū̃ isliye hindī nahī̃ b^hūlī.
VIJAY:	ye to bahut acc^hā hɛ, nahī̃ to yahā̃ hindustānī b^hī hindī b^hūl jāte hɛ̃.
DRIVER:	ye bāt to sac hɛ.

VIJAY:	*Excuse me, what did you say?*
DRIVER:	*I asked if you need to go downtown* (lit. I asked that you need to go downtown).
VIJAY:	*Hey, you can speak Hindi very well* (lit. you can speak very good Hindi).
DRIVER:	*Yes, [I] can speak a little Hindi* (lit. I take speak little little Hindi).
VIJAY:	*Where did you learn Hindi?*
DRIVER:	*At the time of World War II, I was a soldier in the British Army. During that time [I] learned [it] in India.*

VIJAY: *Even now you know Hindi well* (lit. even now good Hindi comes [to you]).

DRIVER: *For a long time I have been learning yoga and meditation; therefore [I] did not forget Hindi.*

VIJAY: *This is very good; otherwise even Indians forget Hindi here* (lit. As regards this, [it] is very good, otherwise Indians also forget go Hindi).

DRIVER: *This is true.*

Vocabulary

to (particle)	तो	as regards
t^{h}oRā	थोड़ा	little, few
bolanā (+/-ne)	बोलना	to speak
bol lenā (+ne)	बोल लेना	to speak for one's benefit
bol letā hū̃	बोल लेता हूँ	(I can) speak
sīk^{h}nā (+ne)	सीखना	to learn
samaya (m.)	समय	time
sɛnik (m.)	सैनिक	soldier
ab^{h}ī b^{h}ī	अभी भी	even now
kāf ī	काफ़ी	enough, sufficient
b^{h}ūlnā (+/-ne)	भूलना	to forget
nahī̃ to	नहीं तो	otherwise
yahā̃	यहाँ	here

Notes

Formulaic expression: māf kījiye, 'forgive me/excuse me'

The English expression 'excuse me' is ambiguous in a number of ways. We pointed out earlier, in Lesson 2, that when the main function of 'excuse me' is to get attention, then it is paraphrased as 'please say' or 'please listen'. In this dialogue, Vijay did not hear the driver at first, and then asked him to repeat his statement; this calls for an apology. Thus Vijay appropriately uses **māf kījiye**. The first part of the expression, **māf**, 'pardoned', is the short adjectival form of the noun **māfī**, 'forgiveness', which is used with the verb **karnā**, 'to do'. (Remember the 'transformer' verbs outlined in the last Lesson.) Thus, this expression is like other conjunct verbs you have encountered in earlier dialogues:

noun	*verb*
māf	**karnā**
pasand	**karnā**
report	**karnā**

The polite imperative form of **māf karnā** is **māf kījiye**. The subject **āp** and the object **mujʰ ko**, 'me' are implied.

The internal obligative: mujʰ ko jānā hɛ 'I need to go'

The Hindi counterpart of the English expression 'you need to go downtown' is

āp	**ko**	***downtown***	**jānā**	**hɛ**
you	to	downtown	to go	is

You need to go downtown.

The internal obligation is expressed by the infinitive form followed by the 'to be' verb form. The subject is always the experiencer subject with the **ko** postposition. In the above sentence the 'to be' verb is in the present tense form. In short, the internal obligatives have the following structure:

subject	*infinitive verb*	*'to be' verb*	
+ ko	**jānā**	**hɛ**	is
		tʰā	was
		hogā	will be

Examples:

āp	**ko**	***downtown***	**jānā**	**hɛ.**	You need to go downtown.
āp	**ko**	***downtown***	**jānā**	**tʰā.**	You needed to go downtown.
āp	**ko**	***downtown***	**jānā**	**hogā.**	You will need to go downtown.

In the case of an intransitive verb, the verb always stays masculine singular. The reason for this is that the verb cannot agree with a subject because it has to be followed by the postposition **ko** and there is no object to agree with either.

Three types of capabilitatives

In the dialogue, you will have noticed the three different ways of saying 'one can speak Hindi'.

āp	**hindī**	**acc^{h}ī**	**bol**	**sakte**	**hɛ̃**
you	Hindi	good	speak	can-present	are

You can speak Hindi well.

Notice the placement of **saknā** in the Hindi sentence. The subject is just plain nominative, as in English. The verb agrees with a subject. It is **saknā** that receives the tense conjugation, and it is preceded by the plain stem form of the verb.

The second way is:

mɛ̃	**t^{h}oRī**	**t^{h}oRī**	**hindī**	**bol**	**letā**	**hū̃.**
I	little	little	Hindi	speak	take-present	am

I can speak Hindi a little.

When one does not have a native-like or full competence in a skill, this construction is used. In other words, this type of expression is used to express 'partial competence' and it usually has quantifiers such as **t^{h}oRā** 'a little/few', with it. Notice the clustering of the two verbs **bol**, 'to speak', and **lenā**, 'to take'. It is the second verb that carries the tense/aspect form. These types of verbs are called 'compound' verbs. We will discuss this class later on in detail. For the time being, just memorize this expression.

The third way is like saying 'Hindi comes to you', as in

āp	**ko**	**ab^{h}ī**	**b^{h}ī**	**hindī**	**ātī**	**hɛ**
you	to	now	even	Hindi	come-present	is

You even now know Hindi (or 'You even now know [how to speak] Hindi. (lit. Hindi even now comes to you.)

In this construction the verb is **ānā**, 'to come' and the subject is an experiential subject. You will remember that experiential subjects are marked with the postposition **ko**. The verb agrees with 'Hindi', which is feminine singular. Unless otherwise modified with a quantifier denoting meagreness, this construction expresses 'full' or 'near complete' competence in a skill, to the extent that it comes to a person without any conscious effort.

This construction– 'Hindi comes to you' – is restricted to skills such as swimming, playing the sitar or any other musical instrument. It cannot be used in expressions such as 'I know John'.

Compare the following two sentences:

us	**ko**	**tɛrnā**	**ātā**	**hɛ**
he/she	to	to swim	come-present	is

[S]he knows [how to] swim. (lit. swimming/to swim comes to him/her)

The verb agrees with the infinitive form **tɛrnā**, which is masculine singular.

mɛ̃	**John**	**ko**	**jāntā**	**hū̃.**
I	John	object	know-present	am

I know John.

However, one cannot say 'John comes to me'.

Focus, emphasis and word order

In the dialogue, Vijay asks the driver

hindī	**āp**	**ne**	**kahā̃**	**sīkʰī?**
Hindi	you	agent	where	learned

Where did you learn Hindi?

The normal word order is as follows:

āp	**ne**	**hindī**	**kahā̃**	**sīkʰī?**
you	agent	Hindi	where	learned

Where did you learn Hindi?

Since Hindi is the centre of the discussion, 'Hindi', which is the object of the sentence, is moved to the beginning of the sentence. If you have the cassettes, you will hear a slight emphasis on the word, 'Hindi'. In other words, an element of a sentence can be pulled out of its normal place in a sentence and placed at the beginning of a sentence to express focus or emphasis.

The particle to 'as regards'

We came across the use of **to** in the sense of 'then'. However, observe that in the following two examples, **to** follows a constituent rather than appearing in the clause-initial position in a 'when–then' type of sentence.

āp	**to**	**bahut**	**acc^{h}ī**	**hindī**	**bol**	**sakte**	**hɛ̃**
you	as regards	very	good	Hindi	speak	can-present	are

As regards you, you can speak very good Hindi.

ye	**to**	**bahut**	**acc^{h}ā**	**hɛ.**
this	as regards	very	good	is

As regards this, this is very good.

The particle **to** is another way of expressing emphasis, but **to** implies some sense of exclusion. The first sentence says 'as regards you, you can speak very good Hindi', and implies that 'others [from your group] cannot speak very good Hindi'.

Compound verb b^{h}ūl jānā 'to forget'

Observe another example of a compound verb in the dialogue:

yahā̃	**hindustānī**	**b^{h}ī**	**hindī**	**b^{h}ūl**	**jāte**	**hɛ̃**
here	Indians	also	Hindi	forget	go-present	are

Here even Indians forget Hindi.

The two verbs are clustered together–**b^{h}ūl** and **jānā**. They share the chore of expressing meaning. **b^{h}ūl**, which is the first verb, is in the form of a stem and conveys the main meaning, whereas **jānā** carries the tense form but does not convey its literal meaning of 'going'. As promised, we will detail this class of verbs later. For the time being satisfy yourself with the 'sharing' nature of Hindi compound verbs.

Dialogue

Can you write Hindi?

Vijay and the driver continue to talk to each other. The topic of the discussion still continues to be the Hindi language

VIJAY: kyā āp ko hindī lik^{h}nī ātī hɛ?

DRIVER: zyādā nahī̃. *army* mẽ kab^{h}ī kab^{h}ī lik^{h}nī paRtī t^{h}ī lekin ab koī zarūrat nahī̃.

VIJAY: hindī mẽ kyõ lik^{h}nā paRtā t^{h}ā?

DRIVER: *secret codes* aur sandeshõ ke liye – xāskar *Europe* jāne vāle sandeshõ ke liye. *Downtown* mẽ kuc^{h} kām hɛ?

VIJAY: bijlī kā bill denā t^{h}ā. āj furasat milī, to socā ki xud vahā̃ jāū̃.

DRIVER: to vo daftar āne vālā hɛ...asal mH aglā *stop* hɛ.

VIJAY: acc^{h}ā, namaskār.

DRIVER: namaskār.

VIJAY: *Do you know [how to] write Hindi* (lit. does to write Hindi come to you)?

DRIVER: *Not much. In the army I had to write sometimes but now [there] is no need [to write in Hindi].*

VIJAY: *Why did [you] have to write in Hindi?*

DRIVER: *For secret codes and messages, especially for messages going to Europe. Do [you] have some work downtown?*

VIJAY: *[I] need to pay the electricity bill* (lit. I need to give the electricity bill) *Today [I] have [some] free time, so I thought I would go myself* (i.e. in person).

DRIVER: *Then [in that case], that office is about to come up...in fact, [it] is the next stop.*

VIJAY: *OK. Goodbye.*

DRIVER: *Bye.*

Vocabulary

lik^{h}nā (+ne)	लिखना	to write
zyādā (invariable)	ज़्यादा	more

kab^{h}ī कभी ever
kab^{h}ī-kab^{h}ī कभी-कभी sometimes
paRnā पड़ना to fall, to lie down, in compound verbs 'to have to'
zarūrat (f.) ज़रूरत need, necessity
sandesh (m.) सन्देश message
xāskar ख़ासकर especially, particularly
jāne vāle जाने वाले going
kām honā (+ko) काम होना to have work
bijlī (f.) बिजली electricity, lighting
furasat (f.) फ़ुरसत free time, spare time, leisure
xud ख़ुद oneself
jānā (-ne) जाना to go
jāū̃ जाऊँ should go
daftar (m.) दफ़्तर office
āne vālā आने वाला about to come
asal mẽ असल में in fact, in reality
aglā (m., adj.) अगला next

Notes

Variation: Hindi lik^{h}nī ātī hɛ or Hindi lik^{h}nā ātā hɛ

In the Standard-Hindi-speaking area, the verb and the preceding infinitive form agree with the object in number and gender, whereas in the Eastern-Hindi speaking area both remain invariable, i.e. masculine singular.

Standard Hindi	*Eastern Hindi*
āp ko hindī lik^{h}nī ātī hɛ. You know how to write Hindi.	**āp ko hindī lik^{h}nā ātā hɛ.** You know how to write Hindi.
āp ko xat lik^{h}ne hɛ̃. you to letters to write are (m.pl)	**āp ko xat lik^{h}nā hɛ.** you to letters to write is (m. sg.)

However, the following sentence in our dialogue

bijlī	**kā**	**bill**	**denā**	**t^hā.**
electricity	of	bill (m. sg.)	to give	was

[I] needed to pay the electricity bill.

remains the same in both dialects because in the Standard Hindi, agreement is with *bill*, which is masculine singular.

The external obligative: muj^h ko jānā paRtā hɛ 'I have to go'

The only difference between the internal and the external obligatives is that in the latter the infinitive is followed by the verb **paRnā**, 'to lie down' instead of the verb **honā,** 'to be'. Semantically, the external obligative expresses 'an external pressure/compulsion to do an act' rather than 'one's own internal need to do an act'. Compare the two types of obligatives:

Internal obligative

āp	**ko**	**hindī**	**lik^hnī**	**hɛ.**
you	to	Hindi (f. sg.)	write (f. sg.)	is

You need to write Hindi.

External obligative

āp	**ko**	**hindī**	**lik^hnī**	**paRtī**	**hɛ**
you	to	Hindi (f. sg.)	to write (f. sg.)	lie down (f. sg.)	is

You have to write Hindi.

In Eastern Hindi the infinitive and the verb form will be in the masculine singular form, i.e. **lik^hnā hɛ** and **lik^hnā paRtā hɛ**, respectively.

Now take a look at the use of the external obligative in our dialogue:

army	**mẽ**	**kab^hī kab^hī**	**lik^hnī**	**paRtī**	**t^hī**
army	in	sometimes	to write (f., sg.)	lie down (f. sg)	was

I had to write sometimes in the army. (lit. I used to have to write sometimes in the army).

The omitted subject **muj^h ko**, 'to me', is experiential and the object is Hindi. The tense form chosen is the past habitual. If the act of compelled writing was carried out only once, the verb **paRnā** would have been in the simple past form, i.e. **paRī**. And the adverb **kab^{h}ī-kab^{h}ī** would have to be dropped.

There is a striking similarity between the verb **paRnā**, 'to lie down' and **paR^{h}nā** 'to read/study'.

Negative-incorporated words: 'nobody', 'nowhere', 'never', etc.

Have a look at the Hindi expression 'now [I have] no need of Hindi writing'.

ab	**koī**	**zarūrat**	**nahī̃**
now	some	need	not

Now (I have) no need.

The negative words such as 'nobody', 'nowhere', 'never' are simply derived from their positive counterparts, and the negative particle **nahī̃** is placed in its original position, i.e. right before the verb.

koī	someone	**nahī̃**	= no one, nobody
kahī̃	somewhere	**nahī̃**	= nowhere
kab^{h}ī	ever	**nahī̃**	= never

The immediate future: the vālā construction

The **vālā** is quite notorious for the meaning it renders and the behaviour it exhibits. It has many faces. Here, we will examine the cases in which the **vālā** follows an infinitive verbal form and thus marks 'immediate future' tense.

vo	**daftar**	**āne**	**vālā**	**hɛ**
that	office (m. sg.)	to come	about	is

That office is about to come up. (i.e. the next stop is that office)

The many faces of **vālā** become evident from the following two facts: (1) it acts like a postposition and exercises peer pressure on the preceding infinitive form, and consequently the infinitive form becomes oblique; and (2) it agrees with the subject in number and gender in the fashion typical of an adjective ending in -**ā**. Now observe one more example of such usage:

gāR*ī*	**jāne**	**vāl*ī***	**t^h*ī***
train (f. sg.)	to go	about (f. sg.)	was (f. sg.)

The train was about to go/leave.

It might be puzzling to see how **vālā** can still be considered as an example of 'immediate future'. However, in this example, the **vālā** still renders 'immediate future' with reference to the past. In short, the structure of the 'immediate future' construction in Hindi is as follows:

subject (nominative)	stem + **ne**	**vālā**	verb 'to be'
		vālī	
		vāle	

The agentive vālā construction

In comparison with the above examples, observe the position of **vālā** in the following phrase. Here its best literal translation is the English agentive suffix -er.

Europe	**jāne**	**vāle**	**sandeshõ**	**ke liye**
Europe	to go	er	messages	for

For the Europe going messages. (lit. for the Europe go-er messages).

Can you guess the meanings of the following phrases?

k^{h}elne vālā and **paR^{h}ne vālī**

The meanings are 'player' and 'reader', respectively. In the former a masculine singular head (e.g. boy) is implied whereas a feminine singular head (e.g. girl) is implied in the latter.

The meaning of the **vālā** phrase is often contextually governed. For example, the phrase

dillī	**vālā**
Delhi	er

means 'the person who lives in Delhi'. However, if the phrase is used in the context of train or vehicle, it can mean either 'the train that goes/is going to Delhi' or a vehicle 'which is made in Delhi'.

Formulaic expressions: 'I have some work', and 'Are you free?'

kyā	**āp ko**	***downtown***	**mẽ**	**kuc^h**	**kām**	**hɛ?**
what	you to	downtown	in	some	work	is

Do you have some work downtown?

āj	**muj^h**	**ko**	**furasat**	**milī.**
today	me	to	free/spare time (f.)	got

Today I was free.

The English expressions such as 'I am busy' and 'I am free' are paraphrased as 'to me the work is' and 'to me the free/leisure/spare time is'. Similarly, the best way to ask, 'Are you free?' is

āp ko furasat hɛ?

and 'are you busy?' is

āp ko kām hɛ?

The subjunctive

The subjunctive expresses the idea of a possibility. Expressions with words such as 'perhaps', and suggestion (e.g. 'Shall we go?'), or permission (e.g. 'May I come in?') usually employ the subjunctive.

mɛ̃	**ne**	**socā**	**ki**	**xud**	**vahā̃**	**jāū̃**
I	agent	thought	that	self	there	go (subjunctive)

I thought that [I] myself would go there.

Verbs such as **cāhnā**, 'to want', **socnā**, 'to think' (which are called non-factive verbs) and **jānnā**, 'to know' (which belongs to the class of factive verbs) select a subjunctive verb form in their subordinate clause, i.e. ***jāū̃.***

The subjunctives are very simple to form. The magic trick is to take any future form and just drop the future ending, i.e. **gā**, **ge** and **gī**. For instance, the corresponding subjunctive form of **ham milẽge**, 'we will meet'; **tum jāoge**, 'you will go', and **mɛ̃ jāū̃gī**, 'I will go', are: **ham milẽ** 'we shall meet', **tum jāo**, 'you would go'; and **mɛ̃ jāū̃** (with rising intonation) 'May I go?' respectively.

The emphatic reflexive xud 'oneself'

The emphatic pronoun **xud** is very similar to English emphatic pronouns. The difference is that the Hindi form **xud** remains invariable, whereas the English emphatic pronouns vary according to their subject. In

mɛ̃ ne **socā ki *mɛ̃ xud* vahā̃ jāū̃**

the emphatic form will always remain unchanged even if the subject of the subordinate class changes.

Dialogue

I am very sick

Professor John Ryder is on his second research trip to rural India. He reaches his village at the beginning of the Monsoon season. Although he took all precautions and shots before leaving for India, he awakens one night with high fever and diarrhoea. He calls Dr Naim's residence. Dr Naim's wife picks up the phone.

JOHN: hɛllo, kyā Dr Naim hɛ̃?
MRS. NAIM: jī nahī̃, koī zarūrī bāt hɛ?
JOHN: merī tabīyat bahut xarāb hɛ.
MRS. NAIM: ek marīz ko dek^{h}ne gaye hɛ̃.
JOHN: kitnī der mẽ lauTẽge?
MRS. NAIM: mere xyāl se jaldī ā jāyẽge.
muj^{h}e apnā Telefon (*telephone*) *number* aur patā de dījiye. āte hī unhẽ b^{h}ej dū̃gī.
JOHN: bahut bahut d^{h}anyavād.

JOHN: *Hello, is Dr Naim [there]?*
MRS. NAIM: *No, is [there] something urgent?*

JOHN:	*[I] am very sick* (lit. my condition/health is very bad).
MRS. NAIM:	*He went to see a patient* (lit. he has gone to see a patient).
JOHN:	*When will he return* (lit. in how much period of time will he return)?
MRS. NAIM:	*I think [he] will come [back] soon* (lit. with my opinion *[he]* will come soon).
	Please give me your address and phone number. As soon as he returns, [I] will send him [to your place].
JOHN:	*Thanks a lot.*

Vocabulary

zarūrī	ज़रूरी	important, urgent, necessary
tabīyat (f.)	तबीयत	health, disposition
xarāb	ख़राब	bad
marīz (m.)	मरीज़	patient
der (f.)	देर	delay, time (period of, slot of)
lauTnā (-ne)	लौटना	to return
lauTẽge	लौटेंगे	will return
xyāl (m.)	ख़्याल	opinion, thought
jaldī	ज़ल्दी	quickly
ā jānā (-ne)	आ जाना	to come (compound verb)
ā jāyẽge	आ जायेंगे	will come (compound verb)
mujʰe	मुझे	to me
patā (m.)	पता	address
de denā (+ne)	दे देना	to give (compound verb)
de dījiye	दे दीजिये	please give (compound verb)
āte hī	आते ही	as soon as (he) comes
unhẽ	उन्हें	him
bʰejnā (+ne)	भेजना	to send
bʰej denā (+ne)	भेज देना	to send (compound verb)
bʰej dū̃gī	भेज दूँगी	[I] will send (compound verb)
dʰanyavād	धन्यवाद	thanks

Notes

Variation

tabīyat can also be spelled with a short **i** (i.e. **tabiyat**).

Present and past perfective forms

ve	**ek**	**marīz**	**ko**	**dek^{h}ne**	**gaye**	**hɛ̃**
he (hon.)	one	patient	obj.	to see (obl.)	gone	are

He went to see a patient (lit. he has gone to see a patient).

kyā	**āp**	**kab^{h}ī̃**	**āgrā**	**gaye**	**hɛ̃?**
what	you	ever	Agra	went	are

Have you ever been (lit. gone) to Agra?

hā̃,	**mɛ̃**	**gayā**	**hū̃.**
yes	I	went	am

Yes, I have been [there]. (lit. yes, I have gone [there]).

hā̃,	**do**	**sāl**	**pɛhɛle**	**mɛ̃**	**gayā**	**t^{h}ā**
yes	two	years	ago	I	went	was

Yes, two years ago I went [there]. (lit. yes, two years ago, I had gone [there].

By adding the 'to be' to the present forms (**hū̃** 'am', **hɛ**, 'is', **hɛ̃**, 'are', and **ho**, 'are' (you), and past forms (**t^{h}ā**, 'was', **t^{h}e**, 'were', **t^{h}ī**, 'was', and **t^{h}ī̃** 'were') to the perfective form, one can get present and past perfective forms, respectively. The present perfect indicates the completed action which has relevance for the present situation and the past perfective shows relevance to the past. That is why the present perfective and past perfective are called 'recent past' and 'remote past'. What is notable is that in the first sentence and the last sentence English will use the simple perfective form but Hindi will use the present and the past perfective, respectively. The past perfect in English is viewed with reference to an event in the past, as in 'When I was in Agra, he had already come'.

Compound verbs

We have already mentioned the compound verbs in Hindi. Observe another example from your dialogue.

mere	**xyāl**	**se**	**ve**	**jaldī**	**ā**	**jāyẽge**
my	opinion	with	he (hon.)	soon	come	go-will

I think he will come [back] soon.

Notice that the two verbs **ā** 'come' and **jā** 'go' are clustered in the verb phrase. The meaning of the sentence is not merely an accumulative or conjunctive meaning rendered by the verbs. In other words, the sentence does not mean 'he will come and go'. On the contrary, the action of coming is being described and the verb **jānā** 'to go' is only a responsible carrier of the tense information. Also, it loses its literal meaning and adds some related but new overtones or emphasis to the first verb. In the case of capabilitative construction with **saknā**, the helping verb adds a clearly observable (literal) meaning; however, as you will see below, this is not usually the case with helping verbs such as **ānā** and **jānā**.

You can view compound verbs as persons wedded to each other or romantically in love with one another, in which both are willing to co-operate with each other to the extent of being dependent on each other in some respects. The compound verb

ā jāyẽge

is composed of two units: the main verb **ā** 'come', which is in the stem form and is totally dependent on the second unit, i.e. the helping verb **jā**, 'go', for the tense information. In addition to supplying the tense information, the other roles the helping verb plays are described below:

jānā as a helping verb

As we already know, the literal meaning of **jānā** is 'to go'. As a helping verb, it refers to the 'transformation of a state or action, completeness or finality'.

simple verbs		*compound verbs*		
ānā	to come	**ā**	**jānā**	to come back, arrive
k^{h}ānā	to eat	**k^{h}ā**	**jānā**	to eat up
pīnā	to drink	**pī**	**jānā**	to drink up
samaj^{h}nā	to understand	**samaj^h**	**jānā**	to understand fully
honā	to be	**ho**	**jānā**	to become
b^{h}ūlnā	to forget	**b^{h}ūl**	**jānā**	to forget completely

denā as a helping verb

The literal meaning of **denā** is 'to give'. When one gives something, the beneficiary of the action is someone other than the subject. That is exactly what is added to the main verb by the helping verb **denā**, i.e. to do an action for others. In the dialogue, the doctor's wife first asks for John's address and telephone number. The expression she uses is the following sentence:

> **muj^{h}e apnā *telephone number* aur patā de dījiye.**
> Give me your telephone number and address.

and then says:

> **āte hī unhẽ b^{h}ej dū̃gī.**
> As soon as he comes, I will send him.

The compound verbs **de denā** and **b^{h}ej denā** are used to highlight the beneficiary of the actions. The simple corresponding verbs **denā**, 'to give' and **b^{h}ejnā**, 'to send', are unable to identify the beneficiary. In the first sentence, the direct beneficiary of the action is the wife herself and in the second sentence John is the beneficiary of the wife's action of sending Dr Naim to his house.

lenā as a helping verb

The verb **lenā** means 'to take'. You can now predict its meaning as a helping verb. It conveys 'doing for oneself', i.e. for the benefit of the subject. For example, in reply to the request for the telephone number and address, John could have answered as follows:

acc^{h}ā **lik^h** **lījiye**
OK write take-imp.
Please write [it] down for your benefit.

The compound verb **lik^h lenā** stresses that Dr Naim's wife is the direct beneficiary of the action of writing down the address and the telephone number.

In the previous dialogue, we have already seen the other meaning (i.e. partial competence) of **lenā** when used as a helping verb with skill verbs.

te hī 'as soon as'

The addition of **te hī** to the verbal stem renders the meaning of 'as soon as', as in

āte hī	**unhẽ**	**b^{h}ej**	**dū̃gī.**
come as soon as	him (honorific)	send	give-will

I will send him as soon as (he) comes (back).

The pitfalls

'I think'

Compare and contrast the Hindi phrase with its English translation:

mere xyāl se... I think....

The Hindi equivalent is either **mere xyāl se** 'with my opinion' or **mere xyāl mẽ** 'in my opinion'. The Hindi verb **socnā**, 'to think', is not acceptable in this context, as in the following sentence:

mɛ̃	**soctā**	**hū̃**
I	think-present	am

The English verb 'to think' is ambiguous: (1) it refers to the process of thinking, as in 'I will think of something' and (2) it expresses an opinion, as in 'I think he is a nice man'. In the latter sense, it is paraphrased as 'in my opinion he is a nice man'. The failure to distinguish between the two types of 'think' is the source of many common errors on the part of English learners of Hindi as a second language.

Compound verbs

Failure to understand the shades in meaning conveyed by compound verbs can take a toll on communication. For example, if a student goes to a professor and requests a letter of recommendation, it makes a significant difference whether the student uses the

recommendation letter	**lik^{h}iye**	
recommendation letter	**lik^h**	**dījiye**
recommendation letter	**lik^h**	**lījiye**

Even though the polite forms are used in all three expressions, the only appropriate choice is the second. The first and the last one have the potential of offending the professor. The first one is polite, but still a command, and the last one claims the professor to be the direct beneficiary of the act of writing a letter of recommendation.

Similarly, be gentle and sensitive with the use of obligatives and capabilitatives.

Coping skills

If you are unsure which form to use, compound or simple verb, the best thing to do is to spell out the beneficiary **mere liye**, 'for me', with simple verbs. By doing this, you cannot totally eliminate the ill-effects of making a bad choice, but you can reduce the damage considerably.

अभ्यास Exercises

Circle the appropriate choice of subject in the following sentences and then translate the sentences into English:

(a) (mɛ̃/muj^h ko/mɛ̃ ne) sitār ātī hɛ.
(b) kyā (āp/āp ko/āp ne) tɛr sakte hɛ̃?
(c) (us ko/vo/us ne) kahā̃ jānā hɛ?
(d) (ve/unhõne/un ko) saŋgīt kab sīk^{h}ā?
(e) vo *salesman* hɛ. (us ko/us ne/vo) bāhar jānā paRtā hɛ.
(f) John ko bahut kām hɛ. isliye (vo/us ko/us ne) kuc^h fursat nahī̃ hɛ.

2

Complete the following sentences by supplying missing parts of the verb:

(a) Bill ko jaldī hɛ kyõki uskī gāRī das minute mẽ jā——— ——hɛ.
(b) Driver jaldī karo, mere dost kī *flight* ā——— ————hɛ.
(c) sardī kā mausam t^{h}ā, jaldī barf gir——— ————thī.
(d) *party* ke liye mɛhmān pahũ——— ——— ——hɛ̃.
(e) shām kā samaya t^{h}ā, and^{h}erā ho——— ——— ——t^{h}ā.
(f) āp kab^{h}ī hindustān ga — ——hɛ̃.

3

Match the duties given on the right with professions given on the left:

(a)	ad^{h}yāpak	us ko *car* calānī hɛ.
(b)	*Doctor*	us ko kapRe d^{h}one hɛ̃.
(c)	gāyak	us ko paR^{h}ānā hɛ.
(d)	*Driver*	us ko lik^{h}nā hɛ.
(e)	d^{h}obī	us ko marīz ko dek^{h}nā hɛ.
(f)	lek^{h}ak	us ko gānā hɛ.

4

Circle the appropriate helping verb in each of the following sentences:

(a) kyā āp mere liye *recommendation letter* lik^{h} (lẽge/dẽge)?
(b) rāt āyī aur and^{h}erā ho (gayā/āyā) t^{h}ā.
(c) mɛ̃ hindī nahī̃ paR^{h} saktā, āp ye xat paR^{h} (lījiye/dījiye).
(d) vo t^{h}oRā t^{h}oRā tɛr (saktā/letā/ātā) hɛ.
(e) us ko bahut acc^{h}ā nācnā (saktā/letā/ātā) hɛ.
(f) mɛ̃ āp ki bāt bilkul b^{h}ūl (āyā/gayā).

5

Write five sentences about the things you hated to do during your childhood, but had to do. The following sentence can serve as a model for your sentences.

bacpan	**mẽ**	**muj^{h}e**	**pālak**	**k^{h}ānī**	**paRtī**	**t^{h}ī.**
childhood	in	to me	spinach (f.)	eat-to	lay-present	was

During my childhood, I had [lit. used] to eat spinach.

6

If you have the recording, listen to the passage. Answer each statement either by saying **sac** (true) or **j^h^ūT^h^** (false)

Now answer each statement either by saying **sac** (true) or **j^h^ūT^h^** (false).

(a)	somvār ko mẽ ne kām kiyā.	**s** (true)	**j^h^** (false)
(b)	maŋgalvār ko mẽ apne dostõ se milā.	**s** (true)	**j^h^** (false)
(c)	bud^h^vār ko g^h^ar se bāhar nahī̃ gayā.	**s** (true)	**j^h^** (false)
(d)	guruvār ko London mẽ rahā.	**s** (true)	**j^h^** (false)
(e)	shukravār ko merī tabīyat T^h^īk nahī̃ t^h^ī.	**s** (true)	**j^h^** (false)
(f)	shanivār ko mẽ ne kām kiyā.	**s** (true)	**j^h^** (false)
(g)	ravivār ko mẽ ne ārām kiyā.	**s** (true)	**j^h^** (false)

8 मुझे चैक कैश करवाने हैं।
I need to get cheques cashed

By the end of this lesson you should be able to:

- learn causatives
- use the present participial forms
- learn more about compound verbs, subjunctives and obligatives
- learn about auxiliary verb deletion with negation
- use conditionals
- highlight contrast
- persuade someone
- advise and caution someone

Dialogue

Be careful what you eat

Finally, Dr Naim reaches John Ryder's house. It is about eleven o'clock at night

JOHN: ādāb arz, Dr Naim.
DR NAIM: ādāb, Ryder sāhib. is bār kaī sāl ke bād mulākāt huī.
JOHN: jī hā̃, koī pā̃c sāl bād.
DR NAIM: tashrīf rak^{h}iye, mɛ̃ āp kā hī intzār kar rahā t^{h}ā. acc^{h}ā, pɛhle batāiye, tabīyat kɛsī hɛ?
JOHN: tabīyat to acc^{h}ī nahī̃, nahī̃ to itnī rāt ko āp ko taklīf na detā.
DR NAIM: taklīf kī bāt kyā hɛ? ye to merā farz hɛ. xɛr, buxār kitnā hɛ?
JOHN: jab ek g^{h}anTe pɛhle mɛ̃ ne *thermometer* lagāyā, to ek sau do *degree* t^{h}ā. ab shāyad kuc^{h} zyādā ho.
DR NAIM: acc^{h}ā, zarā p^{h}ir *thermometer* lagāiye.
(Dr Naim takes John's pulse and temperature.)
DR NAIM: buxār t^{h}oRā baR^{h} gayā hɛ. dast b^{h}ī hɛ̃?
JOHN: jī hā̃, do g^{h}anTe mẽ sāt-āT^{h} bār *bathroom* gayā.
DR NAIM: pic^{h}lī bār āp ne bahut samose k^{h}āye t^{h}e, aur is bār?
JOHN: shām ko kuc^{h} ām khāye.
DR NAIM: merī salāh māniye ek-do mahīne tak āp kuc^{h} parhez kījiye, samose aur ām banda. mɛ̃ ek Tīkā lagātā hū̃ aur ye davāī lījiye. do goliyā̃ har do g^{h}anTe. to kal subā apnī tabīyat ke bāre mẽ batāiye. acc^{h}ā ab ārām kījiye. xudā hāfiz.
JOHN: bahut bahut shukriyā, Doctor sāhib, xudā hāfiz.

JOHN: *Greetings, Dr Naim.*
DR NAIM: *Greetings, Ryder sir, [we] meet again after several years* (lit. this time [our] meeting happened after several years).
JOHN: *After about five years.*
DR NAIM: *Please be seated. I was waiting for you* (lit. I was doing only your wait).
OK. First, tell [me], how you are feeling (lit. how is [your] disposition?)?
JOHN: *As regards my disposition, I am not feeling well;*

	otherwise I would not have bothered you so late at night.
Dr Naim:	*Why talk about trouble* (lit. what is the talk of trouble?)? *This is my duty. Well, how high is the fever?*
John:	*An hour ago when I took the temperature* (lit. an hour ago when put the thermometer), *it was one hundred and two degrees. Now it might be slightly higher.*
Dr Naim:	*OK, again [let's] take [your] temperature* (lit. again put the thermometer [in your mouth]). *(Dr Naim takes John's pulse and temperature.)*
Dr Naim:	*The fever has increased slightly; [do you] have diarrhoea too?*
John:	*Yes, [I] went to the bathroom about six or seven times in the past two hours.*
Dr Naim:	*The last time you ate many samosas, [what about] this time?*
John:	*In the evening [I] ate some mangoes.*
Dr Naim:	*Please take my advice. For about one or two months exercise some caution* (lit. do some abstinence). *No more samosas and mangoes* (lit. samosas and mangoes closed). *I [will] give you an injection and [have you] take this medicine. Two pills every two hours. Then tell me tomorrow morning how you feel. OK. Get some rest. Goodbye.*
John:	*Many many thanks, doctor. Goodbye.*

Vocabulary

ādāb (m.)	आदाब	salutation, greetings
arz (f.)	अर्ज़	request
is bār	इस बार	this time
sāl (m.)	साल	year
ke bād	के बाद	after
mulākāt (f.)	मुलाकात	meeting
mulākāt honā (-ne)	मुलाकात होना	to meet
tashrīf (f.)	तशरीफ़	(a term signifying respect)
tashrīf rak^{h}nā (+ne)	तशरीफ़ रखना	to be seated
tashrīf lānā (-ne)	तशरीफ़ लाना	to grace one's place, welcome, come
intzār (m./f.)	इंतज़ार	wait
(kā/kī) intzār karnā (+ne)	इंतज़ार करना	to wait

pɛhle	पहले	first
itnā (m., adj.)	इतना	so much/many, this much/ many
rāt (f.)	रात	night
taklīf (f.)	तकलीफ़	trouble, bother
taklīf denā (+ne)	तकलीफ़ देना	to bother
farz (m.)	फ़र्ज़	duty
lagānā (+ne)	लगाना	to fix, apply
shāyad	शायद	perhaps
baR^{h}nā (-ne)	बढ़ना	to increase, advance
dasta (m.)	दस्त	diarrhoea
ām	आम	mango, *as* adj. common, general
salāh (f.)	सलाह	advice
salāh mānnā (+ne)	सलाह मानना	to accept/take advice
salāh lenā (+ne)	सलाह लेना	to seek/take advice
mahīnā (m.)	महीना	month
parhez (m.)	परहेज़	abstinence
x se parhez karnā (+ne)	परहेज़ करना	to abstain, avoid
banda	बन्द	closed
banda karnā (+ne)	बन्द करना	to close
banda honā (-ne)	बन्द होना	to be closed
Tīkā lagānā (+ne)	टीका लगाना	to give an injection/a shot
davāī/davā (f.)	दवाई/दवा	medicine
golī (f.)	गोली	tablet, pill; bullet
ārām (m.)	आराम	comfort, rest
ārām karnā (+ne)	आराम करना	to rest
xudā hāfiz	ख़ुदा हाफ़िज़	goodbye

Notes

'We meet again after several years'

Another way of saying 'we meet again after several years' in Hindi is something like 'our meeting took place after several years'.

kaī	**sāl**	**bād**	**hamārī**	**mulākāt**	**huī.**
several	years	after	our	meeting (f.)	happened.

The politeness germ

Note the use of **tashrīf rak^{h}iye** instead of **bɛT^{h}iye**, 'please sit'. As in English, when receiving a guest, usually we will say 'Please have a seat', or 'Please be seated', rather than 'Please sit'. Similarly, it is more polite and much warmer to use **tashrīf rak^{h}iye** rather than **bɛT^{h}iye**, particularly if the listener is a Muslim. In English if the verb 'to sit' is used, it is modified in some form, e.g. 'Please sit down for a while'; the same is true of the Hindi verb **bɛT^h**, 'sit'. If it is used, it needs to precede the polite form of the verb **ā,** 'to come' (e.g. **āiye bɛT^{h}iye** 'Please come (and) sit' or followed by a question tag (e.g. **bɛT^{h}iye na** 'Please sit down, won't you?').

'To wait for x'

The Hindi equivalent of the English 'I was waiting for you' turns out to be

mɛ̃	**āp kā**	**intzār**	**kar**	**rahā**	**t^{h}ā**
I	your	wait (m.)	do	ing	was

i.e, 'I was doing your wait.'

The conditional: counter-factive

The Hindi sentence in our dialogue is as follows:

itnī	**rāt**	**ko**	**mɛ̃**	**āp**	**ko**	**taklīf**	**na**	**detā**
so much	night	at	I	you	to	bother	not	give-would have

The above sentence is a part of the 'if' clause which is implied.

agar	**tabīyat**	**T^{h}īk**	**hotī**	**to...**
if	disposition	fine	were	then...

If my condition were fine...

Notice that the simple present form without the auxiliary verb is used in such counter-factive sentences. The 'if' clause implies that the condition has not been fulfilled; therefore, the action expressed by the 'then' clause did not take place. Consider another example of counter-factives:

agar	**vo**	**ātā,**	**to**	**mɛ̃**	**jātā**
if	he	come-pres.	then	I	go-pres.

If he had come, I would have gone.

agar	**vo**	**kitābẽ**	**likʰtī,**	**to**	**ham**	**bahut**	**xush**	**hote**
if	she	books	write-pres.	then	we	very	happy	be-pres.

Had she written books, we would have been very happy.

Thus, the English verb forms such as 'had come' and 'would have gone' are translated, not as a past tense form, but with the present imperfective without an auxiliary verb.

Formulaic expression

The Hindi expression

taklīf	**kī**	**bāt**	**kyā**	**hɛ**
bother	of	matter	what	is

is not a question sentence. It is equivalent to the English expressions 'do not bother' or 'do not mention'. Thus, the Hindi question word **kyā** is like 'not' in the expression in question. The verb form is always in the simple present, rather than in the imperative form as in English.

Negative particle nā

We have already come across **nahī̃**, 'not'. Another Hindi negative particle is **nā** which occurs in constructions such as 'neither ... nor', counter-factives and polite imperatives. (See p. 83 for more details.)

The subjunctive

ab	**buxār**	**kucʰ**	**zyādā**	**ho**
now	fever (m., sg.)	some	more	be-subjunctive

The fever might be slightly more.

Since the context is the probable increase in fever, the form of the verb 'to be' is in the subjunctive form in Hindi. The verb agrees with **buxār**, 'fever'. Although the verb form **ho** might appear to be in the simple present tense form, it is not, since **tum** is not the subject in the above sentence.

Compound verb with the helping verb jānā

In the expression

buxār	**t^{h}oRā**	**baR^{h}**	**gayā**	**hɛ**
fever	little	increase	went	is

The fever has gone up a little.

the compound verb **baR^{h} jānā** is employed for the reasons explained in the previous lesson.

'Accept my advice'

Hindi paraphrases the English expression 'take my advice' as 'accept my advice'.

merī	**salāh**	**māniye.**
my	advice (f.)	accept–imperative

Please accept my advice.

The substitution of the verb **lenā,** 'take', would produce an odd sentence in Hindi.

Dialogue

Lost in Delhi

Philip Rosenberg is lost in downtown Delhi. He knows that somewhere in the vicinity there is an American Express office where he could cash some traveller's cheques. In fact, he visited that office just two days ago. He does not remember its address either. He inquires from a stranger about its location:

PHILIP: yahā̃ pās koī American Express kā daftar hɛ. mɛ̃ do din pɛhɛle vahā̃ gayā t^{h}ā, lekin āj nahī̃ mil rahā.

STRANGER: āp ko patā mālūm hɛ?

PHILIP: mɛ̃ patā to b^{h}ūl gayā.

STRANGER: mere xyāl se aglī saRak par Amercian Express kā daftar hɛ.
(*pointing to the street*)

PHILIP: (*seemingly puzzled*) vo saRak to sundar hɛ, log use aglī saRak kyõ kɛhɛte hɛ̃?

STRANGER: aglī hindī kā shabda hɛ angrezī kā nahī̃. 'aglī' kā matlab angrezī mẽ 'next' hɛ.

PHILIP: bahut xūb.
(*Philip goes to the cashier's window at the American Express office*)

PHILIP: muj^he kuc^h *traveller's cheque cash* karvāne hɛ̃.

CASHIER: kaun sī *currency* mẽ hɛ̃?

PHILIP: amerīkan *dollars. Exchange rate* kyā hɛ?

CASHIER: ek amrīkan *dollar* tīs rupaye kā hɛ.
(*Philip signs the cheques and the cashier gives him the equivalent amount in rupees*)

CASHIER: kul do sau *dollars.* ye rahe āpke c^he hazār rupaye. gin lījiye.

PHILIP: T^hīk hɛ̃. d^hanyavād.

PHILIP: *[There] is an American Express office nearby. Two days ago I went there. But today I cannot find [it].*

STRANGER: *Do you know the address?*

PHILIP: *I forgot the address.* (lit. as regards the address, I forgot)

STRANGER: *I think the American Express office is on the next* (i.e. 'aglī') *street.*
(lit. in my opinion...)
(pointing to the street)

PHILIP: (Seemingly puzzled) *That street is a beautiful one. Why do people call it 'ugly'?*

STRANGER: *'aglī' is a Hindi word, not English. In English the meaning of 'aglī' is 'next'.*

PHILIP: *[That's] great*!
(Philip goes to the cashier's window at the American Express office)

PHILIP: *I need to get some traveller's cheques cashed.*

CASHIER: *In which currency are they?*

PHILIP: *In American dollars. What is the exchange rate?*

CASHIER:	*One American dollar to thirty rupees.*
	(Philip signs the cheques and the cashier gives him the equivalent amount in rupees.)
Cashier:	*A total of two hundred dollars. Here are your six thousand rupees. Please count it (for your own sake).*
PHILIP:	*That's fine. Thanks.*

Vocabulary

daftar (m.)	दफ़्तर	office
milnā (+ko)	मिलना	to find, to receive
aglā (m., adj.)	अगला	next
shabda (m.)	शब्द	word
angrezī (f.)	अंग्रेज़ी	the English language
angrez (m.)	अंग्रेज़	the English
matlab (m.)	मतलब	meaning
bahut xūb	बहुत ख़ूब	great! splendid!
cash **karnā** (+ne)	कैश करना	to cash
cash **karvānā** (+ne)	कैश करवाना	to get someone to cash
kul	कुल	total
sau	सौ	hundred
<rɛhnā> (-ne)	रहना	to live
rahe	रहे	lived, are
hazār	हज़ार	thousand
ginnā (+ne)	गिनना	to count
gin lenā (+ne)	गिन लेना	to count (for one's benefit)
d^{h}anyavād	धन्यवाद	thanks

Notes

milnā 'I cannot find it'

In the preceding lessons we came across three important usages of the verb **milnā** – namely 'to meet', 'to run into' and 'to be available'. Now observe another use of this verb in the following sentence in your dialogue. Also note its word-for-word translation.

lekin āj nahī̃ mil rahā.
but today not find ing
But today [I] cannot find [it] (lit. but today I am not finding it).

When the verb **milnā** is used to express the meaning 'to find', it takes the experiencer subject. If we insert the implied subject in the above sentence, the form of the Hindi subject will not be the nominative **mɛ̃**, but the experiential subject **mujʰko** or **mujʰe**.

lekin āj mujʰe daftar nahī̃ mil rahā.

Notice that the verb does not agree with the subject. Instead, it agrees with an object, which is **daftar**, 'office', in the above sentence. The gender of **daftar** is masculine. Did you notice the missing element of the verb phrase?

Negation and auxiliary verb deletion

Notice the missing element of the verb in the above sentence.

lekin āj mujʰe daftar nahī̃ mil rahā hɛ.

The auxiliary verb **hɛ** can be optionally deleted in negative sentences. Only the auxiliary verbs of the simple present and present progressive tenses are subject to this optional deletion. Observe some examples:

positive sentences		*negative sentences*	
mɛ̃ jātā hū̃	I go.	**mɛ̃ nahī̃ jātā hū̃**	I do not go
		mɛ̃ nahī̃ jātā	I do not go
mɛ̃ jā rahā hū̃	I am going	**mɛ̃ nahī̃ jā rahā hū̃**	I am not going
		mɛ̃ nahī̃ jā rahā	I am not going
tum jātī ho	you (f.) go	**tum nahī̃ jātī ho**	you (f.) do not go
		tum nahī̃ jātī	you (f.) do not go
tum jā rahī ho	you (f.) are going	**tum nahī̃ jā rahī ho**	you (f.) are not going
		tum nahī̃ jā rahī	you (f.) are not going

Causative verbs

We came across some related verbs such as the following in our earlier dialogues. Note the slight change in the form and the meaning.

paR^h	study, read	**paR^{h}ā**	teach	**paR^{h}vā**	have someone teach
kar	do	—		**karvā**	have someone do
lag	seem, be attached	**lagā**	attach	**lagvā**	cause to be attached

You might already have observed the same base stem in the three verb forms. For the time being, we omit the intricate details about the verb forms – such as the presence of the two forms of **karnā** but three forms of the other two verbs – and proceed to the fundamental points. It is immediately obvious that the verb forms in columns three and five share the verb stem in column one, adding either the suffix **ā** or **vā**, as in

paR^h	+	**ā**	=	**paR^{h}ā**	cause someone to read, teach
paR^h	+	**vā**	=	**paR^{h}vā**	have x to teach y

The two suffixes **ā** and **vā** are the ones that form the causative verbs. The meaning expressed by them can be translated as follows: **ā** expresses 'make someone do something', whereas **vā** means 'have x make y do something'. The English verb 'teach' is a causative verb in Hindi, but in most cases the causative verbs cannot be translated into English that easily. Observe the following examples:

mẽ	**kahānī**	**paR^{h}tā**	**hū̃**.
I	story	read-pres.	am

I read a story.

mẽ	**John**	**ko**	**kahānī**	**paR^{h}ātā**	**hū̃**
I	John	to	story	read-caus.ā-pres.	am

I make John read a story, *or* I teach John a story.

mẽ	**John**	**ko**	**Rām**	**se**	**kahānī**	**paR^{h}vātā**	**hū̃**
I	John	to	Ram	by	story	read-caus. **vā**-pres.	am

I have Ram make John read a story.

Notice that the causative verbs with **vā** always have an indirect agent (e.g. **Ram se**, 'by Ram').

Did you notice the use of the causative verb in our dialogue? The following sentence contains a causative verb:

muj^{h}e	**kuc^{h}**	***traveller's***	***cheque***	***cash***	**karvāne**	**hɛ̃.**
me	some	traveller's	cheques	cash	do-caus. **vā**-inf.	are

I need to [have someone] cash some traveller's cheques.

In this sentence the indirect agent (by someone) is implied because of the causative verb with the suffix **-vā.**

lenā **as a helping verb**

When the cashier hands over the rupees to Philip, he says

gin	**lījiye**
count	take-imp

Please [you] count [for your own benefit].

Had he used the simple verb form instead of the compound verb (i.e. **giniye**), the beneficiary of the action of counting would have remained unspecified. The helping verb **le** indicates subject as the beneficiary.

Reading practice

ek lok-kat^{h}ā

(1) ek gā̃v mẽ ek cor *jail* se b^{h}āg gayā.
(2) *pulis (police)* vālā us ko pakaRne ke liye dauRā.
(3) itne mẽ gā̃v vālõ ne b^{h}āgte cor ko pakaR liyā.
(4) *pulis* vālā zor zor se cillā rahā t^{h}ā, 'pakRo, mat jāne do.'
(5) ye sunte hī̃ gā̃v vālõ ne cor ko c^{h}oR diyā.
(6) jab *pulis* vālā gā̃v vālõ ke pās pahũcā.
(7) to us ko bahut gussā āyā.
(8) gusse mẽ us ne gā̃v vālõ se pūc^{h}ā,
(9) 'tum ne cor ko kyõ c^{h}oR diyā?'
(10) gā̃v vālõ ne javāb diyā.
(11) āp ne hī̃ kahā, 'pakRo mat, jāne do'.

A folk tale

(1) *In a* (lit. one) *village, a thief ran away* (i.e. escaped) *from jail.*
(2) *A policeman ran to catch him.* (lit. ran for catching)
(3) *In the meantime the villagers caught the escaping* (lit. running) *thief.*
(4) *The policeman was screaming very loudly, 'Catch [him]; do not let [him] go.'*
(5) *As soon as the villagers heard this, they left the thief.*
(6) *When the policeman reached the villagers* (lit. reached near the villagers)
(7) *he became very angry.*
(8) *Angrily* (lit. in anger) *he asked the villagers* (lit. asked from the villagers)
(9) *'Why did you leave the thief?'* (i.e. why did you let the thief go?)
(10) *The villagers answered,*
(11) *You yourself said, 'Don't catch [him]; let [him] go.'*

Vocabulary

lok	लोक	people
kat^{h}ā (f.)	कथा	story
lok kat^{h}ā (f.)	लोक-कथा	folk tale
gā̃v (m.)	गाँव	village
b^{h}āgnā (-ne)	भागना	to run
b^{h}āg gayā (compound verb)	भाग गया	to run away
pulis vālā (m.)	पुलिस वाला	policeman
pakaRnā (+ne)	पकड़ना	to catch
dauRnā (-ne)	दौड़ना	to run
itne mẽ	इतने में	in the meanwhile
gā̃v vālā (m.)	गाँव वाला	villager
b^{h}āgte (present participle)	भागते	running
cor (m.)	चोर	thief
pakaRnā (+ne)	पकड़ना	to catch
pakaR liyā (compound verb)	पकड़ लिया	to catch (for one's benefit)
zor se	ज़ोर से	loudly
cillānā (-ne)	चिल्लाना	to scream
mat	मत	not [see notes]

jāne do (compound verb)	जाने दो	let (someone) go.
sunte hī (**sun+te hī** participle)	सुनते ही	as soon as (someone) heard
c^{h}oRnā (+ne)	छोड़ना	to leave
c^{h}oR diyā (compound verb)	छोड़ दिया	left (for someone else's sake)
gussā (m.)	गुस्सा	anger
pūc^{h}nā (+ne)	पूछना	to ask
javāb (m.)	जवाब	answer
javāb denā (+ne)	जवाब देना	to answer, reply

Pronunciation

Compare the pronunciation of the stem **pakaR** पकड़ 'catch', in the following three verbal forms. Note the presence of the stem-final vowel **a** in the first two forms and its absence in the third form which is written as **pakaRo** पकड़ो, but is pronounced as **pakRo**. For further details about when the vowel **a** is retained and under what conditions it is dropped, see script unit 4 in this book.

pak*a*Rne ke liye	पकड़ने के लिये	in order to catch
pak*a*R liyā	पकड़ लिया	caught (for their own benefit)
pakRo	पकड़ो	catch!

Notes

Present participle

In the third line we came across the expression

itne	**mẽ**	**gā̃v**	**vālõ**	**ne**	**b^{h}āgte**	**cor**	**ko**
this much	in	village	-er (p. obl.)	agent	running	thief	to
pakaR	**liyā**						
catch	took						

In the meantime (lit. in this much [time]), the villagers caught the thief.

The phrase **b^{h}āgte cor ko** is in the oblique form of the simple present participial phrase.

b^{h}āgtā	**(huā)**	**cor**
run + present participle	happened	thief (m., sg.)

The running thief, or the thief who is/was/will be running

The composition of the first element is as follows

b^{h}āg	+	**t**	+	**ā**
run	+	present	+	masculine singular

You have probably guessed by now that this is the same form we came across in the simple present tense formation. The only difference is that the auxiliary verb is absent.

The second element is the same form as the simple past tense form of the verb **honā**; remember the forms **huā**, **hue**, **huī** and **huī̃**. The last form (i.e. the feminine plural **huī̃**) does not appear in the participial construction. Why does it fail to appear? The reason will become readily clear from the following explanation. This element is optional; therefore, it can easily be omitted in the conversation. That is the case in our story.

Now compare the participial form with the present tense verb form.

present participle		*simple present tense*		
b^{h}āgtā	**cor**	**cor**	**b^{h}āgtā**	**hɛ**
The running thief		The thief runs		

In the present participial form the verb form ceases to function like a real verb and begins to behave like an adjective. Therefore the verbal adjectives, which are drawn from the simple present tense, are called the 'present participle'. In other words, they are like adjectives ending in **-ā**, but the only difference is that they are derived from verbs.

Like the adjectives ending in **-ā**, these agree in number or gender with the following noun. For example:

b^{h}āgt*ā* laRk*ā*	the running boy	**b^{h}āgt*ī* laRk*ī***	the running girl
b^{h}āgt*e* laRk*e*	the running boys	**b^{h}āgt*ī* laRkiyā̃**	the running girls

The main function of the present participial clause is to denote *'action in progress'*.

Notice that, like adjectives, the present participles do not have any inherent tense reference to time, as is clear from the English translation. The tense is usually supplied by the main verb form in the sentence. If in the third line the verb 'caught' is changed to the present and the future tense, the tense reference of the participial form 'running' will change to present and future, respectively. That is why the alternative English translation of **b^{h}āgtā cor** contains three possible tense references.

Ambiguity and pausing

pakRo	**mat**	**jāne**	**do**
catch	not	go-oblique infinitive	give

The translation of the verb phrase **jāne do** is 'to allow to go' or 'to let go'. The familiar imperative form of the verb **pakaRnā** is **pakRo** which means 'catch'. Depending on the pause, the meaning changes. The pause is indicated by the comma.

pakRo	**mat,**	**jāne**	**do**
catch	not,	go-oblique infinitive	give

Don't catch [him]; let [him] go.

But if the pause is immediately after **pakRo**, then the negative particle **mat** negates the second verb, as in

pakRo,	**mat**	**jāne**	**do**
catch,	not	go-oblique infinitive	give

Catch, don't let [him] go.

The negative particle mat

We have encountered two negative particles – **nahī̃** and **nā** – in the earlier conversation. The third negative marker, **mat**, is primarily restricted to familiar and non-honorific imperatives. In prohibitives, the use of **mat** is particularly noteworthy.

Word order and the contrastive negation

We mentioned earlier that the negative particle is usually placed before the verb. Thus, normally the Hindi equivalent of English 'do not catch' will be

mat pakRo
not catch-imperative (familiar)
Don't catch.

However, the contrastive function is highlighted by the placement of the negative particle in the postverbal position (i.e. after the verb). This is the reason that **mat** is placed after **pakRo** in the expression:

pakRo mat, jãne do Don't catch [him]; let [him] go.

The other reading, 'Catch, do not let [him] go', has conjunctive force rather than contrastive force. Therefore the negative particle appears in its normal preverbal position.

Reading practice

Here is a sample of the opening lines of an old Hindi romantic song. In the song, the lover is imploring his beloved never to forget him. However, the approach is an indirect one. (remember the politeness germ!). Therefore, rather than saying directly not to forget him, he says

ye rātẽ, ye mausam, ye hãsnā, hãsānā
muj^{h}e b^{h}ūl jānā, inhẽ na b^{h}ulānā.

These nights, this weather, this laughter and making [each other] laugh,
[You may] forget me, but never make them forget.

Vocabulary

rāt (f.)	रात	night
mausam (m.)	मौसम	weather
hãsnā (**-ne**)	हँसना	to laugh

hā̃sānā (+ne)	हँसाना	to make someone laugh
b^{h}ūl (-ne)	भूलना	to forget
b^{h}ūl jānā (compound verb)	भूल जाना	to forget fully
b^{h}ulānā (+ne)	भुलाना	to make someone forget

अभ्यास Exercises

1

Match the words or phrases given in the following three columns to make appropriate Hindi sentences.

āiye	kī bāt kyā	rak^{h}iye
taklīf	tashrīā̃	hɛ
shāyad	āp kā intzār	kām zyādā ho
vo	arz	hɛ
ādāb	āp ko daftar mẽ	kar rahī t^{h}ī.

2

Circle the appropriate form of the verb in each of the following sentences:

(a) māf kījiye, mɛ̃ *cheque* b^{h}ejnā
(b^{h}ūl liyā/b^{h}ūl gayā/b^{h}ūl diyā).

(b) mɛ̃ ne k^{h}ānā
(k^{h}ā liyā/k^{h}ā paRā /k^{h}ā diyā).

(c) āp kā buxār
(baR^h liyā/baR^h gayā/baR^h diyā).

(d) āp ne kuc^h javāb nahī̃
(liyā/diyā/āyā/gyā).

(e) āp merī salāh mān
(lījiye/dījiye/āiye).

3

Which job description matches the job?

(a) ad^{h}yāpak	imāratẽ banvātā hɛ.
(b) DākTar (doctor)	kapRe banātā hɛ.
(c) *cashier*	k^{h}ānā banātā hɛ.
(d) darzī	Tīkā lagātā hɛ.

(e) k^{h}ānsāmā — *cheque cash* kartā hɛ.
(f) *driver* — c^{h}ātrõ ko paR^{h}ātā hɛ.
(g) *civil engineer* — *car* calātā hɛ.

4

Ram and Shyam are brothers. Ram believes in self-help and does everything on his own. Shyam, on the other hand, gets someone to do his work. Write about Shyam according to the model given below:

rām ne apnā kām kiyā.	Ram did his work.
shyām ne hilDā se apnā kām karvāyā.	Shyam had Hildā do his work.

(a) Ram: rām ne kār calāī.
Shyam: ____________

(b) Ram: rām xat lik^{h}egā.
Shyam: ____________

(c) Ram: rām g^{h}ar banā rahā hɛ.
Shyam: ____________

(d) Ram: rām kahānī sunā rahā t^{h}ā.
Shyam: ____________

(e) Ram: rām laRkī ko paR^{h}ātā hɛ.
Shyam: ____________

5

Fill out the appropriate present participial form according to the model given below:

calnā: mɛ̃ *caltī* gaR^{h}ī mẽ caR^{h}ā.
b^{h}āgnā: mɛ̃ ne b^{h}āgte kutte ko dek^{h}ā.

(a) hãsnā: muj^{h}e vo ____________ laRkī bahut pasand hɛ.
(b) k^{h}elnā: ____________ bacce bahut sundar lag rahe t^{h}e.
(c) gānā: ____________ ciRiyā uR rahī t^{h}ī.
(d) sitār bajānā: ____________ ____________ ādmī bahut acc^{h}ā hɛ.

(e) tɛrnā: ——— $mac^{h}aliy\tilde{o}$ ko $dek^{h}o$.
(f) ronā: DākTar ne ——— bacce ko Tīkā lagāyā.

6

The pacman has attacked the following text. Consequently, some elements of the following text have been chewed up. Your task is to supply the postpositions or the missing parts of the verb in those places where the three-bullet symbol is left by the pacman.

mɛ̃ *railway station* apne dost ●●● intzār kar rahā $t^{h}\bar{a}$. $t^{h}oR\bar{\imath}$ der bād gāRī āyī aur merā dost gāRī se utrā. ham bahut xush ho kar mile. is bār pā̃c sāl ke bād hamārī mulākāt ●●●. $t^{h}oR\bar{\imath}$ der bād mɛ̃ ne kahā, 'is bār bahut der ke bād yahā̃ āye ho.' usne javāb ●●●, $acc^{h}\bar{\imath}$ bāt $t^{h}\bar{\imath}$ ki agar gāRī der se na ●●●, to mɛ̃ āj $b^{h}\bar{\imath}$ na ●●●.

9 फार्चून कुकी में क्या लिखा है? What's written in the fortune cookie?

By the end of this lesson you should be able to:

- use past participles
- use the participial forms as adverbials
- use the construction 'neither ... nor'
- understand hidden assumptions
- form purpose clauses
- know more about Indian food (particularly curries)
- use the passive construction
- know more on reduplication

Reading practice

Money will come soon

(1) ek din do dost k^{h}ānā k^{h}āne ek cīnī *restaurant* gaye.
(2) k^{h}āne ke bād bɛrā 'fortune cookies' lāyā.
(3) donõ ne apnī apnī *'fortune cookie'* ko k^{h}olā aur apnī apnī kismat ke bāre mẽ paR^{h}ā.
(4) p^{h}ir ek dost ne dūsre se pūc^{h}ā, 'kāgaz par kyā lik^{h}ā hɛ?'
(5) lik^{h}ā hɛ – 'jaldī pɛsā āne vālā hɛ.'
(6) ye to baRī xushī kī bāt hɛ.
(7) to koī lāTrī *(lottery)* xarīdī hɛ?
(8) nahī̃, lekin kal apnā jīvan bīmā karvāyā hɛ.

(1) *One day two friends went to eat in a Chinese restaurant.*
(2) *After eating* (i.e, after they finished eating), *the waiter brought* [*them*] *fortune cookies.*
(3) [*They*] *both opened their fortune cookie*[*s*] *and read about their fortune[s].*
(4) *Then one friend asked the other, 'What is written on the paper?'*
(5) *[It] is written – 'Money is about to come soon.'*
(6) *This is a matter of great happiness.*
(7) *Did [you] buy a lottery ticket?*
(8) *No, but yesterday, I bought life-insurance.*
(lit. I have caused someone to do the life insurance)

Vocabulary

dost (m.)	दोस्त	friend
k^{h}ānā (m.)	खाना	food
k^{h}ānā (+ne)	खाना	to eat
k^{h}āne (ke liye)	खाने (के लिये)	(in order) to eat
cīn	चीन	China
cīnī	चीनी	Chinese
bɛrā (m.)	बैरा	waiter
lānā (-ne)	लाना	to bring
donõ	दोनों	both

k^{h}olnā (+ne)	खोलना	to open
kismat (f.)	किस्मत	fortune, fate
kāgaz (m.)	कागज़	paper
lik^{h}nā (+ne)	लिखना	to write
lik^{h}ā hɛ	लिखा है	is written
jaldī	जल्दी	quickly, hurry
pɛsā (m.)	पैसा	money; one-hundredth of a rupee
āne vālā	आने वाला	about to come
jīvan (m.)	जीवन	life
bīmā (m.)	बीमा	insurance

Notes

Purpose clauses and deletion

In the last lesson, we came across the following expression:

pulis *(police)*	**vālā**	**us ko**	**pakaRne**	**ke liye**	**dauRā.**
police	one/man	him	to catch-obl.	for	ran

The policeman ran to catch him.

Now compare this Hindi expression with the opening line:

ek	**din**	**do**	**dost**	**k^{h}ānā**	**k^{h}āne**	**ek**	**cīnī**
one	day	two	friends	food	to eat-obl.	one	Chinese

restaurant	**gaye.**
restaurant	went.

One day two friends went to a Chinese restaurant to eat food.

You must have observed by now that the underlined infinitive phrases in English, such as 'to catch' and 'to eat', are not translated as plain infinitives such as **pakaRnā** and **k^{h}ānā**. The plain (simple) infinite phrase will yield an ungrammatical sentence in Hindi. As is clear from the Hindi expression **pakaRne ke liye**, 'to catch', the Hindi equivalent of the English purpose clause 'to catch' is paraphrased as 'in order to catch' and therefore, the postposition **ke liye**, 'for, in order to' follows the infinitive phrase **pakaRnā**. The peer group influence of the postposition on the noun makes the noun oblique and, thus, **pakaRnā** changes to **pakaRne**. The postposition can be described as the ghost postposition – **ke liye**.

What causes the retention or deletion of the postposition in the purpose clauses such as those under consideration here? The answer lies in the main verb of the sentence, **dauRā**, 'ran', and **gaye**, 'went'. If the main verb is a motion verb, it is possible optionally to drop the postposition as **k^{h}ane**. Similarly, it is possible to drop **ke liye** in the first sentence:

pulis vālā us ko pakaRne dauRā.

If we replace the main verb in the above sentence with a static (non-motion) verb, the postposition is obligatorily retained, as in

pulis vālā us ko pakaRne ke liye hɛ.	The police are [there] to catch him.

The deletion of the postposition would be ungrammatical; therefore the following sentence is unacceptable.

pulis vālā us ko pakaRne hɛ.

Reduplication and distributive meaning

In Lesson 4, we demonstrated that repetition expresses intensity. In the third sentence the feminine form of the reflexive pronoun **apnā** is repeated:

donõ	**ne**	**apnī**	**apnī**	**'fortune cookie'**	**ko**	**k^{h}olā**
both	agent	self	self	fortune cookie	obj.	opened

Both opened their fortune cookie[s].

apnī is repeated to convey that they opened their respective cookies.

Past participle: adjectival and adverbial use

In Lesson 8 we introduced the present participles. Compare the phrase **b^{h}āgte cor ko**, 'the running thief', with **b^{h}āge cor ko**. The later form is called the past participial form and can be translated into English as 'the escaped thief'.

Now compare the difference between the present forms and their corresponding past participial forms and the difference in meaning rendered by the two forms:

Present Participle		*Past Participle*	
bʰāg*tā* cor	the running thief	**bhāg*ā* cor**	the escaped thief
bolt*ī* laRkī	the speaking girl	**bol*ī* bāt**	the spoken matter
likʰ*te* laRke	the writing boys	**likʰ*e* shabda**	the written words

(the boys who are/were/will be writing.)

Notice the composition of the past participial form:

Stem	+	*past participial marker*
bʰāg	+	**ā**
run	+	past-masculine singular
bol	+	**ī**
speak	+	past-feminine singular
likʰ	+	**e**
write	+	past-masculine plural

You have probably guessed by now that the past participle is the same form as that we came across in the simple past tense formation. The only difference is that the feminine singular form is used for both singular and for plural forms.

The second element (optional) remains the same both in the present and the past participial forms, i.e. **huā**, **hue** and **huī**.

As stated earlier, in the participle the verb form ceases to function as a real verb and begins to behave like an adjective. Therefore, the verbal adjectives which are drawn from the simple past tense are called the 'past participle'. In other words, they are like adjectives ending in **ā**: the only difference is that they are derived from verbs.

Like the adjectives ending in **ā**, they agree in number or gender with the following noun. Note the gender number agreement in the above examples.

Unlike the present participle, which denotes *'action in progress'*, the past participle indicates a *state*.

Note the difference in meaning between the present participle and its corresponding past participial form:

present participle	*past participle*
bɛT^{h}tā laRkā The boy who is [in the process of] sitting.	**bɛT^{h}ā laRkā** The seated boy.
sotī laRkiyā̃ The girls who are in the process of sleeping.	**soī laRkiyā̃** The sleeping girls.

The present participial form **sotī** indicates the dozing off stage prior to sound sleep, whereas the corresponding past participle indicates the state of sound sleep.

Adverbials

So far we have discussed the adjectival use of participles. Participial forms when placed before verbs mark adverbial usage. Note the translation of the sentence given in quotes in sentence 4 of the reading passage.

kāgaz	**par**	**kyā**	**lik^{h}ā**	**hɛ?**
paper	on	what	written	is

What is written on the paper?

Superficially it appears as if **lik^{h}ā hɛ** is the present perfect form of the verb **lik^{h}**, which should be translated as 'has written', but this is not the case. The main verb is **hɛ**, while **lik^{h}ā** is the past participial form used as an adverb without the optional element **huā**. In short,

lik^{h}ā **hɛ** = **lik^{h}ā huā** **hɛ**

Since the main verb is **hɛ** and **lik^{h}ā** is the past participle, the translation is 'is written' rather than 'has written'. The insertion of the optional element disambiguates it from the present perfect form of the verb **lik^{h}**. In passing, it should be mentioned that the verb phrase in sentence 7 of the passage, **xarīdī hɛ**, is a real present perfect form of the verb **xarīd**, 'buy'; therefore its literal translation is 'has bought'.

Dialogue

'Spice up your life'

Bill Hassett and his wife, who are visiting India for the first time, are invited by Bill's Indian partner for dinner. Bill's partner's wife, Jyotsna Singh, asks her guests about the type of food they would prefer. Bill suggests to his wife, 'Honey, as is said in English: "Spice up your life." Why don't we both spice up our lives in the literal sense and try the spicy food?' Therefore, with the intention of enjoying spicy food, he tells Jyotsna Singh:

BILL: hindustānī *curry* ab^{h}ī tak ham ne nahī̃ k^{h}āyī.

JYOTSNA: āp ko masāledār k^{h}ānā pasand hɛ yā *curry*?

BILL: donõ mẽ farka kyā hɛ?

JYOTSNA: amrīkā mẽ curry ek *dish* kā nām hɛ lekin hindustān mẽ ɛsī bāt nahī̃.

BILL: hamāre yahā̃ *curry* kā matlab 'koī masāledār hindustānī dish' hɛ.

JYOTSNA: hindustān mẽ na to *curry* hameshā masāledār hotī hɛ aur na hī hindustān mẽ *curry powder* aksar biktā hɛ. *curry* aksar tarī vālī hotī hɛ aur ye mā̃s, sabzī, macc^{h}lī yā p^{h}al kī banī hotī hɛ.

BILL: are! binā masāle kī *curry*. ye to ham ne kab^{h}ī nahī̃ sunā t^{h}ā.

JYOTSNA: to ab āp ko kaun sī *curry* pasand hɛ?

BILL: ām ke ām aur guT^{h}līyõ ke dām. *curry* ke bāre me patā lag gayā aur aslī *curry* cak^{h}ne kā maukā b^{h}ī mil jāyegā. acc^{h}ā, ham ko tez masāledār mā̃s kī *curry* bahut pasand hɛ. (*They laugh at the unexpected turn of the conversation; the proverb has added a lighter touch to the conversation, and they continue to talk ...*)

BILL: *So far, in India we have not eaten curry.*

JYOTSNA: *Do you like spicy food or curry?*

BILL: *What is the difference between the two?*

JYOTSNA: *In America, curry is the name of a dish, but such is not the case in India.*

BILL: *In our place* (i.e. in America) *curry is a spicy Indian dish.*

JYOTSNA: *In India, curry is not always spicy nor is curry powder*

	usually sold [*commercially*]. *Curry is usually liquefied and is made of meat, vegetables, fish or fruit.*
BILL:	*Wow! Curry without spices. This we have (lit. had) never heard of* [*before*].
JYOTSNA:	*So, which curry do you like?*
BILL:	[*This is like*] *earth's and heaven's joy combined.* [*Now*] *I have come to know about curry and will get an opportunity to taste a genuine curry. Well, we like very spicy meat curry very much.*

(They laugh at the unexpected turn of the conversation; the proverb has added a lighter touch to the conversation, and they continue to talk...)

Vocabulary

curry (f.)	करी/कढ़ी	curry (*see Notes)
masālā (m.)	मसाला	spice
masāledār (adj.)	मसालेदार	spicy
yā	या	or
farka (m.)	फर्क	difference
hamāre yahā̃	हमारे यहाँ	at our place (house, country, etc.)
na ... na	न ... न	neither...nor
matlab (m.)	मतलब	meaning
hameshā	हमेशा	always
aksar	अकसर	often, usually
tar	तर	wet
tarī (f.)	तरी	liquid
mā̃s (m.)	माँस	meat
sabzī (f.)	सब्जी	vegetable
macc^{h}lī (f.)	मछली	fish
p^{h}al (m)	फल	fruit
bannā (-ne)	बनना	to be made
banī	बनी	made
binā	बिना	without
kab^{h}ī	कभी	ever

kab^{h}ī nahī̃	कभी नहीं	never
ām (m.); (adj.)	आम	mango (n.); common (adj.)
guT^{h}lī (f.)	गुठली	stone (of a fruit)
dām (m)	दाम	price
ām ke ām aur ... ... guT^{h}līyõ ke dām	आम के आम और ... ... गुठलियों के दाम	earth's joy and heaven's combined
patā lagnā (+**ko**)	पता लगाना	to come to know
aslī	असली	real, genuine
cak^{h}nā (+**ne**)	चखना	to taste
maukā (m.)	मौका	opportunity
tez	तेज़	fast, quick, sharp, strong

Pronunciation

The English word 'curry' is a derivative of the Hindi word **kaR^{h}ī.** Note the presence of the retroflex **R^{h}** in the Hindi word.

Notes

Curry powder/curry

In the authentic Indian tradition, the English word 'curry' simply does not exist. It is part of the vocabulary of English-educated bilinguals. The Hindi word **kaR^{h}ī** is restricted to a vegetarian curry which is made out of chick-pea flour. The chances are that Hindi speakers will not use the term, curry, to refer to the dishes mentioned above. Therefore, do not be surprised if this term is not understood in the native Indian context. Indians will capture this concept by specifying the degree of spiciness and by qualifying a dish with words such as **tarī vālī sabzī** or **tarī vālā mā̃s/goshta.** Curry is actually a blend of ground herbs and spices adapted by British settlers in India from the traditional spice mixtures of Indian cuisine. The basic ingredients of commercial curry powder are turmeric (which imparts the characteristic yellow colour), cumin, coriander and cayenne pepper. Curry powder is primarily made for foreign consumption.

Focus and word order

The normal word order of the opening sentence of the above dialogue is as follows:

ham	**ne**	**hindustānī**	***curry***	**ab^{h}ī tak**	**nahī̃**	**k^{h}āyī.**
we	agent	Indian	curry	yet	not	ate

We have not eaten Indian curry yet.

The two elements of the above sentence – time adverb and the object – are placed in the sentence in the initial position, as they are being singled out for emphasis.

hindustānī	**curry**	**ab^{h}ī tak**	**ham**	**ne**	**nahī̃**	**k^{h}āyī.**
Indian	curry	yet	we	agent	not	ate

As yet, it is the Indian curry [that] we have not eaten.

'Neither ... nor' and emphatic particles

Note the use of the emphatic particles with **na...na**, 'neither...nor'. Also, observe the placement of the phrase **hindustān mẽ** in the 'neither' and 'nor' clause.

hindustān	**mẽ**	**na**	**to**	***curry***	**hameshā**	**masāledār**
India	in	not	emp.par.	curry	always	spicy

hotī	**hɛ**	**aur**	**na**	**hī**	**hindustān**	**mẽ**
be-pres.	is (aux.)	and	not	emp. par.	India	in

curry powder	**aksar**	**biktā**	**hɛ.**
curry powder	often	be sold-pres.	is

As regards curry in India, it is not always spicy and curry powder is not often sold in India.

The emphatic particles **to** and **hī** are more intimately tied to curry and curry powder, respectively, as shown:

hindustān	**mẽ**	**na**	***curry***	**to**	**hameshā**	**masāledār**
India	in	not	curry	emp.part.	always	spicy

hotī	**hɛ**	**aur**	**na**	**hindustān**	**mẽ**	***curry powder***
be-present	is (aux.)	and	not	India	in	curry powder

hī	**aksar**	**biktā**	**hɛ**
emp.part.	often	be sold-pres.	is

The movement of the emphatic particles from their original position after the negative particle **na** renders the emphatic counterpart of the normal 'neither...nor' construction.

Past participle: adverbial

The verb **hotī hɛ** is the generic construction explained in Lesson 4. Can you find the past participle in the following sentence?

ye	**mā̃s**	**sabzī**	**macc^{h}lī**	**yā**	**p^{h}al**	**kī**
this	meat	vegetable	fish	or	fruit	of

banī	**hotī**	**hɛ**
make-past.ppl.	be-pres.	is (aux.)

Yes, **banī** is the past participial form of the verb **bannā**, 'to be made'. It can be followed by the optional element **huī**. However, in the following sentence

ham	**ne**	**kab^{h}ī**	**nahī̃**	**sunā**	**t^{h}ā**
we	agent	ever	not	heard	was

We had never heard of [it].

sunā is not a past participle. In combination with the auxiliary, **t^{h}ā**, it renders the past perfect form of the verb **sunnā**, 'to hear/listen to'.

Compound verbs with jānā 'to go'

As explained in Lesson 7, the helping verb **jānā** expresses 'transformation' and/or 'finality or completeness'. Both semantic shades can be witnessed in the following conjunct sentence:

curry	**ke bāre mẽ**	**patā**	**lag**	**gayā**	**aur**	**aslī**	*curry*
curry	about	address	strike	went	and	genuine	curry

cak^{h}ne	**kā**	**maukā**	**b^{h}ī**	**mil**	**jāyegā**
taste	of	opportunity	also	get	go-will

The verbs **patā lagnā**, 'to come to know', and **milnā** 'to get', are subjected to the compound verb construction, and the helping verb **jānā**, 'to go', loses its literal meaning.

'The opportunity to...'

Note the word-for-word translation of the English expression, 'we will get the chance to taste the genuine curry'.

ham	**ko**	**aslī**	*curry*	**cak^{h}ne**	**kā**	**maukā**	**mil**	**jāyegā**
we	to	genuine	curry	taste	of	opportunity	get	go-will

The expression 'to get the opportunity to do x' requires the experiential subject; therefore, the subject **ham**, 'we', is followed by the postposition **ko**. Since a Hindi verb never agrees with a subject that is followed by a postposition, the verb in the above sentence agrees with **maukā**, 'opportunity', which is masculine singular. Also, the genitive **kā** agrees with **maukā.**

Dialogue

āg! āg! *'Fire! Fire!'*

The following week, Mr and Mrs Hassett again come to the Singhs' residence for dinner. They converse with each other on a wide variety of subjects. Finally, the delicious smell of the food begins to overpower their conversation. In the meanwhile, the hostess announces that dinner is served.

BILL: vāh! vāh! shāndār xushbū ā rahī hɛ, aur intazār karnā mushkil hɛ.

JYOTSNA: āiye, to k^{h}ānā shurū kiyā jāye. ye hɛ, āp kī pasand – tez mirca vālī *chicken curry.*

(*Bill takes a lot of curry while Mrs Hassett takes only a little bit. After taking the first substantial bite:*)

BILL: (*fanning his mouth*) Ohhh! ... āg! ... āg!

JYOTSNA: kyõ kyā huā?

BILL: ye to *curry* nahī̃ hɛ! ye to jwālāmuk^{h}ī hɛ!! aur mɛ̃ apnā āg buj^{h}āne kā sāmān b^{h}ī nahī̃ lāyā.

JYOTSNA: āg buj^{h}āne kā sāmān ye hɛ – agar bahut mirca lag rahī hɛ to kuc^{h} dahī lījiye.

(*After a while Bill's mouth cools down.*)

BILL: sac, amrīkā [America] mẽ tez masāledār k^{h}ānā itnā tez nahī̃ hotā.

JYOTSNA: hā̃, ye to hindustān hɛ. yahā̃ 'tez' kā matlab 'bahut tez' hɛ. ham log bahut tez k^{h}āte hɛ̃ lekin hindustān mẽ sab^{h}ī log itnā tez k^{h}ānā nahī̃ k^{h}ā sakte.

BILL: galat-fahamī dūr karne ke liye shukriya. mɛ̃ ab samaj^{h} gayā ki 'tez' xatarnāk shabda hɛ.

BILL: *Wow! Wow! The splendid fragrance [of food] is coming; [It] is difficult to wait any longer* (i.e. I cannot wait more).

JYOTSNA: *Please come, let's start eating* (lit. eating should be started). *This is your favourite – hot chicken curry* (lit. sharp pepper one chicken curry).

(Bill takes a lot of curry while Mrs Hassett takes only a little bit. After taking the first substantial bite:)

BILL: (*fanning his mouth*) *Oh...h...h..! Fire!... Fire!*

JYOTSNA: *Why? What happened?*

BILL: *This is not curry* (lit. as regards this, this is not curry)*! This is a volcano* (lit. as regards this, this is a volcano)*!! And I did not bring my fire extinguisher* (lit. fire extinguisher = the stuff/tools to extinguish fire).

JYOTSNA: *This is [your] fire extinguisher – If [it] is very hot* (lit. if very much pepper striking you), *then take some yogurt.*

(After a while Bill's mouth cools down.)

BILL: *True, in America the spicy food is not so spicy.*

JYOTSNA: *Yes, this is India* (lit. as regards this, this is India). *Here, 'hot' means 'very hot'. We eat very hot food, but not all people can eat such hot [food] in India.*

BILL:	*Thanks for dispelling [my] misconception. Now I [fully] understand* (lit. now I understood) *that 'tez' is a dangerous word.*

Vocabulary

vāh! vāh!	वाह ! वाह !	Wow! Bravo!
shāndār	शानदार	grand, splendid
xushbū (f.)	खुशबू	fragrance (lit. happy smell)
shurū karnā (+ne)	शुरू करना	to begin
shurū kiyā jāye	शुरू किया जाये	should be started
mirca (f.)	मिर्च	chili peppers
oh	ओह	exclamation of pain/sorrow
āg (f.)	आग	fire
jwālāmuk^{h}ī (m.)	ज्वालामुखी	volcano
buj^{h}ānā (+ne)	बुझाना	to extinguish
sāmān (m.)	सामान	baggage, goods, stuff, tools
lānā (-ne)	लाना	to bring
dahī (m./f.)	दही	yogurt
sac (m.)	सच	truth, true
<itnā>	इतना	this/so much/many
galat	ग़लत	wrong
galat-fahamī (f.)	ग़लतफहमी	misconception, misunderstanding
dūr	दूर	far, distant
dūr karnā (+ne)	दूर करना	to dispel, to eliminate
<xatrā> (m.)	ख़तरा	danger
xatarnāk	ख़तरनाक	dangerous
shabda (m.)	शब्द	word

Pronunciation

Words such as **xatrā** and **itnā** are written as **xatarā** and **itanā**, respectively. The omitted vowel of **xatrā** surfaces in **xatarnāk**.

Notes

Ambiguity

The following expression in the opening line of the above dialogue is ambiguous.

aur	**intazār**	**karnā**	**mushkil**	**hɛ**
and	wait	to do	difficult	is

'[It] is difficult to wait any longer', or 'and [it] is difficult to wait'.

In other words, **aur** can be interpreted either as a conjunction marker or a modifier of **intazār.**

Passive construction

The English expression, 'let's begin eating', is paraphrased as 'eating should be done'.

k^{h}ānā	**shuru**	**kiyā**	**jāye**
eating	begin	did	go-subjunctive

The verb phrase is in the passive subjunctive form. The passive construction in Hindi takes the compound verb construction in the sense that it involves a main verb and the helping verb. The only difference is that the main verb, rather than being in a stem form, is in the past form.

Passive		
main verb (past form)	*helping verb (**jānā** + tense)*	
kiyā	**jāye**	should be done
paR^{h}ā	**jātā hɛ**	is read
paR^{h}ā	**gayā**	was read
paR^{h}ā	**jāyegā**	will be read
bolā	**jā rahā hɛ**	is being spoken/told

In other words, the passive is formed by using the main verb in the past form. The helping verb is always **jānā,** 'to go', which undergoes tense conjugation like any other helping verb in the compound verb construction.

Like English passive subjects, which are appended with 'by', Hindi passive subjects are attached to the postposition **se**, 'from, by'. Here is a list of pronominal forms with the postposition **se**.

mɛ̃ + se = muj^h se	by me	**ham + se = ham se**	by us
tū + se = tuj^h se	by you	**tum + se = tum se**	by you
		āp + se = āp se	by you (honorific)
vo + se = us se	by him/her	**ve + se = un se**	by them

Since the passive subject is always followed by the postposition **se**, the passive verb can never agree with it; instead it agrees with the object as in

muj^h	**se**	**kitāb**	**paR^h*ī***	**gay*ī***
me	by	book (f.)	read-past-feminine	passive-go + past-feminine-singular

The book was read by me.

If the feminine object **kitāb**, 'book', is replaced by the masculine object **xat**, 'letter', the passive verb form will be in the masculine singular form.

muj^h	**se**	**xat**	**paR^h*ā***	**gay*ā***
me	by	letter (m.)	read-past-masculine	Passive-go + past-masculine-singular

The letter was read by me.

One important difference between Hindi and English is that the transitive as well as intransitive verbs can be made passive in Hindi, while only the transitive verbs can be made passive in English. See the grammar section for more details.

Omitted subject

agar	**[āp**	**ko]**	**bahut**	**mirca**	**lag**	**rahī**	**hɛ**	**to**	**[āp]**
If	[you	to]	very	pepper	strike	ing	is	then	(you)

kuc^h	**dahī**	**lījiye**
some	yogurt	take

The omitted subject of the first clause is experiential while it is simple nominative in the second clause.

The past participle and the passive construction

You must have discovered by now that there is no neat correspondence between the English and Hindi passives. The English passive construction can be paraphrased in one of the following three ways. First, those instances where English and Hindi both use the passive construction to express the target idea. For example, English expressions such as 'it is said' and 'it is heard' will be translated by means of Hindi passive, as in:

kahā	**jātā**	**hɛ**
say-past	passive-go-present	is
[It] is said		

sunā	**jātā**	**hɛ**
hear-past	passive-go-present	is
[It] is heard		

As mentioned in Lesson 2, Hindi is a 'pro-drop' language and the English dummy 'it' is not translated.

Second, English passives are sometimes translated as past participal forms in Hindi. Consider sentence 4 in the Reading practice at the beginning of this chapter:

kāgaz	**par**	**kyā**	**likʰā**	**hɛ**
paper	on	what	written (past.ppl.)	is
What is written on the paper?				

Compare the English sentence with its corresponding Hindi sentence. The Hindi sentence does not use the passive construction. Instead, the past participial form of the verb **likʰnā** is used in the corresponding Hindi sentence.

Third, Hindi intransitive verbs are translated as passive in English.

intransitive		*transitive*	
biknā	to be sold	**becnā**	to sell
bannā	to be made	**banānā**	to make
kʰulnā	to be opened	**kʰolnā**	to open

Since English does not have intransitive verbs corresponding to those in Hindi, the Hindi intransitive verbs are best translated by means of the English passive. For example, a common billboard sight in India is:

yahā̃	**kitābẽ**	**biktī**	**hɛ̃**
here	books	be sold-pres.	are

Books are sold here.

Notice that the English meaning does not correspond to the Hindi structure. In Hindi, the intransitive verb **biknā** is conjugated in the simple present tense form. Thus the Hindi sentence is in its active form, as opposed to the passive form in English.

Negation and auxiliary deletion

The present auxiliary verb is dropped with negative sentences in the following two sentences:

amrīkā	**mẽ**	**tez**	**masāledār**	**kʰānā**	**itnā**
America	in	sharp	spicy	food	so much

tez	**nahī̃**	**hotā**	**[hɛ]**
sharp	not	be-present	is [aux]

In America the hot food is not so hot.

and

lekin	**hindustān**	**mẽ**	**sabʰī**	**log**	**itnā**	**tez**
but	India	in	all + **hī**	people	so much	sharp

kʰānā	**nahī̃**	**kʰā**	**sakte**	**[hɛ̃]**
food	not	eat	can-present	are

But in India not everybody can eat such hot food.

अभ्यास Exercises

1

Match the places with the purposes for which people visit them. Then write complete sentences according to the model presented below, matching the appropriate places with the purposes for which people visit them.

place		*purpose*	
pustakālaya	library	kitābẽ paR^{h}ne	to read books

sentence

log pustakālaya kitābẽ paR^{h}ne jāte hɛ.
People go to the library to read books.

Do not attempt to translate the English place names into Hindi.

	place	*purpose*
(a)	laundromat	*beer* pīne
(b)	restaurant	*film* dek^{h}ne
(c)	cinema	tɛrne
(d)	college	paR^{h}ne
(e)	swimming pool	k^{h}ānā k^{h}āne
(f)	bar	davāī lene
(g)	pharmacy	kapRe d^{h}one

2

Change each present participial phrase into its corresponding past participial form in the following sentences:

(a) vo bɛT^{h}te hue bolā.
(b) John sote hue hãs rahā t^{h}ā.
(c) ye shɛhɛr sota sā lagtā hɛ.
(d) laRkī rotī huī g^{h}ar āyī.
(e) aurat ne *swimming pool* par leTte hue kahā.

3

Which participial forms modify/match the noun?

lik^{h}ā	bāt
sunī	xat
hãstā	laRkā

b^{h}ūle	gāRī
caltī	log
b^{h}āgtī	billī

4

Change the following sentences into their corresponding passive forms:

(a) John ne ek kahānī paR^{h}ī.
(b) ham log k^{h}ānā k^{h}ā rahe hɛ̃.
(c) tum kyā karoge?
(d) mɛ̃ ne *chicken curry* banāyī.
(e) Bill hindustān mẽ paR^{h}egā.
(f) kyā āp ne gānā gāyā?

5

Circle the appropriate form of the subject, verb etc. given in brackets in the following sentences:

(a) (ham ko/ ham/ham ne) vahā̃ jāne kā maukā (milā/mile).
(b) (John ne/John ko /John) hindustān (jānā/jāne) kā maukā aksar miltā hɛ.
(c) ye sunhɛra maukā (t^{h}ā/t^{h}ī).
(d) (āp ko/āp) kitāb lik^{h}ne kā maukā kab (milegī/milegā).
(e) is kāgaz mẽ kyā (lik^{h}ā/lik^{h}ī) hɛ?
(f) billī ko maukā (milā/milī) aur vo dūd^h pī gayī.
(g) ye bahut (acc^{h}ā maukā/acc^{h}e mauke) kī bāt hɛ.

10 भारतीय त्यौहार Indian festivals

By the end of this lesson you should be able to:

- use various types of relative clauses
- use complex sentences
- know more about Hindi passives
- get cultural information about the festivals of India
- distinguish between the scholarly and formal Sanskritized style and informal Persianized style

Reading practice

Divali, the festival of lights

In this lesson we will describe some Indian festivals and various symbols that underlie the colourful mosaic of the culture and spirit of India. You will notice a slight shift in the style, which is more Sanskritized now. This style is preferred in formal, literary, scholarly and cultural endeavours. The Persianized style is preferred in informal and conversational situations.

(1) 'dīvālī' shabda sanskrita ke 'dīpāvalī' shabda se āyā hɛ.
(2) dīpāvalī yā dīvālī kā art^{h}a hɛ 'dīpakõ kī paŋkti'.
(3) ye b^{h}ārata kā sab se prasidd^{h}a tyauhāra hɛ.
(4) dīvālī aktūbar (*October*) yā navambar (*November*) ke mahīne mẽ ātī hɛ.
(5) ye tyauhāra acc^{h}āī kī burāī par aur prakāsha kī and^{h}kāra par vijaya kā pratīka hɛ.
(6) ye rājā rāma kī rākshasa rāvaN par vijaya kī xushī mẽ manāyā jātā hɛ.
(7) kahā jātā hɛ ki jab caudā varsha ke banvāsa aur rāvaNa par vijaya pāne ke bād rājā rāma apane rājya, Ayod^{h}yā, lauT rahe t^{h}e, tab har g^{h}ar ne xushī mẽ diye jalāye.
(8) isliye dīvālī kī rāt ko āj tak har g^{h}ar mẽ diye jalāye jāte hɛ̃.
(9) āp is tyauhāra ko 'b^{h}ārata kā *Christmas*' kah sakte hɛ̃. ye tyauhār b^{h}ārata se bāhar – Singapore, Nepal, Trinidad, Fijī ādi kaī deshõ mẽ b^{h}ī manāyā jātā hɛ.
(10) dīvālī kī rāt ko log paTāxe aur p^{h}ul-j^{h}aRiyā̃ calāte hɛ̃ aur har g^{h}ar mẽ 'lakshmī pūjana' hotā hɛ.
(11) jɛse *Christmas* sirf īsāī hī nahī̃ manāte, vɛse dīvālī sirf hinduõ kā tyauhār nahī̃ hɛ. āj-kal lagb^{h}aga sab^{h}ī d^{h}armõ ke log dīvālī manāte hɛ̃.

(1) *The word 'dīvālī' originated* (lit. came from = originate) *from the Sanskrit word 'dīpāvalī'.*
(2) *The meaning of 'dīpāvalī' or 'dīvālī' is 'a row of lamps'.*
(3) *This is the most famous festival of India.*
(4) *Divali comes in the month of October or November.*

(5) *This festival is a symbol of victory of 'good' over 'evil', and 'light' over 'darkness'.*

(6) *This* [*festival*] *celebrates* (lit. is celebrated in) *the glory* (lit. happiness) *of King Rama's victory over the demon* [*king*] *Ravana.*

(7) [*It*] *is said that when, after the fourteen years of exile and after obtaining the victory over Ravana, King Rama was returning to his kingdom, Ayodhya, then every house lit lamps in happiness* [*because of his return.*]

(8) *Therefore, on* [*the*] *Divali night until today, lamps are lit in every house.*

(9) *You could* (lit. can) *call this festival 'the Christmas of India'. This festival is also celebrated in many countries outside India – Singapore, Nepal, Trinidad, Fiji etc.*

(10) *On* [*the*] *Divali night, people light firecrackers and fireworks; and the goddess Lakshmi is worshipped* (lit. the worship of Lakshmi happens/occurs).

(11) *Just as* [*not*] *only the Christians celebrate Christmas,* [*similarly*] *Divali is not the festival of the Hindus alone. Nowadays people of almost every religion celebrate Divali.*

Vocabulary

dīvālī	दीवाली	the festival of lights/lamps
<sanskrita> (f.)	संस्कृत	Sanskrit
art^{h}a (m.)	अर्थ	meaning
dīpak/diyā (m.)	दीपक/दिया	an earthen lamp
paŋkti (f.)	पंक्ति	line, row
<b^{h}ārata> (m.)	भारत	the official name of India
<prasidd^{h}a>	प्रसिद्ध	famous
<tyauhāra> (m.)	त्यौहार	festival
acc^{h}āī (f.)	अच्छाई	good (n.), quality, ideal
burāī (f.)	बुराई	evil
<prakāsha> (m.)	प्रकाश	light
<and^{h}kāra> (m.)	अन्धकार	darkness
<vijaya> (f.)	विजय	victory
<pratīka> (m.)	प्रतीक	symbol
rājā (m.)	राजा	king, emperor

<rāma> (m.)	राम	Lord Rama (proper name)
<rākshasa> (m.)	राक्षस	demon
<rāvaNa> (m.)	रावण	the demon king, Ravana
manānā (+ne)	मनाना	to celebrate (festival, holiday), persuade
<caudā>	चौदह	fourteen
varsha (m.)	वर्ष	year
<banvāsa> (m.)	बनवास	exile, residence in forest
pānā (+ne)	पाना	to find, obtain
rājya (m.)	राज्य	kingdom
ayod^{h}yā (f.)	अयोध्या	Ayodhya, a place name
lauTnā (-ne)	लौटना	to return
jalānā (+ne)	जलाना	to light, to burn; to kindle
ādi	आदि	etc.
kaī	कई	several
<desha> (m.)	देश	country
paTāxā (m.)	पटाख़ा	a firecracker
p^{h}ul-j^{h}aRī (f.)	फुलझड़ी	a kind of firework which emits flower like sparks
calānā (+ne)	चलाना	to drive, to manage (business), to light/ play firecrackers
lakshmī (f.)	लक्ष्मी	Lakshmi, the goddess of wealth, fortune, prosperity
<pūjana> (n.)	पूजन	worship
jɛse (ki)	जैसे (कि)	as, as if
īsāī	ईसाई	a Christian
vɛse	वैसे	like that, similarly
hindu/hindū	हिन्दु	a Hindu
<lagb^{h}aga>	लगभग	about, approximately, almost
<d^{h}arma> (m.)	धर्म	religion

Pronunciation

With the exception of **caudā**, all the words enclosed with the symbol < > are written with the word-final vowel **a.** However, in the colloquial pronunciation, the final **a** is dropped. Since the above passage is written in the high and formal style, the word-final **a** is indicated.

The numeral **caudā,** ‘fourteen’, is written **caudah** (चौदह).

Notes

Sanskritized vs. Perso-Arabic style

The style differences in Hindi primarily involve vocabulary. The high or formal literary style is often equated with borrowing from Sanskrit, and the colloquial style usually borrows from Arabic and Persian sources. The simple substitution of the Perso-Arabic words for the corresponding Sanskrit words will yield the informal colloquial style of Hindi.

Sanskrit	*Perso-Arabic*	
art^{h}a	**matlab**	meaning
b^{h}ārata	**hindustān**	India
prasidd^{h}a	**mashhūr**	famous
varsha	**sāl**	year
lagb^{h}aga	**karīb**	about, approximately

Agentless passives

The Hindi equivalent of the English sentence ‘this festival is celebrated’ is:

ye	**tyauhār**	**manāyā**	**jātā**	**hɛ.**
this	festival (m.)	celebrate-past	passive-go-present	is

This festival is celebrated.

Hindi tends to omit the passive subject. The opening clause of sentence 7 of the reading practice further exemplifies this point. Note the omission of the passive subject (‘by x’) in the following paragraph.

kahā	**jātā**	**hɛ.**
say-past	passive-go-present	is

[It] is said.

Generic passive subjects such as ‘by people’ are understood in these sentences.

Relative clauses

The relative clause relates two clauses. The relative clause contains a relative pronoun which begins with the sound **j-** in Hindi, while in English a relative pronoun begins with a **wh-**word. For example, the English sentence 'The people who live in India celebrate Divali' is paraphrased as 'which/who people live in India, those people celebrate Divali'. So the Hindi sentence would be

jo	**log**	**b^{h}ārat**	**mẽ**	**rɛhɛte**	**hɛ̃**
who	people	India	in	live-present	are

ve	**[log]**	**dīvālī**	**manāte**	**hɛ̃**
those	people	Divali	celebrate-present	are

The people who live in India celebrate Divali.

The **jo-**clause is called the relative clause and is linked to the correlative clause. The second repeated noun (**log**, 'people') can be dropped, and the final result is as follows:

jo log b^{h}ārat mẽ rɛhɛte hɛ̃ ve dīvālī manāte hɛ̃.

The list of the relative and correlative pronouns is given below:

	simple		*oblique*		
	singular	*plural*	*singular*	*plural*	
relative	**jo**	**jo**	**jis**	**jin**	who/which
correlative	**vo**	**ve**	**us**	**un**	

The correlative pronouns are the same as the third person pronouns. Observe one more example of Hindi relative clauses:

jis	**tyauhār**	**kā**	**nām**	**dīvālī**	**hɛ,**	**vo**	**prasidd^{h}a**	**hɛ**
which-obl	festival	of	name	Divali	is	that	famous	is

The festival called Divali is famous.

Other types of relative clauses found in Hindi and their markers are as follows:

	relative		*correlative*	
place	**jahā̃**	where, in which place	**vahā̃**	there, in that place
time	**jab**	when	**tab**	then
manner	**jɛse**	as, in which manner	**vɛse**	in that manner
directional	**jid^har**	in which direction	**ud^har**	in that direction
kind	**jɛsā**	as/which kind	**vɛsā**	that kind
quantity	**jitnā**	as much/many as	**utnā**	that much/many

The relative clauses of kind and quantity behave like 'green' types of adjectives which agree with their following noun in number and gender.

The instance of a time relative clause can be found in sentence 7 of this unit:

jab...	**rājā**	**rāma**	**apne**	**rājya**	**lauT**	**rahe**	**t^he**
when	king	Rama	own	kingdom	return	ing	was

tab	**har**	**g^har**	**ne**	**xushī**	**mẽ**	**diye**	**jalāye**.
then	every	house	agent	happiness	in	lamps	lit

When King Rama was returning to his kingdom, then every house lit lamps in happiness.

Sentence 11 exemplifies the manner relative clause:

jɛse	***Christmas***	**sirf**	**īsāī**	**hī**	**nahī̃**	**manāte,**
as	Christmas	only	Christians	emp.part.	not	celebrate-present

vɛse	**dīvālī**	**sirf**	**hinduõ**	**kā**	**tyauhār**	**nahī̃**	**hɛ**
in that manner	Divali	only	Hindus	of	festival	not	is

As not only the Christians celebrate Christmas, [similarly] Divali is not the festival of the Hindus alone.

Reading practice

Holi, the festival of colours

(1) holī b^hārat kā ek aur raŋg-biraŋgā tyauhār hɛ.

(2) ye vasanta ritu mẽ ātā hɛ.
(3) is samaya gā̃võ mẽ fasal kaTne ke bād har g^har mẽ bahut anāj ā jātā hɛ.
(4) isliye ye tyauhār xush-hālī kā sandesh lātā hɛ.
(5) is din log bahut utsāha se ek dūsre par raŋg p^hẽkte hɛ̃.
(6) bacce pickārī se raŋgīn pānī Dālte hɛ̃, jab ki baRe log sūk^he raŋga se k^helte hɛ̃ jis ko 'gulāl' kɛhte hɛ̃.
(7) hālā̃ ki is din har tarā kā raŋga lagāyā jātā hɛ, lāl raŋga sarva-priya hɛ kyõki lāl raŋga 'prema' kā pratīka hɛ.
(8) holī ke din b^hārat mẽ *'Carnival'* jɛsā vātāvaraNa hotā hɛ. ye baRī d^hūm-d^hām se brindāvan mẽ manāyā jātā hɛ jahā̃ shrī krishna pale t^he.
(9) holī ke bāre mẽ kaī prācīn kahāniyā̃ pracalit hɛ̃ jo man kī pavitratā par zor detī hɛ̃.
(10) is din log baRī prasannatā se ek dūsre ko gale lagāte hɛ̃ aur shatrutā b^hūl kar shatrū ko b^hī mitra banā lete hɛ̃.

(1) *Holi is another colourful Indian festival* (lit. festival of India.)
(2) *It falls during spring* (lit. it comes during the spring season).
(3) *At this time after the harvesting* (lit. cutting) *of the crop, every house is full of grain* (lit. in every house, a lot of grain comes).
(4) *Therefore, this festival brings the message of prosperity.*
(5) *On this day people throw colour on each other with great enthusiasm.*
(6) *The children throw coloured water with a water-gun while the elders play with the dry colour which is called 'gulāl'.*
(7) *Although on this day all kinds of colours are used,* [*the*] *red* [*colour*] *is the favourite because it is the symbol of love.*
(8) *On the day of Holi generally* [*there*] *is a carnival-like atmosphere in India. This* [*festival*] *is celebrated with great joy in Brindavan where Lord Krishna was brought up.*
(9) [*There*] *are several stories prevalent about Holi which emphasize the purification of the mind.*
(10) *On this day people embrace each other with great joy and, forgetting enmity* (lit. and having forgotten enmity) [*they*] *make even their enemies* [*their*] *friends.*

Vocabulary

holī (f.)	होली	the festival of colours
raŋg (m.)	रंग	colour
raŋg-biraŋgā	रंग-बिरंगा	colourful
<vasanta>	बसन्त	spring
ritu (f.)	ऋतु	season
gā̃v (m.)	गाँव	village
fasal (f.)	फसल	crop
kaTnā (-ne)	कटना	to be cut
(ke) bād	के बाद	after
anāj (m.)	अनाज	grain, corn
xush-hālī (f.)	खुश-हाली	prosperity
sandesh (m.)	सन्देश	message
lānā (-ne)	लाना	to bring
utsāh (m.)	उत्साह	enthusiasm, joy, zeal
ek dūsre se	एक दूसरे से	with one another, each other
pʰẽknā (+ne)	फेंकना	to throw
pickārī (f.)	पिचकारी	a syringe-shaped water-gun made of wood or metal
raŋgīn	रंगीन	colourful
pānī (m.)	पानी	water
Dālnā (+ ne)	डालना	to put in, throw
jab ki	जब कि	while
sūkʰā (m. adj.)	सूखा	dry
kʰelnā (+/-ne)	खेलना	to play
kɛhte hɛ̃	कहते हैं	is called
hālā̃ ki	हालांकि	although
lagānā (+ ne)	लगाना	to attach, to stick
lāl	लाल	red
srava-priya	सर्व-प्रिय	loved by all, the favourite
prema (m.)	प्रेम	love
jɛsā	जैसा	as
vātāvaraNa (m.)	वातावरण	atmosphere, environment
dʰūm-dʰām se	धूमधाम से	with pomp and show
<brindāvan>	बृंदावन	Brindavan, the place where Lord Krishna was brought up
shrī krishna	श्रीकृष्ण	Lord Krishna

palnā (**-ne**)	पलना	to be brought up
prācīn	प्राचीन	ancient
pracalit honā (**-ne**)	प्रचलित होना	to be prevalent
man (m.)	मन	mind
pavitratā (f.)	पवित्रता	purification, holiness
zor denā (**-ne**)	ज़ोर देना	to emphasize
prasannatā (f.)	प्रसन्नता	happiness, joy
gale lagānā	गले लगाना	to embrace
shatrutā (f.)	शत्रुता	enmity, hostility
b^{h}ūlnā (**+/-ne**)	भूलना	to forget
shatru (m.)	शत्रु	enemy
mitra (m.)	मित्र	friend

Reading practice

Rakshāband^{h}an or *rākhī, 'the festival of love and protection'*

(1) rakshāband^{h}an kā dūsrā nām rāk^{h}ī b^{h}ī hɛ.

(2) ye b^{h}āī-bɛhɛn ke aTūT prem ko yād dilātā hɛ.

(3) is din har bɛhɛn apne b^{h}āī ko ek sunharā d^{h}āgā bā̃d^{h}tī hɛ̃.

(4) is d^{h}āge kā art^{h}a hɛ ki b^{h}āī apnī bɛhɛn ko vacan detā hɛ ki vo hameshā us kī rakshā karegā.

(5) yahā̃ tak ki videshī b^{h}āī b^{h}ī purāne samaya se is vacan ko pūrā karate rahe hɛ̃.

(6 solvī shatābdī mẽ gujarāt ke sultān ne citauRa par ākramaNa kiyā.

(7) citauRa kī rānī karaNavatī ne parājit hone se pɛhɛle dillī ke mugal samrāT humāyī ke pās rāk^{h}ī b^{h}ejī.

(8) jab tak humāyī apnī apnāyī bɛhɛn ko bacāne ke liye citauRa pahũcā tab tak rānī jauhar rachā cukī t^{h}ī.

(9) lekin humāyī ne p^{h}ir b^{h}ī gujarāt ke sultān ko harāya aur rānī karNavatī ke beTe ko, jis ko laRāī ke samaya c^{h}ipākar citauRa se bāhar b^{h}ej diyā gayā t^{h}ā, rājya kā uttarād^{h}ikārī banāyā.

(1) *Rakshabandhan's other name is Rakhi.*

(2) *This [festival] reminds [us] of the unbreakable love between brother and sister.*

(3) *On this day every sister ties [bracelets of] golden thread [on] her brother['s wrist].*

(4) *The meaning of this [thread] is that the brother vows to his sister that he will defend and always protect her.*

(5) *Even foreign brothers have been fulfilling this vow since olden times.*

(6) *In the sixteenth century the Sultan of Gujarat attacked Chitaur.*

(7) *The queen of Chitaur, Karnavati, sent Rakhi to Humayun, the Mogul king of Delhi before her defeat.*

(8) *By the time Humayun reached Chitaur to save his [now] adopted sister, Queen Karnavati had immolated herself.*

(9) *Still, Humayun defeated the Sultan of Gujarat and made the son of Queen Karnavati the heir of the kingdom, who [had been] sent secretly out of Chitaur at the time of battle [with the Sultan of Gujarat].*

Vocabulary

rakshāband^{h}an (m.)	रक्षा-बन्धन	'the festival of love and protection'
aTūT	अटूट	unbreakable
yād dilānā (+ne)	याद दिलाना	to remind
sunharā (m., adj.)	सुनहरा	golden
d^{h}āgā (m.)	धागा	(bracelets of) thread
bā̃d^{h}nā (+ne)	बाँधना	to tie
art^{h}a (m.)	अर्थ	meaning
vacan (m.)	वचन	promise
rakshā karnā (+ne)	रक्षा करना	to protect, to defend
yahā̃ tak ki	यहाँ तक कि	to the point, to the extent that
videshī (m.)	विदेशी	foreigner
pūrā (m. adj.)	पूरा	complete, whole, full
pūrā karnā (+ne)	पूरा करना	to complete
<solvī̃>	सोलहवीं	sixteenth
shatābdī (m.)	शताब्दी	century
gujarāt	गुजरात	the state of Gujarat
sultān (m.)	सुलतान	a sultan, king, emperor
citauRa	चित्तौड़	Chitaur, a very famous historical place in Rajasthan

ākramaNa karnā (+ne)	आक्रमण करना	to attack
rānī (f.)	रानी	queen
parājit honā (-ne)	पराजित होना	to be defeated
mugal	मुग़ल	the Moguls
samrāT (m.)	सम्राट	king, emperor
b^{h}ejnā (+ne)	भेजना	to send
apnāyī	अपनायी	adopted
bacānā (+ne)	बचाना	to save
tab tak	तब तक	by then
jauhar rachānā	जौहर रचाना	When defeat seemed certain, Rajput women immolated themselves while Rajput men performed a deliberate battle to the death, leaving the enemy with an empty victory. The Rajputs are from the colourful and glamorous desert state in the north-west of India.
cū̃ki	चूँकि	because
harānā (+ne)	हराना	to defeat
laRāī (f.)	लड़ाई	fight, battle, war
c^{h}īpākar	छिपाकर	secretly
rājya (m.)	राज्य	kingdom
uttarād^{h}ikārī (f.)	उत्तराधिकारी	heir, inheritor
banānā (+ne)	बनाना	to make

Observation exercise

b^{h}ārtīya swāstikā *'The Indian Swastika'*

Speaking of festivals, perhaps I should point out that one should not draw the wrong conclusions if one sees a *swastika* sign on the occasion of a festivity or even posted permanently on shops or products. In India, particularly among the Hindus and Jains, the symbol is an integrated aspect of spiritual, social and commercial life. The Nazis' symbol was borrowed from India and was twisted in meaning. The original Indian *swastika* is the symbol of universal prosperity and well-being of humanity. The original Indian *swastika* is shown below:

You will have noticed that in the Indian *swastika,* the four lines point to the four directions and it has a cross-section point in the middle. This cross-section point symbolizes an individual. The symbol states: 'Wherever I am there should be prosperity around me in all four directions.' Thus this symbol is created and re-created in the spirit of world peace and prosperity in India every day. Never lose sight of its intrinsic symbolic meaning. If the word *swastika* still causes shock waves in the West, then imagine the resentment of Indians whose most spiritual and auspicious symbol has been deformed in the West, to the extent that they feel totally betrayed. In short, the Indian *swastika* is not *twisted* but is straight. Furthermore, it is usually accompanied by an expression beginning with **shub^{h}a** (शुभ), which means 'auspicious'.

अभ्यास Exercises

1

Match the passive statements given in the right-hand column with the three festivals given in the left-hand column.

dīvāīī	shatruõ ko b^{h}ī mitra banāyā jātā hɛ.
holī	diye jalāye jāte hɛ̃.
rakshāband^{h}an	d^{h}āgā bā̃d^{h}ā jātā hɛ.
	paTāxe calāye jāte hɛ̃.
	rājā rāma ke apne rājya lauTne kī xushī mẽ manāyā jātā hɛ.
	gulāl lagāyā jātā hɛ.
	raŋg se k^{h}elā jātā hɛ.

2

Translate the sentences given in the right-hand column in question 1 into English.

3

Read the following relative clause statements and then identify the festival associated with each statement:

(a) vo tyauhār jo akTūbar ke mahīne mẽ ātā hɛ.
(b) vo tyauhār jo b^{h}āī aur bɛhɛn kā hɛ.
(c) vo tyauhār jis mẽ bɛhɛn b^{h}āī ko d^{h}āgā bā̃d^{h}tī hɛ.
(d) vo tyauhār jis din log ek-dūsre par raŋg p^{h}ẽkte hɛ̃.
(e) vo tyauhār jis din rājā rāma ayod^{h}yā lauTe t^{h}e.

1 पहला पाठ – लिपि Script unit 1

The first letter of the Devanagari script is अ **<u>a</u>**.

When the preceding sound is a consonant, it is absorbed into the consonant; thus, it is not written separately (as in the Hindi word **par**, 'on/at'). In all other situations, however, it is written separately (e.g., **ab**, 'now').

Look at the following combinations of consonants with vowel अ **a** and try to read them aloud first. You may need to refer to the consonant chart on page 11.

letters				*word*		*pronunciation*
प	+	र	=	पर		
pa	+	**ra**	=	**par** ~~**a**~~	on/at	**par**
अ	+	ब	=	अब		
a	+	**ba**	=	**ab** ~~**a**~~	now	**ab**
क	+	ल	=	कल		
ka	+	**la**	=	**kal** ~~**a**~~	yesterday/ tomorrow	**kal**

Notice with preceding **b**, **p** and **k**, the independent shape of the vowel does not appear. The vowel in such cases is absorbed into the consonant. This is the reason that the Hindi script is called a 'syllabic' script, i.e. a consonant letter such as क stands for **k** + **a**. Each consonant letter is not written separately, as is the case with the roman script. So **k** + **a** *cannot* be written as क + अ.

Of course, there are ways to write a consonant without a vowel; however, we will learn to write such consonants at a later stage.

If you thought that the vowel -**a** at the end of a word is absorbed into the preceding consonant, but is *not* pronounced (i.e. silent) in Standard Hindi speech, you are right. So a word written as पर **para**, 'on/at', is actually pronounced **par**. Some dialects of Hindi do not drop the word-final **a** in pronunciation.

Combinations of three or more consonants follow the same pattern.

letters						*word*		*pronunciation*
स	+	ड़	+	क	=	सड़क		
sa	+	**Ra**	+	**ka**	=	**saRak~~a~~**	road	**saRak**
म	+	ग	+	र	=	मगर		
ma	+	**ga**	+	**ra**	=	**magar~~a~~**	but	**magar**
अ	+	ग	+	र	=	अगर		
a	+	**ga**	+	**ra**	=	**agar~~a~~**	if	**agar**

अभ्यास Exercises

1

Read aloud the following Hindi words. Feel free to consult the consonant chart on page 11. However, resist the temptation to transcribe and write every letter before you pronounce the word. Treat this as an exercise in simple arithmetic addition. The difference is that you have words rather than numbers here.

(a) अमन (b) असल (c) जलन (d) कलम (e) कमल (f) गरम (g) जब (h) कब (i) तब (j) सब

2

Write the following words in the Hindi script. Assume that the word-final vowel **a** is dropped.

(a) **kaT** (b) **gal** (c) **cal** (d) **namak** (e) **sabak** (f) **parak**^{h} (g) **sadar** (h) **calan** (i) **man** (j) **pal** (k) **garam**.

2 दूसरा पाठ – लिपि Script unit 2

In script unit 1, we learned how to use the independent form of short अ **a** and its absorption into the preceding consonant.

Now, let us learn to combine dependent forms of the vowel symbols. The independent and the dependent forms of Hindi vowels are given below:

independent		*dependent* (**matra**) (following a consonant)	*position*
अ	**a**	zero	—
आ	**ā**	ा	after a consonant
इ	**i**	ि	before a consonant
ई	**ī**	ी	after a consonant
उ	**u**	ु	under a consonant
ऊ	**ū**	ू	under a consonant
ए	**e**	े	top of a consonant
ऐ	**ɛ**	ै	top of a consonant
ओ	**o**	ो	after a consonant
औ	**au**	ौ	after a consonant

Now let us consider the following three dependent vowel symbols:

ा	long	**ā**
ि	short	**i**
ी	long	**ī**

As mentioned above, ा and ी are placed after a consonant, whereas ि is placed before a consonant, as shown on the next page:

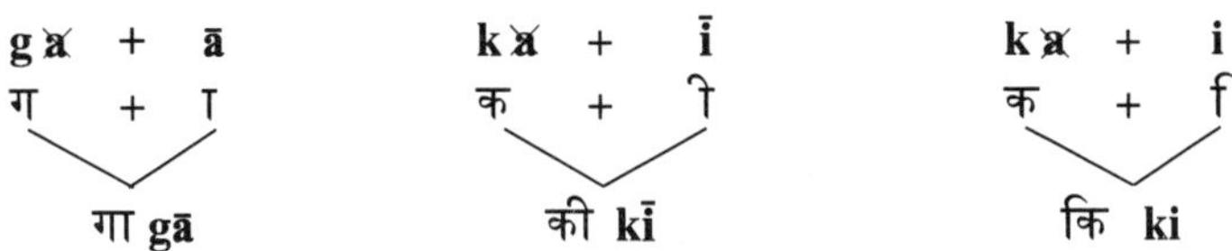

Notice that when a dependent form of the vowel is joined to a consonant, the invisible short **a** is actually *absorbed*. As mentioned in script unit 1, the word-final short **a** is silent.

bā	+	**ta̸**	**ba**	+	**tā**	**tī**	+	**na̸**
बा	+	त	ब	+	ता	ती	+	न
	बात **bāt**			बता **batā**			तीन **tīn**	
	thing, matter			tell			three	

Now look at the following examples:

bā	+	**rī**	**ca**	+	**nā**	**gi**	+	**rā**
बा	+	री	च	+	ना	गि	+	रा
	बारी			चना			गिरा	
	turn			chick pea			fell	

Observe the following three-syllable words:

ka	+	**hā**	+	**nī**	**ma**	+	**sā**	+	**lā**
क	+	हा	+	नी	म	+	सा	+	ला
		कहानी					मसाला		
		story					spice		
ki	+	**d^{h}a**	+	**ra̸**	**kī**	+	**ma**	+	**ta̸**
कि	+	ध	+	र	की	+	म	+	त
		किधर					कीमत		
		where, which direction					price		

Now let us turn our attention to the next four dependent vowel forms:

ु	ू	े	ै
u	**ū**	**e**	**ɛ**

These vowel symbols are either placed above or below a consonant symbol, as shown below:

तु	तू	ते	तै
tu	**tū**	**te**	**tɛ**

Read the following words (in what follows the absence of the word-final short **a** is assumed):

cu	+	**k**			
चु	+	क	=	चुक	finish
pū	+	**c**^{h}			
पू	+	छ	=	पूछ	ask
je	+	**l**			
जे	+	ल	=	जेल	jail
pɛ	+	**sā**			
पै	+	सा	=	पैसा	money

Exceptions

When ु and ू are joined to र **ra**, they are joined to the middle joint of the र, as shown below:

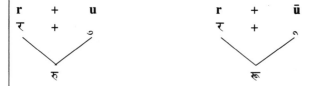

It is incorrect to place ु and ू below the र, as in र्ु **ru** and र्ू **rū**. Also, notice the difference in the shape of ु. With र the symbol of the dependent vowel **u** becomes ु.

Now here are the last two dependent vowel forms:

ो	ौ
o	**au**

They are placed to the *right* of a consonant, as with the vowels such as **ā** or **ī**, as shown below:

c^{h}o	+	**Tā**			
छो	+	टा	=	छोटा	small
cau	+	**k**			
चौ	+	क	=	चौक	crossing

Observe some more examples of the vowels in question:

pa	+	**rau**	+	**sī**			
प	+	ड़ौ	+	सी	=	पड़ौसी	neighbour
hau	+	**sa**	+	**lā**			
हौ	+	स	+	ला	=	हौसला	courage
po	+	**shā**	+	**ka**			
पो	+	शा	+	क	=	पोशाक	dress
ni	+	**co**	+	**Ra**			
नि	+	चो	+	ड़	=	निचोड़	squeeze, essence

अभ्यास **Exercises**

1

Read the following Hindi words aloud and transcribe them. Note that your transcription should take into account the word-final absence of the short vowel **a**.

(a) भारी	(b) बड़ा	(c) कितना	(d) काला	(e) भारत
(f) गाड़ी	(g) किनारा	(h) गीत	(i) गायब	(j) चावल
(k) चाहना	(l) चिड़ियाघर	(m) ज़रा	(n) जीवन	(o) जापान
(p) चोर	(q) मोर	(r) फूल	(s) भूत	(t) चौथा
(u) डौल	(v) पुलिस	(w) हाथी	(x) सितार	(y) शाम

2

Write the following words in the Devanagari script:

jab ki	kī	bāzār	rājā	rānī
pahcān	nayī	banāras	kānapur	mātā
pitā	kab^{h}ī	milan	zamīn	kār
mahīnā	sāl	din	cār	sāt
saverā	rāt	dopahar	k^{h}ol	sau
sonā	cāy	pānī	pati	b^{h}ālū

3

The following words are written incorrectly in Hindi. Look at the transcriptions, and write the correct forms in Hindi:

correct	*incorrect*	*correct*	*incorrect*
rupayā	रुपया	Dar	दर
rūk^{h}ā	रुखा	nām	नाभ
kar	कअर	t^{h}ān	यान
ki	कि	g^{h}ar	धर
aur	आर	Dāl	ड़ार

3 तीसरा पाठ – लिपि
Script unit 3

In this unit we will learn how to use the independent vowel forms and the nasalized vowels. In the last lesson we showed that the dependent counterparts are used with a preceding consonant. In all other cases, the independent form is used. Here is once again the list of the independent vowels. These vowels are also called ‘main’ vowels:

अ	आ	इ	ई	उ	ऊ	ए	ऐ	ओ	औ
a	**ā**	**i**	**ī**	**u**	**ū**	**e**	**ɛ**	**o**	**au**

When a word begins with a vowel, the independent form of the vowel is used, as in

ā	+	**m**			
आ	+	म	=	आम	mango, common

but not the dependent form

ा + म = ~~ाम~~

Similarly:

i	+	**d^{h}a**	+	**r**			
इ	+	ध	+	र	=	इधर	in this direction, here

but not

ि + ध + र = ~~धिर~~

You will also observe the same in the following example:

au	+	**r**			
औ	+	र	=	और	and

but not

ौ + र = ~~ौर~~

If the *preceding sound* is a vowel, the independent form of a vowel is used, e.g.:

ā	+	**i**	+	**e**			
आ	+	इ	+	ए	=	आइए	please come

but not any of the following ways:

ा	+	ि	+	ए	=	~~ाएि~~
ा	+	ि	+	े	=	~~ाि~~
आ	+	ि	+	े	=	~~आि~~

Now you should be able to distinguish between the following two words:

K + **ī** → की (of)

Ka + **ī** → कई (several)

Notice that the independent form of **ī**, ई is used in **kaī** *because its preceding sound is a vowel.*

Nasalized vowels

In our transcription, vowel nasalization is indicated by a tilde ~ over the transliterated vowel.

In Hindi, the two symbols used to mark vowel nasalization are: *candrabindu* ('moon dot') ँ and *bindu* (dot) ं. The former is used either over the headstroke of the vowel itself or over the headstroke of the consonant to which the vowel is attached. If any part of the vowel is written above the headstroke, then the dot is used rather than the moon dot. Observe the following examples:

nasalized vowel	*independent vowel*	*dependent vowel*
ā̃	आँ	ाँ
ī̃	ईं	ीं
ū̃	ऊँ	ुँ
ẽ	एँ	ेँ
ɛ̃	ऐं	ैं
õ	ओं	ों
ā̃ū̃	औं	ौं

Now examine the usage of the nasalized vowels in the following words:

h	+	**ā̃**				**h**	+	**ū̃**			
ह	+	ाँ	=	हाँ	yes	ह	+	ुँ	=	हूँ	am
ā̃	+	**k^{h}**	=	**ā̃k^{h}**		**m**	+	**ā̃**	=	**mā̃**	
आँ	+	ख	=	आँख	eye	म	+	ाँ	=	माँ	mother
ū̃	+	**T**	=	**ū̃T**		**m**	+	**ẽ**	=	**mẽ**	
ऊँ	+	ट	=	ऊँट	camel	म	+	ें	=	में	in
ā̃ū̃	+	**d^{h}ā**	=	**ā̃ū̃d^{h}ā**		**m**	+	**ɛ̃**	=	**mɛ̃**	
औं	+	धा	=	औंधा	overturned	म	+	ैं	=	मैं	I

अभ्यास **Exercise**

Write the following expressions in Hindi. Since they are useful, their English translations are also provided.

(a) t^{h}ānā vahī̃ hɛ.
The police station is right there.

(b) āp merī madad kar sakte hɛ̃?
Can you help me?

(c) mɛ̃ vahā̃ kɛse jāū̃?
How shall I get there?

(d) ye merī galatī nahī̃.

This is not my mistake.

(e) yahā̃ xatrā hɛ.
There is danger here.

(f) bacāo!
(Help!) (lit. save!)

(g) ye (written as yah) bahut zarūrī hɛ.
This is very urgent.

(h) Dāk-k^{h}ānā kahā̃ hɛ?
Where is the post office?

(i) kis k^{h}iRkī par jāū̃?
Which window should I go to?

(j) TikaT (*ticket*) kitnā lagegā?
How much postage will [it] take?

(k) tār amrīkā *(America)* b^{h}ejanā cāhatā hū̃.
[I] want to send a telegram to America.

4 चौथा पाठ – लिपि
Script unit 4

Conjunct letters

In script unit 1 we mentioned that since the Devanagari script is a syllabic script, every consonant symbol contains an invisible अ **a** in it. Now let us learn to write consonants without this vowel. Such consonants are also called 'half' consonants.

The simplest way to drop the अ **a** is to place the sign ् called 'hal' or 'halant'. For example, if you want to write the word **kyā**, just put the 'halant' sign under क् and then go on to write the next syllable. How ever, Hindi speakers tend to prefer special conjunct symbols over the 'hal' sign. These special conjuncts are described below:

If a consonant has a right vertical stroke, the vertical line is dropped, as in

full consonant		*conjunct consonant (half consonant)*		*word with a conjunct*		
ख़	**xa**	ख़्	**x**	सख़्त	**saxta**	hard
ग	**ga**	ग्	**g**	अग्नि	**agni**	fire
च	**ca**	च्	**c**	अच्छा	**acc^{h}ā**	good
ज	**ja**	ज्	**j**	ज्यों	**jyõ**	as
ण	**Na**	ण्	**N**	ठण्डा	**T^{h}aNDā**	cold
त	**ta**	त्	**t**	त्यौहार	**tyauhār**	festival
न	**na**	न्	**n**	अन्धा	**and^{h}ā**	blind
स	**sa**	स्	**s**	सस्ता	**sastā**	cheap

Notice the placement of the dependent form of the vowel **i** ि which is placed before the conjunct letter ग् but is pronounced after **n**.

The consonants that contain the stroke ा in the middle have the following forms:

क	**ka**	क्	**k**	क्या	**kyā**	what
फ़	**fa**	फ़्	**f**	हफ़्ता	**haftā**	week

For all other letters, either the 'halant' sign is used or the conjunct letter is on the top of the full consonant letter, as in:

ट् **T**	+	ट **Ta**	ट् + ट	**T+Ta**	*or*	ट्ट	
			पट्‌टी	**paTTī**	*or*	पट्टी	bandage
ड् **D**	+	ड **Da**	ड् + ड	**D+Da**	*or*	ड्ड	
			अड्‌डा	**aDDā**	*or*	अड्डा	station (bus)

With the emergence of new printing technology, the 'halant' form is gaining more prominence.

Exceptions

Once again, र, **ra**, is notorious and needs special attention. The symbol for the conjunct र is र्, as in

ka	+	**r**	+	**ma**	=	**karma**	fate	
क	+	र्	+	म	=	कर्म	but not	र्कम

The conjunct **r** is placed at the very end of the syllable it precedes, e.g.

va	+	**r**	+	**mā**	=	**varmā**		a last name
व	+	र्	+	मा	=	वर्मा	but not	र्वमा Varma

When र is the second member of the conjunct, it is realized ्र. Note the following clusters with **r**:

p	+	**ra**	=	**pra**
प्	+	्र	=	प्र
t	+	**ra**	=	**tra**
त्	+	्र	=	त्र
sh	+	**ra**	=	**shra**
श्	+	्र	=	श्र

With ट **Ta** and ड **Da**, ‸ is added rather than ्र :

T	+	**ra**	=	**Tra**	
ट्	+	्र	=	ट्र	but not ~~ट्र~~
D	+	**ra**	=	**Dra**	
ड्	+	्र	=	ड्र	but not ~~ड्र~~

Long consonants

With the exception of **tta**, the long consonants follow the conjunct formation rules described above.

t	+	**ta**	=	**tta**	
त्	+	त	=	त्त	but not ~~त्त~~

Nasal consonants

In script unit 3 we showed that the moon dot and the simple dot can express vowel nasalization. However, the dot has yet another function. When it appears over either a short vowel or a consonant, it shows the presence of a homorganic nasal consonant. 'Homorganic' means the sound produced by the same speech organ. The consonants listed in each of the five groups in the consonant chart are homorganic. For example, the five consonant sounds listed in the fifth column – **ŋ**, **ñ**, **N**, **n** and **m** – are homorganic to the rest of the velar, palatal, retroflex, dental and labial consonants, respectively.

When the dot is placed either over a short vowel or a consonant, it indicates the corresponding homorganic conjunct nasal consonant of the following consonant. Therefore, the dot can also be written with a conjunct nasal consonant, as in:

अंग	=	अङ्ग	**aŋg**	limb
पंच	=	पञ्च	**pañc**	juror
ठंड	=	ठण्ड	**T^{h}aND**	cold
हिंदी	=	हिन्दी	**hindī**	the Hindi language
खंबा	=	खम्बा	**k^{h}ambā**	pole

The hide and seek game of a

We mentioned in the chapter on the Hindi writing system and pronunciation that the Devanagari script is a phonetic script and the words are primarily written the way they are pronounced. However, one should keep in mind that language is a living thing; it keeps changing and even the most scientific script cannot keep up with all the change. We have already discussed the case of the word-final silence of **a** in script units 1 and 2. Now do some detective work and see another situation in which **a** is *written but not pronounced.*

word	*pronunciation*		*word*	*pronunciation*	
सड़क	**saRak**	**saR*a*k**	सड़कें	**saR*a*k+ẽ**	**saRkẽ**
road			roads		
औरत	**aurat**	**aur*a*t**	औरतें	**aur*a*t+ẽ**	**aurtẽ**
woman			women		
लड़क	**laRak**	**laR*a*k**	लड़का	**laR*a*k+ā**	**laRkā**
child			boy (male child)		
लड़क	**laRak**	**laR*a*k**	लड़की	**laR*a*k+ī**	**laRkī**
child			girl (female child)		
समझ	**samaj**^{h}	**sam*a*j**^{h}	समझा	**sam*a*j**^{h}**+ā**	**samj**^{h}**ā**
understand			understood		

If you noticed that the penultimate (second to last) vowel **a** is dropped before a suffix, then your observation is correct. Now examine the following words:

word	*pronunciation*		*word*	*pronunciation*	
सड़क	**saRak**	**saR*a*k**	सड़कपन	**saR*a*k+pan**	**saR*a*kpan**
road			'roadness'		
औरत	**aurat**	**aur*a*t**	औरतपन	**aur*a*t+pan**	**aur*a*tpan**
woman			womanhood		
लड़क	**laRak**	**laR*a*k**	लड़कपन	**laR*a*k+pan**	**laR*a*kpan**
child			childhood		
समझ	**samaj**^{h}	**sam*a*j**^{h}	समझदार	**sam*a*j**^{h}**+dār**	**sam*a*j**^{h}**dār**
understand			intelligent		

The set of data presented above indicates that the penultimate **a** is dropped in pronunciation if the suffix begins with a vowel. Otherwise it is retained.

अभ्यास Exercises

1

Write the following expressions in Hindi. Since they are useful, English translations are also provided.

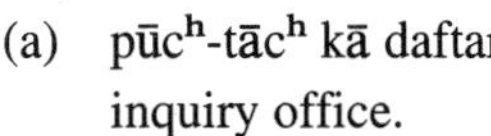

(a) pūc^{h}-tāc^{h} kā daftar
inquiry office.

(b) mɛ̃ rāstā b^{h}ūl gayī hū̃.
I (f.) am lost (lit. I have lost my way).

(c) mɛ̃ rāstā b^{h}ūl gayā hū̃.
I (m.) am lost (lit. I have lost my way).

(d) taŋg mat karo.
Do not bother me.

(e) mɛ̃ kunjī D^{h}ū̃D^{h} rahā hū̃.
I am looking for my key.

(f) nahī̃ mil rahī.
[I] can't find [it].

(g) ciTT^{h}ī havāī Dāk se b^{h}ejiye.
Please send [this] letter by air mail.

(h) kyā āp yah sāmān sīd^{h}e bambaī b^{h}ej sakte hɛ̃?
Can you send this baggage straight to Bombay?

(i) sāmān ke liye rasīd dījiye.
Please give [me] a receipt for this baggage.

(j) merā sāmān nahī̃ āyā.
My baggage did not arrive [by this flight].

2

Transcribe the following sentences. Some words used in these expressions are from English but have been written the way they are pronounced by the Hindi speakers. If you have the cassettes, you can listen to their pronunciation. Otherwise after transcribing the sentences, read the sentences and practise their pronunciation on your own.

(a) हम एक हफ़्ता दिल्ली में रहेंगे।
We will stay in Delhi for a week.

(b) मैं यहाँ छुट्टी पर हूँ।
I am here on a vacation.

(c) हम यहाँ काम से आये हैं।
We (m.) came here on a business trip (lit. we have come here with work).

(d) यह मेरा पासपोर्ट है।
This is my passport.

(e) क्या इस सामान पर ड्यूटी लगेगी?
Will this baggage (or things) require duty?

(f) ये चीज़ें मेरे अपने इस्तेमाल के लिये हैं।
These things are for my own [personal] use.

(g) मेरे पास ड्यूटी-वाला सामान नहीं है।
I have nothing to declare (lit. I do not any thing that requires duty).

(h) मेरे पास कुछ गिफ़्ट्स हैं।
I have some gifts.

(i) इस में सिर्फ कपड़े और किताबें हैं।
There are only clothes and books in this [bag].

(j) इस के अलावा और कोई चीज़ नहीं है।
Besides this [I] have nothing else [to declare for duty].

3

Note the presence or absence of the word-medial **a** in the following words. Take a lead from the Roman transcription and practise the pronunciation.

(a)	सड़क	saR*a*k	सड़कें	saRkẽ
(b)	औरत	aur*a*t	औरतें	aurtẽ
(c)	लड़क	laR*a*k	लड़का	laRkā
(d)	लड़कपन	laR*a*kpan	लड़की	laRkī
(e)	समझ	sam*a*j^{h}	समझा	samj^{h}ā
(f)	समझदार	sam*a*j^{h}dār	समझी	samj^{h}ī

5 पाँचवाँ पाठ – लिपि Script unit 5

You must have heard the expression 'it is not what you say that matters but how you say it'. In this chapter we will consider some 'how to' aspects of the script and pronunciation together with some other questions, such as significant and insignificant variations.

Syllables

The vowel and consonant segments can be combined into units which are called syllables. A syllable refers to the smaller unit of a word. The syllable boundary is indicated by the symbol #, as follows.

Between successive vowels

word		*syllabification*	
जाओ	**jāo**	जा # ओ	**jā # o**
आइए	**āie**	आ # इ # ए	**ā # i # e**
नई	**naī**	न # ई	**na # ī**
खाए	**k^{h}āe**	खा # ए	**k^{h}ā # e**

Between vowels and consonants

word		*syllabification*	
जाता	**jātā**	जा # ता	**jā # tā**
सोना	**sonā**	सो # ना	**so # nā**
पता	**patā**	प # ता	**pa # tā**

Between consonants

word		*syllabification*	
इच्छा	**icc^{h}ā**	इच # छा	**ic # c^{h}ā**
सड़कें	**saRkẽ**	सड़ # कें	**saR # kẽ**
आदमी	**ādmī**	आद # मी	**ād # mī**

Stress

Stress means loudness, a change in volume to express a wide variety of meanings such as emotions, contrast, focus and change in grammatical categories. This term is interchangeably used with 'accent' by some linguists. It refers to the most prominent part of a syllable or word. As in English, stress distinguishes some nouns from verbs in Hindi, as in

noun			*verb*		
गला	***ga*lā**	neck	गला	**ga*lā***	cause to melt
तला	***ta*lā**	sole	तला	**ta*lā***	cause to fry

The stressed syllable is in italics. However, stress is not usually distinctive in Hindi. Therefore, whether one places stress on the first syllable or on the second, the meaning will not be affected, nor will the quality of the pronunciation of the vowel:

su*nā**   **su*nā

This tendency is different from English, where the vowel in the non-stressed syllable is reduced, such as in A*la*ska, where one witnesses a difference between the pronunciation of the *a* in the middle position (i.e. stressed syllable) and in the word-initial and final position (i.e. unstressed syllables). This is why stress is not as distinctive and crucial in Hindi as in English. Therefore Hindi is often characterized as a 'syllable-timed' language like French, where the syllables are pronounced in a steady flow, resulting in a 'machine-gun' effect.

The predominant pattern in Hindi is to stress the penultimate syllable, as in:

ki*rā*yā	rent
***jā*nā**	to go
***cī*tā**	leopard
***in*du**	a name
***ru*ci**	interest
ka*nik*ā	a female name

Since short vowels are not stressed in English, chances are you will not hear stress on the syllables with short vowels.

The long vowel receives stress and thus takes precedence over the penultimate-syllable rule, e.g.

***tā*riNī**	a female name
sir*kā*	vinegar

Also, note that if there is more than one long syllable, the stress falls on the first syllable. The other intricate aspects of the stress system in Hindi are beyond the scope of this introductory book. At the level of word-compounding, the stress is usually placed at the second word, as in

bāt-*cīt*	conversation
bol-*cāl*	colloquial

In information-type questions, the question-word is usually stressed.

āp	***kyā***	**karẽge?**
you	what	do-will

What will you do?

āp	**ye**	***kyõ***	**karẽge?**
you	this	why	do-will

Why would you do this?

āp	***kahā̃***	**jāẽge?**
you	where	go-will

Where will you go?

Intonation pattern

Take, for example, the word **acc^{h}ā**, 'good, okay', which can be pronounced with different intonation in different contexts. When **acc^{h}ā** is uttered in the following five contexts: in a response to an inquiry 'what kind of person is x?'; in a statement expressing surprise, e.g. 'is that so?'; as an expression of agreement, disagreement, or detachment, it will be produced with different intonations. Intonation is the rise and fall of the pitch of the voice. Hindi exhibits the following four main intonation patterns:

rising ↗

falling ↘

rising, falling and rising ∿↗

neutral or level —

Rising intonation

As in English, the intonation rises towards the end of the sentence in yes-no type of question:

kyā	**āp**	**vahā̃**	**jāẽge?** ↗
what	you	there	go-will

Will you go there?

In exclamatory sentences the intonation rises sharply:

vo	**pās**	**ho**	**gayā!** ↗
he	pass	be	went

He passed [the exam!]

Falling intonation

Statements, prohibitives and information questions show this intonation pattern:

laRkā	**acc^{h}ā**	**hɛ** ↘
boy	good	is

The boy is good.

cigreT	**pinā**	**manā**	**hɛ**
cigarette	drinking	prohibited	is

Smoking is prohibited.

āp	**kahā̃**	**jāẽge**
you	where	go-will

Where will you go?

Rising–falling and rising

In tag-questions intonation rises at the beginning of the verb and falls at the end of the verb, and then rises slightly again while the tag marker is pronounced:

āp	**āyẽge**	**na**
you	come-will	tag

You will come, won't you?

Neutral or level

The ordinary imperative sentences are uttered with a neutral or level intonation:

tum jāo.
You go.

Linguistic variation

As mentioned in the chapter on the Hindi writing system and pronunciation, Hindi is spoken in the vast region of South Asia and outside South Asia. It is therefore natural to expect linguistic variation in the regions. Some regional pronunciation differences are already pointed out in the treatment of the description of Hindi vowels and borrowed consonant sounds. One can easily see some variation regarding the pronunciation of word-final and medial pronunciation of **a**. In the Eastern and Southern varieties of Hindi, the vowel **a** is retained in both positions. However, the **a** is optional in many words of Perso-Arabic origin even in Standard Hindi, as shown on the next page:

कुरसी	**kur*a*sī**	कुर्सी	**kursī**	chair
सरदी	**sar*a*dī**	सर्दी	**sardī**	winter, cold
गरमी	**gar*a*mī**	गर्मी	**garmī**	summer, hot
नज़दीक	**naz*a*dīk**	नज़्दीक	**nazdīk**	near
कतल	**qatal**	कत्ल	**qatla**	murder

Another important source of variation is the consonant **h**. The preceding stressed vowel **a** becomes **ɛ** if **h** is followed by a non-vowel sound. For example:

कह	**k*a*h**	but pronounced	**kɛh**.
रहना	**r*a*hnā**	but pronounced	**rɛhnā**.
वह	**v*a*h**	but pronounced	**vo**.
यह	**y*a*h**	but pronounced	**ye**.

The stressed vowel is in italics. The only exceptions are the third person singular pronouns which are pronounced as **vo** and **ye**, respectively.

When the preceding vowel is unstressed, the **h** is dropped but the vowel becomes long, as in

वजह	**v*a*jah**	but pronounced	**vajā**
तरह	**t*a*rah**	but pronounced	**tarā**

If the **h** is preceded by **a** and followed by **u**, the **h** is dropped and the merger of the two vowels either results in **au** (as in c*au*ght) or **o**. For example, **bahut** is pronounced either as **baut** or **bot**.

In many dialects, the **h** is produced with the script pronunciation (i.e. pronounced the way it is written).

Verb forms: more than one spelling

Some verb forms ending in **ā** and **e** can be written with more than one spelling. For example, the subjunctive, past and imperative forms of the verb can be written with the following variations:

verb	*past*		*subjunctive*		*Imperative*			
jā to go	**gaye**		**jāe**		**jāo**		**jāiye**	
जा	गए	**gae**	जाए	**jāe**	जाओ	**jāo**	जाइए	**jāie**
	गये	**gaye**	जाये	**jāye**	जावो	**jāvo**	जाइये	**jāiye**
			जाय	**jāy**				

The phonetic considerations are primarily responsible for the variation in the traditional spellings.

अभ्यास Exercises

1

Mark the syllable boundary in the following words, using the symbol #:

(a) āiye
(b) aurtẽ
(c) paR^{h}tā
(d) suno
(e) namaste
(f) milẽge
(g) sunkar
(h) ādmī

2

Read through the following questions and answers, and try to imagine the intonation patterns involved in them. It would be helpful to seek the assistance of a native speaker.

(a) yes–no type

question	kyā vo *pās* ho gayā?	Did he pass [the exam]?
answer:	hã.	

(b) information question

question:	kaun sā *grade* milā?	What grade did he get?
answer:	'A' grade.	

(c) statement

vo acc^{h}ā laRkā hɛ.	He is a good boy.

(d) Surprise

statement:	vo pās ho gayā.	He passed the exam.
reply:	acc^{h}ā!	(with rising intonation) implying 'Is that so? I do not believe you.'

(e) agreement

suggestion:	āo, *film* dek^{h}ne calẽ.	Come, let's go and see a film.
agreement:	acc^{h}ā.	Okay.

(f) detached

suggestion: āo, *film* dek^{h}ne calẽ.	Come, let's go and see a film.
agreement: acc^{h}ā.	Okay.

(g) normal commands

darvāzā band karo.	Close the door.

3

Note the stressed syllable in each of the following words:

(a)	ki*rā*yā	rent
(b)	*jā*nā	to go
(c)	*cī*tā	leopard
(d)	*in*du	a name
(e)	*ru*ci	interest
(f)	ka*ni*kā	a female name
(g)	*tā*riNī	a female name
(h)	sir*kā*	vinegar

6 छठा पाठ – लिपि Script unit 6

In this unit dialogues and reading-practice exercises are presented in the Devanagari script.

Lesson 1

Hindu-Sikh greetings

मोहन (मो०) सरिता (स०)

मो:	नमस्ते जी।
स:	नमस्ते। क्या हाल है?
मो:	ठीक है और आप?
स:	मैं भी ठीक हूँ। हुकम कीजिये?
मो:	हुकम नहीं, विनती है।
	(The conversation continues for some time.)
मो:	अच्छा, नमस्ते।
स:	नमस्ते।

Muslim greetings

तहसीन सिद्दिकी (त०) रज़िया अरीफ़ (र०)

त:	सलाम, रज़िया जी।
र:	सलाम, सब ख़ैरियत है?
त:	मेहरबानी है, और आप के मिज़ाज कैसे हैं?
र:	अल्लाह का शुक्र है।
	(The conversation continues for some time.)
त:	अच्छा, ख़ुदा हाफ़िज़।
र:	ख़ुदा हाफ़िज़।

Lesson 2

Small-talk

मुकेश भार्गव (मु०)   अनूप पटेल (अ०)

मु:	कहिये, आप का नाम डाक्टर अनूप पटेल है न?
अ:	जी हाँ, मेरा नाम अनूप पटेल है।
	(extending his hand to shake hands)
मु:	मेरा नाम मुकेश है।
अ:	मिल के बड़ी खुशी हुई। आप का पूरा नाम क्या है?
मु:	मुकेश भार्गव है।
अ:	आप क्या करते हैं?
मु:	मैं *स्टाक ब्रोकर* हूँ। आप *मैडीकल डाक्टर* हैं?
अ:	जी नहीं, मैं *मैडीकल डाक्टर* नहीं हूँ। दूसरा डाक्टर हूँ।

Where are you from?

कनिका भाटिया (क०)   सुनीता दिवान (सु०)

क:	आप कहाँ की हैं?
सु:	मैं दिल्ली की हूँ और आप?
क:	मैं बनारस में रहती हूँ।
सु:	आप के कितने भाई बहनें हैं?
क:	हम चार भाई और दो बहनें हैं।
सु:	मेरा एक भाई और बहन है।

This is my address

कनिका भाटिया (क०)   सुनीता दिवान (सु०)

सु:	यह मेरा पता है।
क:	यह पता बहुत बड़ा है।
सु:	हाँ, बड़ा शहर, बड़ा पता।
क:	छोटा शहर, छोटा पता।
	(both laugh)
सु:	अच्छा, फिर मिलेंगे।
क:	अच्छा, मिलेंगे।

Lesson 3

Buying a saree

मेगन ऐशली (मे०) अनिता शर्मा (अ०) राजेन्द्र सिंह (रा०)

अ: ज़रा नये फैशन की साड़ियाँ दिखाइये।
रा: कौन-सी साड़ी चाहिये? रेशमी या सूती?
अ: रेशमी।
रा: ये देखिये, आज-कल इसका बहुत रिवाज़ है।
देखिये, सिल्क कितना अच्छा है!
(Rajendra shows a number of sarees. Anita asks Meghan about her choice.)
अ: मेगन, आप को कौन-सी साड़ी पसन्द है?
मे: ये पीली।
अ: इसका दाम क्या है?
(turning to Rajendra to ask the price)
रा: बारह सौ रुपये।
अ: ठीक बताइये, ये बाहर से आयी हैं।
रा: आज-कल इतना दाम है... अच्छा ग्यारह सौ।
अ: अच्छा, ठीक है।

Booking a flight

जॉन स्मिथ (जॉ०) एजेन्ट (ए०)

जॉ: जयपुर की एक टिकट चाहिये।
ए: कौन-से दिन के लिये?
जॉ: कल के लिये।
ए: कम्प्यूटर पर देखता हूँ, है या नहीं।
जॉ: सुबह की फ़्लाइट चाहिये।
ए: टिकट है।
जॉ: तो दीजिये। फ़्लाइट कब चलती है?
ए: सुबह दस बजे।
जॉ: मेरे पास कैश नहीं है।
ए: तो क्रैडिट कार्ड दीजिये।

A visit to the doctor

कुशवंत सिंह (कु०) चरन चतुर्वेदी (च०)

कु: डाक्टर साहिब, मुझे कुछ बुख़ार है।
च: कब से है?
कु: कल रात से।
च: सिर-दर्द भी है?
कु: जी हाँ।
(putting the thermometer into Kushwant's mouth)
च: थरमामीटर लगाइये।
(after taking the thermometer from Kushwant's mouth)
च: थोड़ा बुख़ार है... यह दवाई दिन में दो बार लीजिये... जल्दी ठीक हो जायेंगे।

'Tell me why' column

सवाल: हिन्दुस्तानी औरतें बिन्दी क्यों लगाती हैं?

(a) सिंगार
(b) शादी-शुदा है।
(c) दोनों

जवाब: दोनों

Humour column

इंस्पैक्टर inspector (इं) चोर thief (चो०)

इ: तुम्हारा नाम?
चो: बैनरजी।
(now turning to the other)
इं: तुम्हारा नाम?
चो: चैटरजी।
(inspector talking to both thives)
इं: चोरी करते हो और नाम के साथ जी लगाते हो।
(turning to his assistant)
इं: इन का नाम लिखिये, बैनर और चैटर।

Lesson 4

What are your hobbies?

प्रो० जेम्ज़ जोन्ज़ (प्रो०) य. मलिक (य०)

य:	क्या आप भारत जाते हैं?
प्रो:	जी हाँ, कई बार।
य:	आप को हिन्दुस्तानी खाना पसन्द है?
प्रो:	जी हाँ, तन्दूरी चिकन, डोसा... वैसे समोसा भी बहुत पसन्द है।
य:	आप के शौक क्या-क्या हैं?
प्रो:	मुझ को तैरने का शौक है, इस के अलावा भारतीय संगीत का भी शौक है।
य:	गाने का भी?
प्रो:	ज़रूर, मेरे गाने से मेरे बच्चे हैड फ़ोन लगाते हैं।
य:	वाह! वाह!

Indian films

सुहास रंजन (सु०) अकबर अली (अ०) अजीत सिंह (अ०)

सु:	खलनायक मेरी मन-पसन्द फिल्म है।
अ:	वह कैसे?
सु:	गाने बहुत अच्छे हैं, कहानी और ऐकटिंग भी शानदार है।
अ:	हिन्दी फिल्में तो मुझ को बिल्कुल पसन्द नहीं। सिर्फ़ फ़ार्मूला।
सु:	लेकिन यह फ़ार्मूला फिल्म नहीं, इस का अन्दाज़ और है।
अ:	सब हिन्दी फिल्में एक-सी होती हैं, लड़का लड़की से मिलता है, दोनों में प्यार होता है, फिर खलनायक आता है ...
	(Suhas interrupts)
सु:	और दोनों की शादी होती है। जी नहीं, यह ऐसी फिल्म नहीं।
अ:	तो पश्चिम की नकल होगी।
सु:	तो आप के ख़्याल में सिर्फ़ पश्चिमी फिल्में अच्छी होती हैं?
अ:	मैं यह नहीं कहता, पुरानी हिन्दी फिल्में अच्छी होती हैं।
	(Ajit Singh listens patiently to this discussion, and then intervenes.)
अजीत:	फिल्म की बात पर महाभारत क्यों?

'Tell me why' column

सवाल:	क्या हिन्दुस्तानी लोग कहते हैं: 'I love you'.
जवाब:	(a) आँखों से, लेकिन शब्दों से नहीं (b) सिर्फ़ शब्दों से
ठीक जवाब:	(a)
सवाल:	हिन्दुस्तानी शब्दों से कहते हैं: 'I love you'.
जवाब:	(a) कभी नहीं (b) कभी कभी
ठीक जवाब:	(b)
सवाल:	हिन्दुस्तानी शब्दों से कैसे कहते हैं: 'I love you'.
जवाब:	(a) मैं तुम से प्यार करता हूँ (b) मुझ को तुम से प्यार है
ठीक जवाब:	(b)

What do you eat for breakfast?

राकेश सेठ (रा०) डाक्टर (डा०)

डॉ:	राकेश जी, नाश्ते में आप क्या खाते हैं?
रा:	दस समोसे।
डॉ:	और, क्या पीते हैं?
रा:	मुझे चाय बहुत अच्छी लगती है। सवेरे बहुत चाय पीता हूँ।
डॉ:	आप को शरीर की बिमारी नहीं। दिमाग की बिमारी है इसलिये आप किसी साकिऐट्रिसट के पास जाइये।

Lesson 5

I want to go to India

सुमन कुमार (सु०) एजेन्ट (ए०)

ए:	क्या सेवा कर सकती हूँ?

सु: हिन्दुस्तान के लिये टिकट चाहिये।
ए: सिर्फ़ अपने लिये?
सु: परिवार के लिये।
ए: कितने लोग हैं?
सु: चार — दो बड़े और दो बच्चे।
ए: बच्चों की उमर बारह से कम है?
सु: लड़की की उमर बारह है और लड़के की छह।
ए: कब जाना चाहते हैं?
सु: क्रिसमस में।
ए: पीक सीज़न है, टिकट महँगी होगी।
सु: कोई बात नहीं।

Thinking about India

अल नसीरी (अ०) सुमन कुमार (सु०)
अ: भई, किस दुनिया में हो?
सु: हिन्दुस्तान के बारे में सोच रहा था।
अ: क्यों, सब ठीक है न?
सु: हाँ, क्रिसमस ब्रेक में हिन्दुस्तान जा रहे हैं।
अ: अकेले या परिवार के साथ?
सु: बीबी बच्चे यानी कि पूरी ट्राइब के साथ।
अ: हाँ भाई, नहीं तो बीबी तलाक के लिये कहेगी। कहाँ जाओगे?
सु: दिल्ली, आगरा और जयपुर।
अ: आगरा कैसे जाओगे?
सु: हवाई जहाज़ से।
अ: हवाई जहाज़ से जाना बेकार है।
सु: क्यों?
अ: हवाई जहाज़ से गाड़ी में कम समय लगता है।

The train to Agra

अल नसीरी (अ०) सुमन कुमार (सु०)
अ: आगरा के लिये सब से अच्छी गाड़ी ताज ऐक्सप्रेस है।
सु: ताज ऐक्सप्रेस कहाँ से चलती है?
अ: नयी दिल्ली से, सवेरे सात बजे।
सु: और आने के लिये?

अ: वही गाड़ी शाम को वापस आती है।
सु: लेकिन हम लोग रात को ताज महल देखना चाहते हैं।
अ: हाँ, ताज रात को और भी सुन्दर लगता है।
सु: तो एक रात आगरा रुकेंगे, अगले दिन दिल्ली लौटेंगे।
अ: चाँदनी रात, ताज महल और बीबी साथ ... मज़ा कीजिये।

'To build castles in the air'

1. एक दिन देश में अकाल पड़ेगा।
2. मैं आटा बेचूँगा।
3. और कुछ जानवर ख़रीदूँगा।
4. तो मैं अमीर बनूँगा।
5. एक दिन मेरी शादी होगी।
6. फिर मेरा बच्चा होगा।
7. अब मैं आराम से किताबें पढ़ूँगा।
8. बच्चा मेरे पास आयेगा।

Lesson 6

Someone has picked my pocket

अदिति चैटरजी (अ०) सुमन चैटरजी (सु०)

सु: हैलो।
अ: हैलो, डैड, मैं अदिति बोल रही हूँ।
सु: कहाँ से बोल रही हो?
अ: न्यू यॉर्क से।
सु: क्यों, अभी शिकागो नहीं पहुँची?
अ: नहीं।
सु: क्या बात है? परेशान लग रही हो। सब ठीक-ठाक है न।
अ: मैं तो ठीक हूँ, लेकिन मेरा पासपोर्ट, मेरे पैसे और ट्रैवलरज़ चैक्स गुम हो गये।
सु: क्या!
अ: किसी ने मेरी जेब काटी — ऐसा लगता है।
सु: सच!
अ: हाँ।

My passport is lost

अदिति चटरजी (अ०) अफ़सर

अ:	मेरा पासपोर्ट गुम गया है। नया पासपोर्ट चाहिये।
अफ़सर:	कब गुमा?
अ:	आज, करीब पाँच घंटे पहले।
अफ़सर:	आप को मालूम है कि कहाँ गुमा?
अ:	जी हाँ, कैनैडी हवाई अड्डे में।
अफ़सर:	कैसे?
अ:	जब इम्मिग्रेशन से बाहर आई, तो मेरे पास था। फिर, शिकागो की फ़्लाइट के लिये दूसरे टर्मिनल गयी, तब भी था। जब काऊन्टर पर पहुँची, तो देखा, पासपोर्ट, टिकट, पैसे और ट्रैवलरज़ चैक्स पर्स में नहीं थे।
अफ़सर:	पुलिस में रिपोर्ट की?
अ:	जी हाँ, यह देखिये।
अफ़सर:	अच्छा, यह फार्म भरिये, एक-दो महीने में नया पासपोर्ट आप को मिल जायेगा।
अ:	इस से जल्दी नहीं मिल सकता?
अफ़सर:	जी नहीं, पहले रिपोर्ट हिन्दुस्तान जायेगी और क्लियरैन्स के बाद ही पासपोर्ट मिल सकता है।
अ:	शुक्रिया।
अफ़सर:	कोई बात नहीं।

Visiting an astrologer

जान कारनी (जॉ०) ज्योतिषी (ज्यो०)

जॉ:	मैं अपने भूत के बारे में जानना चाहता हूँ।
ज्यो:	अपने फरिश्ते के बारे में पूछिये, भूत के बारे में क्यों?
जॉ:	मेरा मतलब है कि पिछले जन्म के बारे में।
ज्यो:	पत्रे के बिना मुश्किल है।
जॉ:	तो मेरे बचपन के बारे में बताइये।
ज्यो:	ये लाइनें बताती हैं कि आप का बचपन बहुत अच्छा था...सुन्दर परिवार...बड़ा घर...यह ठीक है?
जॉ:	जी हाँ, ...लेकिन...
ज्यो:	लेकिन पिछले पाँच साल अच्छे नहीं थे।
जॉ:	पिता जी के मरने के बाद बहुत मुश्किलें आईं।
ज्यों:	यह बड़े अफ़सोस की बात है।

Lesson 7

You can speak Hindi!

विजय मिश्रा (वि०)   ड्राइवर

वि:	माफ़ कीजिये, आप ने क्या कहा?
ड्राइवर:	मैंने पूछा कि डाउन टाउन जाना है।
वि:	अरे! आप तो बहुत अच्छी हिन्दी बोल सकते हैं।
ड्राइवर:	हाँ, मैं थोड़ी-थोड़ी हिन्दी बोल लेता हूँ।
वि:	हिन्दी आप ने कहाँ से सीखी?
ड्राइवर:	दूसरी वर्ड वार के समय में ब्रिटिश आर्मी में सैनिक था। उस समय हिन्दुस्तान में सीखी।
वि:	अभी भी अच्छी हिन्दी आती है।
ड्राइवर:	काफ़ी समय से योग और मैडीटेशन सीख रहा हूँ इसलिये हिन्दी नहीं भूली।
वि:	यह तो बहुत अच्छा है, नहीं तो यहाँ हिन्दुस्तानी भी हिन्दी भूल जाते हैं।
ड्राइवर:	यह बात तो सच है।

Can you write Hindi?

विजय मिश्रा (वि०)   (ड्राइवर)

वि:	क्या आप को हिन्दी लिखनी आती है?
ड्राइवर:	ज़्यादा नहीं। आर्मी में कभी-कभी लिखनी पड़ती थी लेकिन अब कोई ज़रूरत नहीं।
वि:	हिन्दी में क्यों लिखना पड़ता था?
ड्राइवर:	सीक्रेट कोड और सन्देशों के लिये — ख़ासकर योरुप जाने वाले सन्देशों के लिये। डाउन टाउन में कुछ काम है?
वि:	बिजली का बिल देना था। आज फ़ुरसत मिली, तो सोचा कि खुद वहाँ जाऊँ।
ड्राइवर:	तो वह दफ़्तर आने वाला है ... असल में अगला स्टाप है।
वि:	अच्छा, नमस्कार।
ड्राइवर:	नमस्कार।

I am very sick

जॉन रायडर (जॉ०)　डाक्टर नाइम की पत्नी (प०)

जॉ: हैलो, क्या डा० नाइम हैं?
प: जी नहीं, कोई ज़रूरी बात है?
जॉ: मेरी तबीयत बहुत ख़राब है।
प: एक मरीज़ को देखने गये हैं।
जॉ: कितनी देर में लौटेंगे?
प: मेरे ख़्याल से जल्दी आ जायेंगे। मुझे अपना टैलीफ़ोन नम्बर और पता दे दीजिये। आते ही उन्हें भेज दूँगी।
जॉ: बहुत-बहुत धन्यवाद।

Lesson 8

Be careful what you eat

जॉन रायडर (जॉ०)　डाक्टर नाइम (डा०)

जॉ: आदाब अर्ज, डाक्टर नाइम।
डॉ: आदाब, रायडर साहिब। इस बार कई साल के बाद मुलाकात हुई।
जॉ: जी हाँ, कोई पाँच साल बाद।
डॉ: तशरीफ़ रखिये, मैं आप का ही इन्तज़ार कर रहा था। अच्छा, पहले बताइये, तबीयत कैसी है?
जॉ: तबीयत तो अच्छी नहीं, नहीं तो इतनी रात को आप को तकलीफ़ न देता।
डॉ: तकलीफ़ की क्या बात है? यह तो मेरा फ़र्ज है। ख़ैर, बुख़ार कितना है?
जॉ: जब एक घंटे पहले थर्मामीटर लगाया, तो एक सौ दो डिग्री था अब शायद कुछ ज़्यादा हो।
डॉ: अच्छा, ज़रा फिर थर्मामीटर लगाइये।
(Dr Naim takes John's pulse and temperature.)
डॉ: बुख़ार थोड़ा बढ़ गया है। दस्त भी है?
जॉ: दो घंटे में सात बार बाथरूम गया।
डॉ: पिछली बार आप ने बहुत समोसे खाये थे, और इस बार?
जॉ: शाम को कुछ आम खाये।
डॉ: मेरी सलाह मानिये एक-दो महीने तक आप कुछ परहेज़ कीजिये, समोसे और आम बन्द। मैं एक टीका लगाता हूँ और यह दवाई

लीजिये। दो गोलियाँ हर दो घंटे। तो कल सुबह अपनी तबीयत के बारे में बताइये। अच्छा, अब आराम कीजिये। ख़ुदा हाफ़िज़।

जॉ: बहुत बहुत शुक्रिया, डाक्टर साहिब। ख़ुदा हाफ़िज़।

Lost in Delhi

फिलिप रोज़नबर्ग (फ़ि०) अजनबी (अ०) कैशियर (कै०)

फि: यहाँ पास कोई अमरीकन ऐक्सप्रैस का दफ़्तर है। मैं दो दिन पहले वहाँ गया था, लेकिन आज नहीं मिल रहा।

अ: आप को पता मालूम है?

फि: मैं पता तो भूल गया।

अ: मेरे ख़्याल से अगली सड़क पर अमरीकन ऐक्सप्रैस का दफ़्तर है *(pointing to the street)*

फि: *(seemingly puzzled)* वह सड़क तो सुन्दर है, लोग उसे अगली सड़क क्यों कहते है?

अ: अगली हिन्दी का शब्द है अंग्रेजी का नहीं। 'अगली' का मतलब अंग्रेज़ी में 'next' है।

फि: बहुत खूब।

(Philip goes to the cashier's window at the American Express office)

फि: मुझे कुछ ट्रैवलरज़ चैक कैश करवाने हैं।

कै: कौन-सी करन्सी में हैं?

फि: अमरीकन डालर। ऐक्सचेंज रेट क्या है?

कै: एक अमरीकन डालर तीस रुपये का है।

(Philip signs the cheques and the cashier gives him the equivalent amount in rupees)

कै: कुल दो सौ डालरज़। ये रहे आप के छह हज़ार रुपये। गिन लीजिये।

फि: ठीक है। धन्यवाद।

A folk-tale

एक लोक-कथा

१. एक गाँव में एक चोर जेल से भाग गया।

२. पुलिस वाला उस को पकड़ने के लिये दौड़ा।

३. इतने में गाँव वालों ने भागते चोर को पकड़ लिया।
४. पुलिस वाला ज़ोर ज़ोर से चिल्ला रहा था, 'पकड़ो मत, जाने दो।'
५. यह सुनते ही गाँव वालों ने चोर को छोड़ दिया।
६. जब पुलिस वाला गाँव वालों के पास पहुँचा,
७. तो उस को बहुत गुस्सा आया।
८. गुस्से में उस ने गाँव वालों से पूछा,
९. 'तुम ने चोर को क्यों छोड़ दिया?'
१०. गाँव वालों ने जवाब दिया,
११. आप ने ही कहा, 'पकड़ो मत, जाने दो।'

Lesson 9

Money will come soon

१. एक दिन दो दोस्त खाना खाने एक चीनी रैस्टोरैन्ट गये।
२. खाने के बाद बैरा 'फार्चून कुकी' लाया।
३. दोनों ने अपनी-अपनी 'फार्चून कुकी' को खोला और अपनी-अपनी किस्मत के बारे में पढ़ा।
४. फिर एक दोस्त ने दूसरे से पूछा, 'कागज़ पर क्या लिखा है?'
५. लिखा है — 'जल्दी पैसा आने वाला है।'
६. यह तो बड़ी खुशी की बात है।
७. तो कोई लाटरी खरीदी है?
८. नही, लकिन अपना जीवन बीमा करवाया ह।

'Spice up your life'

बिल हैसट (बि०) ज्योत्सना सिंह (ज्यो०)

बि:	हिन्दुस्तानी 'करी' अभी तक हम ने नहीं खायी।
ज्यो:	आप को मसालेदार खाना पसन्द है या 'करी'?
बि:	दोनों में फ़र्क क्या है?
ज्यो:	अमरीका में 'करी' एक डिश का नाम है लेकिन हिन्दुस्तान में ऐसी बात नहीं।
वि:	हमारे यहाँ 'करी' का मतलब 'कोई मसालेदार डिश' है।
ज्यो:	हिन्दुस्तान में न तो 'करी' हमेशा मसालेदार होती है और न ही 'करी पाउडर' अक्सर बिकता है। 'करी' अक्सर तरी वाली

होती है और माँस, सब्ज़ी, मच्छी या फल की बनी होती है।

बि: अरे! बिना मसाले के 'करी' — यह तो हम ने कभी नहीं सुना था।

ज्यो: तो अब आप को कौन-सी 'करी' पसन्द है?

बि: आम के आम और गुठलियों के दाम। 'करी' के बारे में पता लग गया और असली 'करी' चखने का मौका भी मिल जायेगा। अच्छा, हम को तेज़ मसालेदार माँस की 'करी' बहुत पसन्द है।

'Fire! Fire!'

बि: वाह! वाह! शानदार खुशबू आ रही है, और इन्तज़ार करना मुश्किल है।

ज्यो: आइये, खाना शुरू किया जाये। यह है आप की पसन्द — तेज़ मिर्च वाली चिकन करी

(Bill takes a lot of curry while Mrs Hassett takes only a little bit. After taking the first substantial bite:)

बि: *(fanning his mouth)* ओहहह! आग! ... आग!

ज्यो: क्यों, क्या हुआ?

बि: यह तो 'करी' नहीं है! यह तो ज्वालामुखी है!! और मैं अपना आग बुझाने वाला सामान भी नहीं लाया।

ज्यो: आग बुझाने वाला सामान यह है — अगर बहुत मिर्च लग रही है तो दही लीजिये।

(After a while Bill's mouth cools down.)

बि: सच, अमरीका में तेज़ मसालेदार खाना इतना तेज़ नहीं होता।

ज्यो: हाँ, यह तो हिन्दुस्तान है। यहाँ 'तेज़' का मतलब 'बहुत तेज़' है। हम लोग बहुत तेज़ खाते हैं लेकिन हिन्दुस्तान में सब लोग इतना 'तेज़' नहीं खा सकते।

बि: गलत-फ़हमी दूर करने के लिये शुक्रिया। मैं अब समझ गया कि 'तेज़' ख़तरनाक शब्द है।

Lesson 10

Divali, the festival of lights

१. दीवाली शब्द संस्कृत के दीपावली शब्द से आया है।

२. दीपावली या दीवाली का अर्थ है — दीपकों की पंक्ति।
३. यह भारत का सबसे प्रसिद्ध त्यौहार है।
४. दीवाली अक्तूबर या नवम्बर के महीने में आती है।
५. यह त्यौहार अच्छाई की बुराई और प्रकाश की अंधकार पर विजय का प्रतीक है।
६. यह राजा राम की राक्षस रावण पर विजय की खुशी में मनाया जाता है।
७. कहा जाता है कि जब चौदह वर्ष के बनवास और रावण पर विजय पाने के बाद राजा राम अपने राज्य, अयोध्या, लौट रहे थे, हर घर ने खुशी के दिये जलाये।
८. इसलिये दीवाली की रात को आज तक हर घर में दिये जलाये जाते हैं।
९. आप इस त्यौहार को भारत का क्रिसमस कह सकते हैं। यह त्यौहार भारत से बाहर — सिंगापुर, नेपाल, त्रिनिदाद, फ़ीजी आदि कई देशों में मनाया जाता है।
१०. दीवाली की रात को लोग पटाख़े और फुलझड़ियाँ जलाते हैं और हर घर में लक्ष्मी पूजन होता है।
११. जैसे क्रिसमस सिर्फ ईसाई ही नहीं मनाते, वैसे दीवाली सिर्फ हिन्दुओं का त्यौहार नहीं है। आज-कल लगभग सभी धर्मों के लोग दीवाली मनाते हैं।

Holi, the festival of colours

१. होली भारत का एक और रंग-बिरंगा त्यौहार है।
२. यह बसन्त ऋतु में आता है।
३. इस समय गाँवों में फ़सल कटने के बाद हर घर में बहुत अनाज आ जाता है।
४. इसलिये यह त्यौहार खुशहाली का सन्देश लाता है।
५. इस दिन लोग बहुत उत्साह से एक दूसरे पर रंग फेंकते हैं।
६. बच्चे पिचकारी से रंगीन पानी डालते हैं, जब कि बड़े लोग सूखे रंग से खेलते हैं, जिसको गुलाल कहते हैं।
७. हालाँकि इस दिन हर तरह का रंग लगाया जाता है, लाल रंग सर्व-प्रिय है क्योंकि लाल रंग प्रेम का प्रतीक है।
८. होली के दिन भारत में कारनीवल जैसा वातावरण होता है। यह बड़ी धूम-धाम से वृंदावन में मनाया जाता है जहाँ श्रीकृष्ण पले थे।
९. होली के बारे में कई प्राचीन कहानियाँ प्रचलित हैं जो मन की पवित्रता पर ज़ोर देती है।
१०. इस दिन लोग बड़ी प्रसन्नता से एक-दूसरे को गले लगाते हैं और शत्रुता भूल कर शत्रु को भी मित्र बना लेते है।

Rakshābandʰan or Rākhī, the festival of love and protection

१. रक्षाबन्धन का दूसरा नाम राखी भी है।
२. यह भाई-बहन के अटूट प्रेम को याद दिलाता है।
३. इस दिन हर बहन अपने भाई को सुनहरा धागा बाँधती है।
४. इस धागे का अर्थ है कि भाई अपने बहन को वचन देता है कि वह हमेशा उस की रक्षा करेगा।
५. यहाँ तक कि विदेशी भाई भी पुराने समय से इस वचन को पूरा करते रहे हैं।
६. सोलहवीं शताब्दी में गुजरात के सुलतान ने चित्तौड़ पर आक्रमण किया।
७. चित्तौड़ की रानी कर्णवती ने पराजित होने से पहले दिल्ली के मुग़ल सम्राट हुमायूँ के पास राखी भेजी।
८. जब तक हुमायूँ अपनी अपनायी बहन को बचाने के लिये चित्तौड़ पहुँचा तब तक रानी जौहर रचा चुकी थी।
९. लेकिन हुमायूँ ने फिर भी गुजरात के सुलतान को हराया और रानी कर्णवती के बेटे को, जिस को लड़ाई के समय छिपाकर चित्तौड़ से बाहर भेज दिया गया था, राज्य का उत्तराधिकारी बनाया।

हिन्दी लेखन अभ्यास
Hindi handwriting practice

a	अ	=	उ अ
ā	आ	=	अ आ
i	इ	=	इ
ī	ई	=	ई
u	उ	=	उ
ū	ऊ	=	उ ऊ
e	ए	=	ए

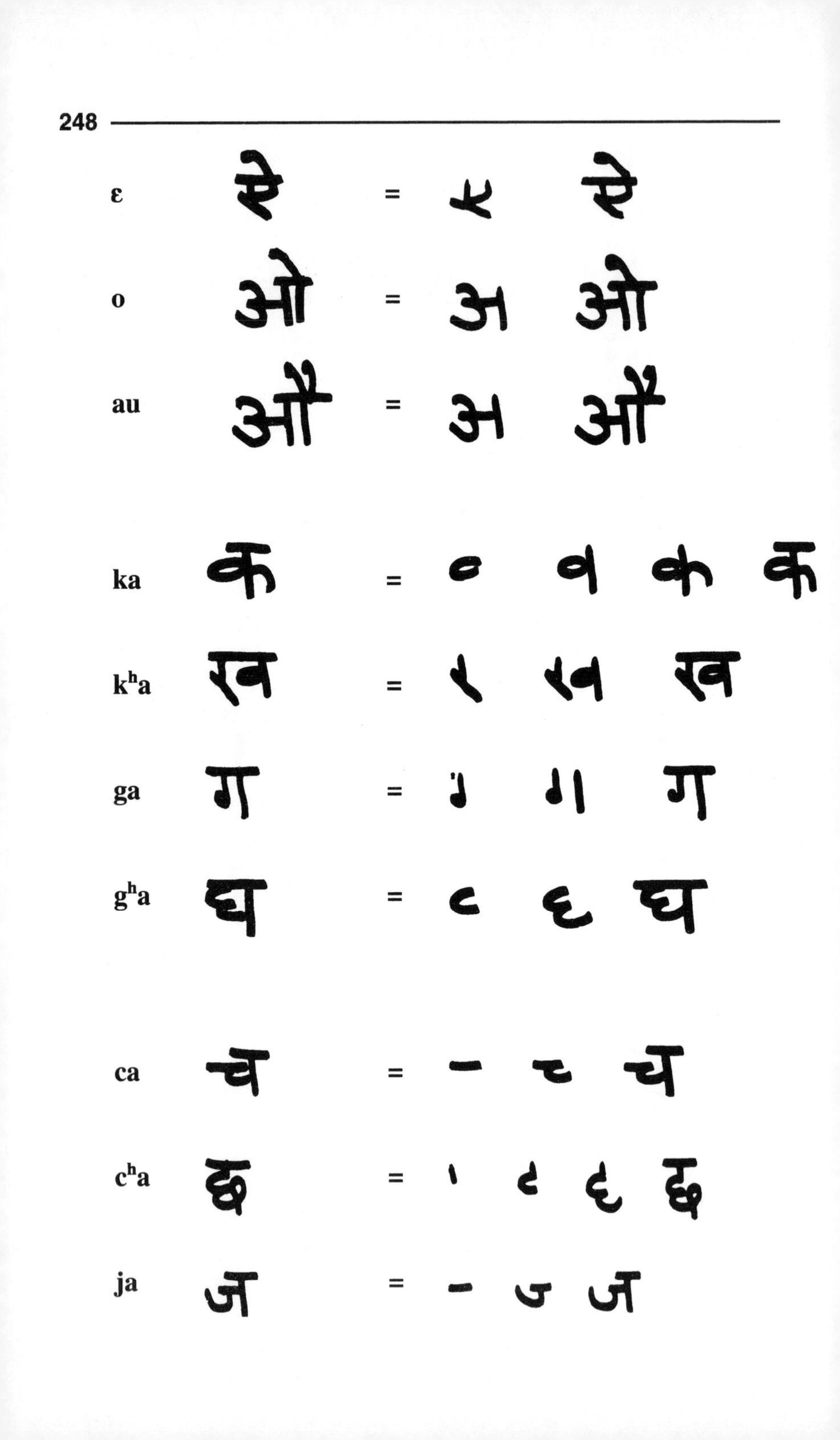

ε ऐ = ऐ

o ओ = अ ओ

au औ = अ औ

ka क = क

k^ha ख = ख

ga ग = ग

g^ha घ = घ

ca च = च

c^ha छ = छ

ja ज = ज

j^ha झ = … झ

Ta ट = … ट

T^ha ठ = ठ

Da ड = … ड

D^ha ढ = … ढ

Na ण = … ण

t त = … त

t^ha थ = … थ

da द = … द

d^ha ध = … ध

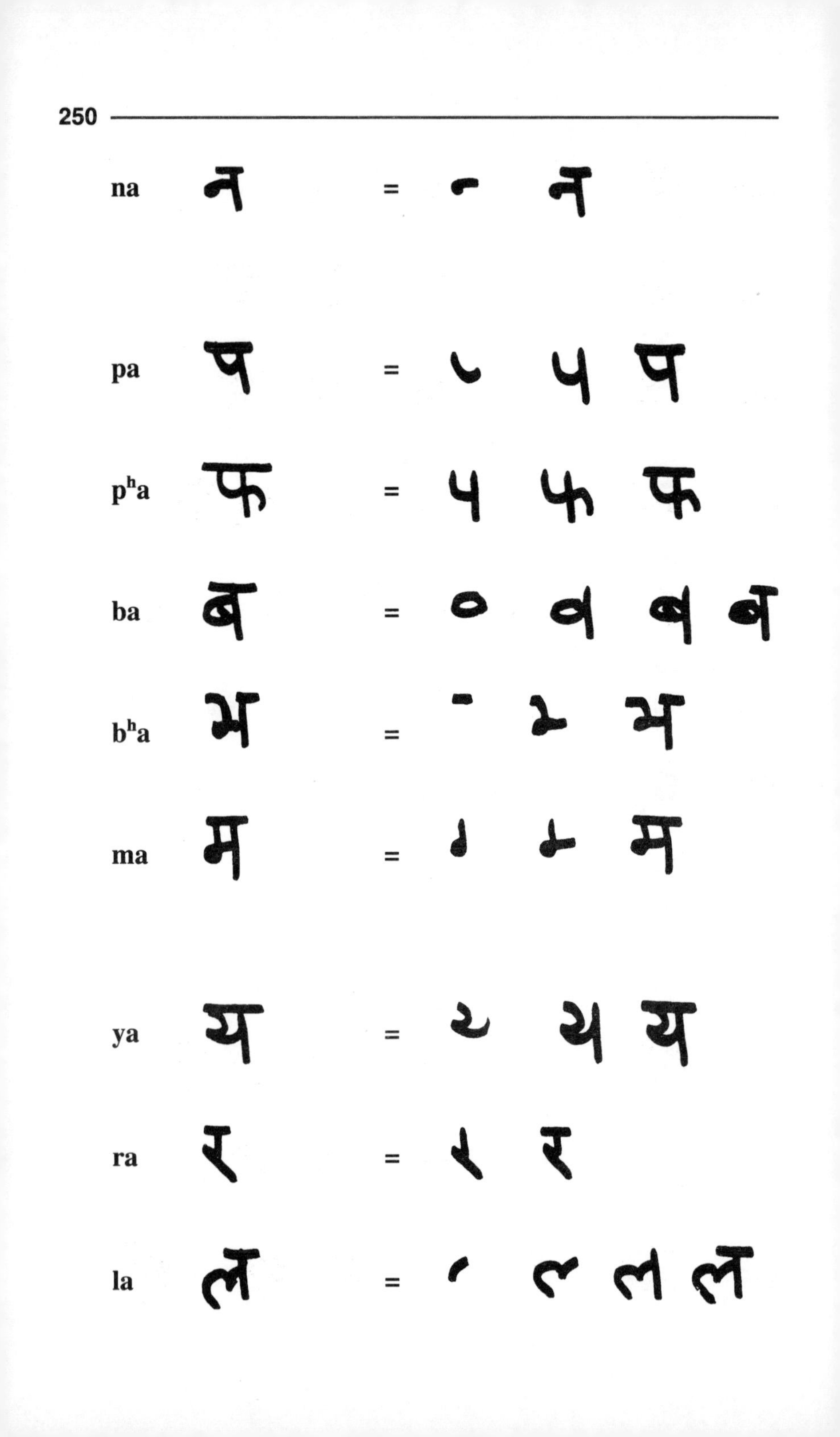

na न = न

pa प = प

p^{h}a फ = फ

ba ब = ब

b^{h}a भ = भ

ma म = म

ya य = य

ra र = र

la ल = ल

wa/va	व = व
sha	श = श
sHa	ष = ष
sa	स = स
ha	ह = ह
Ra	ड़ = ड ड़
R^ha	ढ़ = ढ ढ़
ksha	क्ष = क्ष
tra	त्र = त्र
gya	ज्ञ = ज्ञ

ka क

kā का = क का

ki कि = क कि कि कि

kī की = क की की

ku कु = क कु कु

kū कू = क कू

ke के = क के के

kε कै = क कै कै

ko को = क का को को

kau कौ = क का कौ कौ

kri कृ = क कृ

pa प

pā	पा
pi	पि
pī	पी
pu	पु
pū	पू
pe	पे
pɛ	पै
po	पो
pau	पौ
pri	पृ
ra	र
rā	रा

ri	रि				
rī	री				
ru	रु	=	र	र	रु
rū	रू	=	र	र	रू
re	रे				
rɛ	रै				
ro	रो				
rau	रौ				
amara	अमर	=	अमर		अमर
ũ̃t	ऊँट	=	ऊ	ऊँ	ऊँट

Reference grammar

Nouns

Nouns are inflected for gender, number and case.

Gender

There are two genders in Hindi, masculine and feminine. The gender system is partly semantically based and partly phonologically based. The rule of thumb is that inflected nouns ending in **-ā** are usually assigned masculine gender whereas the nouns ending in **-ī** are feminine. The semantic criterion (logical sex) takes precedence over the phonological criterion. Overall, the gender is unpredictable. **rastā**, 'path', is masculine but **rāh**, 'path', is feminine. **dāR^{h}ī**, 'beard', is feminine and so is **senā**, 'army'. Although **ādmī** ends in **-ī**, it is masculine, and **mātā** ends with **-ā** but is feminine. The class of masculine nouns that *do not* end in **-ā** and the feminine nouns that *do not* end in **-ī** are affectionately called 'nerd' nouns in this book.

People of the male sex take masculine gender while those of the female sex are assigned feminine gender. Therefore, nouns such as **laRkā**, 'boy', and **ādmī**, 'man', are masculine whereas **laRkī**, 'girl', and **aurat**, 'woman', are feminine. The same is true of some non-human animate nouns. Nouns such as **kuttā**, 'dog', **g^{h}oRā**, 'horse', **bandar**, 'monkey', and **bɛl**, 'ox', are masculine and **kutiyā**, 'bitch', **g^{h}oRī**, 'mare', **bandarī**, 'female monkey', and **gāy**, 'cow', are feminine.

Nouns denoting professions are usually masculine, as **b^{h}aŋgī**, 'sweeper'.

Some animate nouns (species of animals, birds, insects, etc.) exhibit unigender properties in the sense that they are either masculine or feminine. For example, **macc^{h}ar**, 'mosquito', **kīRā**, 'insect', **cītā**, 'leopard', and **ullū**, 'owl', are masculine in gender and nouns such as **ciRiyā**, 'bird', **koyal**, 'cuckoo', **titlī**, 'butterfly', **makk^{h}ī**, 'fly', **mac^{h}lī**, 'fish', are feminine. To specify the sex of animate nouns, words such as **nar**, 'male', and **mādā**, 'female', are prefixed to yield compound nouns such as **mādā-macc^{h}ar**, 'female-mosquito', or **nar-ciRiyā**, 'male bird'.

In the case of inanimate nouns, abstract, collective and material nouns, gender is partly determined by form and partly by semantics. On many occasions both criteria fail to determine the gender. The names of the following classes of nouns are usually masculine:

trees – **pīpal** (the name of a tree), **sāgvān**, 'teak', **devdār**, 'eucalyptus', **cīR**, 'pine', **ām**, 'mango' (however, **imlī**, 'tamarind' is feminine);

minerals and jewels – **lāl**, 'ruby', **sonā**, 'gold', **koyalā**, 'coal', **hīrā**, 'diamond' (however, **cā̃dī**, 'silver', is feminine);

liquids – **tel**, 'oil', **dūd^h**, 'milk', **pānī**, 'water' (however, **sharāb**, 'wine/liquor', is feminine);

crops – **d^{h}ān**, 'rice', **bājrā**, 'millet', **maTar**, 'pea';

mountains and oceans – **himālaya**, 'Himalayas', **hindmahāsāgar**, 'Indian Ocean';

countries – **hindustān**, 'India', **pākistān**, 'Pakistan', **amrīkā**, 'America';

gods, demons and heavenly bodies – **brahmā**, 'Brahma', **sūraj**, 'sun';

days and months (Native calendar) – **somvār**, 'Monday', **vaisāk^h**, 'Vaisakh';

body parts – **sir**, 'head', **kān**, 'ear', **hāt^h**, 'hand' (however, **ā̃k^h**, 'eye', **zabān**, 'tongue', are feminine); and

abstract nouns – **prem**, 'love', **gussā**, 'anger', **suk^h**, 'comfort' (however, some abstract nouns, including a synonym of **prem**, **mohabbat**, are feminine)

Number

Like English, Hindi has two ways of indicating number: singular and plural. However, there are some differences between the Hindi and the English ways of looking at the singularity or plurality of objects. Words such as **pajāmā,** पजामा, 'pyjamas', and **kẽcī,** कैंची, 'scissors', are singular in Hindi but plural in English. Similarly, 'rice' is singular in English but it is both singular and plural in Hindi.

Masculine nouns ending in **-ā** change to **-e** in their plural form. The other group (the 'nerd group') of masculine nouns that does not end in **-ā**, remains unchanged. Therefore they follow the following patterns.

Masculine nouns

Pattern I: ending in ā → e

बेटा	**beTā**	son	बेटे	**beTe**	sons
लड़का	**laRkā**	boy	लड़के	**laRke**	boys

Exceptions: **rājā,** king; **pitā,** father – remain unchanged.

Pattern II: non-ending in ā → *remain unchanged*

आदमी	**ādmī**	man	आदमी	**ādmī**	men
गुरु	**guru**	teacher	गुरु	**guru**	teachers

Feminine nouns

Similarly, feminine nouns also exhibit two patterns. Singular feminine nouns ending in **-ī** (including those ending in **i** or **iyā**) change to **iyā̃** in their plural forms, while feminine nouns not ending in **-ī** add **ẽ** in the plural.

Pattern I: ending in ī → iyā̃

बेटी	**beTī**	daughter	बेटियाँ	**beTiyā̃**	daughters
लड़की	**laRkī**	girl	लड़कियाँ	**laRkiyā̃**	girls
चिड़िया	**ciRiyā**	bird	चिड़ियाँ	**ciRiyā̃**	birds

Pattern II: not ending in ī → *add* ẽ

किताब	**kitāb**	book	किताबें	**kitābẽ**	books
माता	**mātā**	mother	माताएँ	**mātāẽ**	mothers
बहू	**bahū**	bride	बहुएँ	**bahuẽ**	brides

Note that feminine nouns ending in long **ū** shorten the vowel before the plural ending.

Direct and oblique case

Some nouns or noun phrases show 'peer pressure' under the influence of a postposition, i.e. they change their shape before a postposition. The form of the noun that occurs before a postposition is called the *oblique* case. The regular non-oblique forms are called *direct* form, as shown above.

Masculine singular nouns that follow pattern I change under the influence of postpositions. The word-final vowel **ā** changes to **e** in the oblique case. However, all plural nouns change and end in **õ** before postpositions. The following examples illustrate these rules.

Masculine nouns

Pattern I: ending in - ā

	direct			*oblique* (before postpositions)		
singular	बेटा	**beTā**	son	बेटे को	**beTe ko**	to the son (i.e. **ā** → **e**)
plural	बेटे	**beTe**	sons	बेटों से	**beTõ se**	by the sons (i.e. **e** → **õ**)

Pattern II: not ending in - ā *('nerd nouns')*

	direct			*oblique* (before postpositions)		
Singular	आदमी	**ādmī**	man	आदमी में	**ādmī mẽ**	in the man (i.e. no change)
Plural	आदमी	**ādmī**	men	आदमियों में	**ādmiyõ mẽ**	in the men (i.e. **õ** added; slight change in the vowel **ī** which becomes **i** and the semivowel **y** intervenes)

Feminine nouns

Pattern I: ending in -ī

	direct			*oblique* (before postpositions)		
Singular	बेटी	**beTī**	daughter	बेटी पर	**beTī par**	on the daughter
					(i.e. no change)	
Plural	बेटियाँ	**beTiyā̃**	daughters	बेटियों पर	**beTiyõ par**	on the daughters
					(i.e. **ā̃** changes to **õ**)	

Pattern II: not ending in -ī ('nerd nouns')

	direct			*oblique* (before postpositions)		
Singular	किताब	**kitāb**	book	किताब में	**kitāb mẽ**	in the book
					(i.e. no change)	
Plural	किताबें	**kitābẽ**	books	किताबों में	**kitābõ mẽ**	in the books
					(i.e. **ẽ** changes to **õ**)	

Articles

Hindi has no equivalents to the English articles *a, an* and *the*. This gap is filled by means of indirect devices such as the use of the numeral **ek** for the indefinite article, and the use of the postposition **ko** with an object to fulfil the function of the definite article.

Pronouns

Although the case system of pronouns is essentially the same as that of nouns, pronouns have more case forms in the oblique case than nouns, as exemplified below by the difference in pronominal form with different postpositions.

Personal: singular

direct	*oblique*			
	general oblique	*oblique* + **ko** (e.g. me)	*oblique* + **kā** (e.g. my)	*oblique* + **ne** (agentive past)
mɛ̃ I मैं	**muj^h** मुझ	**muj^h ko = mujhe** मुझ को = मुझे	**merā** मेरा	**mɛ̃ ne** मैं ने
tū you तू	**tuj^h** तुझ	**tuj^h ko = tuj^he** तुझ को = तुझे	**terā** तेरा	**tū ne** तू ने
vo he/she वह	**us** उस	**us ko = use** उस को = उसे	**us kā** उस का	**us ne** उस ने
ye this यह	**is** इस	**is ko = ise** इस को = इसे	**is kā** इस का	**is ne** इस ने

Personal: plural

direct	*oblique*			
	general oblique	*oblique* + **ko**	*oblique* + **kā**	*oblique* + **ne**
ham we हम	**ham** हम	**ham ko = hamẽ** हम को = हमें	**hamārā** हमारा	**ham ne** हम ने
tum you तुम	**tum** तुम	**tum ko = tumhẽ** तुम को = तुम्हें	**tumhārā** तुम्हारा	**tum ne** तुम ने
āp you आप	**āp** आप	**āp ko** आप को	**āp kā** आप का	**āp ne** आप ने
ve they वे	**un** उन	**un ko = inhẽ** उन को = उन्हें	**un kā** उन का	**unhõne** उन्होंने
ye these ये	**in** इन	**in ko = inhẽ** इन को = इन्हें	**in kā** इन का	**inhõne** इन्होंने

Other pronouns: singular

direct	*oblique*			
	general oblique	*oblique* + **ko**	*oblique* + **kā**	*oblique* + **ne**
kaun who? कौन	**kis** किस	**kis ko = kise** किस को = किसे	**kis kā** किस का	**kis ne** किस ने
jo who जो	**jis** जिस	**jis ko = jise** जिस को = जिसे	**jis kā** जिस का	**jis ne** जिस ने
kyā what क्या	**kis** किस	**kis ko = kise** किस को = किसे	**kis kā** किस का	– –
koī someone कोई	**kisī** किसी	**kisī ko** किसी को	**kisī kā** किसी का	**kisī ne** किसी ने

Other pronouns: plural

direct	*oblique*			
	general oblique	*oblique* + **ko**	*oblique* + **kā**	*oblique* + **ne**
kaun who? कौन	**kin** किन	**kin ko=kinhẽ** किन को = किन्हें	**kin kā** किन का	**kinhõne** किन्होंने
jo who जो	**jin** जिन	**jin ko=jinhẽ** जिन को = जिन्हें	**jin kā** जिन का	**jinhõne** जिन्होंने

Adjectives

Adjectives can be classified into two groups: 'green' (**harā**) and 'red' (**lāl**). Like some masculine nouns, green adjectives end in **ā**. They change their form (or agree) with the following nouns in terms of number and gender and show the signs of 'peer pressure' before a postposition. Red adjectives that do not end in **-ā** remain invariable. The following endings are used with the green adjectives when they are inflected for number, gender and case.

Pattern I: the green (harā) adjectives

	direct		*oblique*	
	singular	*plural*	*singular*	*plural*
masculine	**-ā**	**-e**	**-e**	**-e**
feminine	**-ī**	**-ī**	**-ī**	**-ī**

Example:

direct		*oblique*	
acc^{h}ā laRkā अच्छा लड़का	good boy	**acc^{h}e laRke se** अच्छे लड़के से	by a/the good boy
acc^{h}e laRke अच्छे लड़के	good boys	**acc^{h}e laRkõ se** अच्छे लड़कों से	by good boys
acc^{h}ī laRkī अच्छी लड़की	good girl	**acc^{h}ī laRkī sū̃** अच्छी लड़की से	by a/the good girl
acc^{h}ī laRkiyā̃ अच्छी लड़कियाँ	good girls	**acc^{h}ī laRkiyõ se** अच्छी लड़कियों से	by good girls

Pattern II: the red (lāl) adjectives

direct		*oblique*	
sundar laRkā सुन्दर लड़का	handsome boy	**sundar laRke se** सुन्दर लड़के से	by a/the handsome boy
sundar laRke सुन्दर लड़के	handsome boys	**sundar laRkõ se** सुन्दर लड़कों से	by handsome boys

sundar laRkī	beautiful girl	**sundar laRkī se**	by a/the beautiful girl
सुन्दर लड़की		सुन्दर लड़की से	
sundar laRkiyā̃	beautiful girls	**sundar laRkiyõ se**	by beautiful girls
सुन्दर लड़कियाँ		सुन्दर लड़कियों से	

Possessive pronouns (listed under oblique pronouns + **kā**), the reflexive pronoun **apnā,** 'self', and *participles* behave like green adjectives; therefore they are inflected in number, gender and case.

Postpositions

The Hindi equivalent of the English prepositions such as *to, in, at, on* etc., are called postpositions because they follow nouns and pronouns rather than precede them as in English.

Simple postpositions

Simple postpositions consist of one word. Here is the list of some important simple postpositions:

kā	का	of (i.e. possessive marker)
ko	को	to; also object marker
mẽ	में	in
par	पर	on, at
se	से	from, by, object marker for some verbs.
tak	तक	up to, as far as
ne	ने	agent marker for transitive verbs in simple past, present perfect and past perfect tenses
vālā	वाला	-er (and wide range of meanings)

Two postpositions, **kā** and **vālā,** also change like green adjectives; all others act like the red adjectives.

Compound postpositions

Compound postpositions consist of more than one word. They behave exactly the same way as simple postpositions, i.e. they are the source of peer pressure and thus require nouns or pronouns to be in the oblique case. Examples of some most frequent compound postpositions are given below:

***ke**-type*			***kī**-type*		
ke bāre mẽ	के बारे में	about	**kī taraf**	की तरफ	towards
ke āge	के आगे	in front of	**kī jagah**	की जगह	instead of
ke sāmne	के सामने	facing	**kī tarah**	की तरह	like
ke pahle	के पहले	before	**kī bajāy**	की बजाय	except for
ke bād	के बाद	after			
ke nīce	के नीचे	below			
ke ūpar	के ऊपर	above			

Notice that most of the compound postpositions begin with either **ke** or **kī**, but never with **kā**.

Question words

In English, the question words such as *who*, *when*, and *why* begin 'wh-' (exception *how*); the Hindi question words begin with the **k** sound. Some of the most common question words are listed below.

Pronouns

kyā	क्या	what	see pronouns for oblique forms
kaun	कौन	who	see pronouns for oblique forms
kaun-sā	कौन-सा	who	**kaun** remains invariable but **sā** changes like the green adjectives

Possessive pronouns

See oblique + **kā** forms of **kyā** and **kaun** in the section on pronouns.

Adverbs

kab	कब	when
kahā̃	कहाँ	where
kyõ	क्यों	why
kɛsā	कैसा	how, of what kind
kitnā	कितना	how much, how many

The last two adverbs, **kɛsā** and **kitnā,** are changeable and behave like the green adjectives.

Question words and word order

In Hindi it is not usual to move question words such as *what*, *how* and *where* to the beginning of the sentence. The question words usually stay in their original position, i.e. somewhere in the middle of the sentence. The only exception is the yes–no questions where the Hindi question word **kyā** is placed at the beginning of the sentence.

Verbs

The Hindi concept of time is quite different from the 'unilinear' concept found in English. In other words, time is not viewed as smoothly flowing from the past through the present into the future. It is possible to find instances of the present or future within the past. For example, the English expression 'he said that he was going' will turn out to be as 'he said that he is going' in Hindi. Similarly, the concept of habituality is also different in Hindi. It is possible to say in English 'I always went there'; however, in Hindi one has to use past habitual instead of English simple past to indicate a habitual act. Therefore the translational equivalent of the English sentence 'I always go there' will be 'I always used to go there' in Hindi.

Infinitive, gerundive or verbal nouns

nā is suffixed to the verbal stem to form the infinitive (or gerundive or verbal noun) form of the verb. **nā** follows the stem in Hindi rather than preceding it.

Simple infinitive

stem		stem+**nā**		
pī	पी	**pīnā**	पीना	to drink, drinking
kar	कर	**karnā**	करना	to do, doing
jā	जा	**jānā**	जाना	to go, going

The infinitive marker **ā** becomes **e** in the oblique case.

Causative verbs

Intransitive, transitive and detransitive verbs are made causative by a productive process of suffixation. Two suffixes **ā** (called the 'first causative' suffix) and **vā** (termed the 'second causative' suffix) are attached to the stem of a verb, and are placed before the infinitive marker **nā**. The process of causativization brings about some changes in some stems (as in **de**, 'to give'); Here are examples of some causative verb types.

Type 1

No changes occur in the verbal stem.

intransitive		*transitive*		*causative*	
uRnā	to fly	**uRāNā**	to fly X	**uRvāNā**	to cause Y to fly X
उड़ना		उड़ाना		उड़वाना	
paknā	to be cooked	**pakāNā**	to cook X	**pakvāNā**	to cause Y to cook X
पकना		पकाना		पकवाना	

Type 2

The stem-vowel of the intransitive verb undergoes either a raising or a shortening process in its corresponding transitive and causative forms.

intransitive		*transitive*		*causative*	
jāgnā	to wake	**jagānā**	to awaken X	**jagvānā**	to cause Y to awaken X
जागना		जगाना		जगवाना	
(i.e. **ā** → **a**)					
leTnā	to lie down	**liTānā**	to lay down	**liTvānā**	to cause Y to lay down X
लेटना		लिटाना		लिटवाना	
(i.e. **e** → **i**)					
j^{h}ūlnā	to swing	**j^{h}ulānā**	to swing X	**j^{h}ulvānā**	to cause Y to swing X
झूलना		झुलाना		झुलवाना	
(i.e. **ū** → **u**)					

Type 3

The stem-vowel of the transitive verb undergoes either a raising or a shortening process in its corresponding intransitive and causative forms.

In cases where the stem is disyllabic, it is the second vowel that undergoes such changes. The distinction between the causative marker **-vā** and its corresponding transitive marker **-ā** is neutralized, the two causal suffixes occur in free variation.

Type 3a

intransitive		*transitive*		*transitive (with -**ā**)/ causative*	
marnā	to die	**mārnā**	to kill	**marānā/ marvānā**	to cause Y to kill
मरना		मारना		मराना/मरवाना	
(i.e. **a** → **ā**)					
pisnā	to be ground	**pīsnā**	to grind X	**pisānā/ pisvānā**	to cause Y to grind X
पिसना		पीसना		पिसाना/पिसवाना	
(i.e. **i** → **ī**)					

pujnā पुजना (i.e. **u** → **ū**)	to be worshipped	**pūjnā** पूजना	to worship X	**pujānā/ pujvānā** पुजाना/पुजवाना	to cause Y to worship X
k^{h}ulnā खुलना (i.e. **u** → **o**)	to be/ become opened	**k^{h}olnā** खोलना	to open X	**k^{h}ulāNā/ k^{h}ulvānā** खुलाना/खुलवाना	to cause Y to open X

Type 3b

Transitive verbs show one of the following tendencies: a new semantic distinction between the derived and the base transitive forms is created as shown by the gloss in set A; derived transitive and causative verbs undergo one level of causativization as is the case with set B.

Set A

transitive		*transitive (with -**ā**)*		*causative*	
paR^{h}nā पढ़ना	to read	**paR^{h}ānā** पढ़ाना	to teach	**paR^{h}vānā** पढ़वाना	to cause Y to teach X
bolnā बोलना (i.e. **o** → **u**)	to speak	**bulānā** बुलाना	to call	**bulvānā** बुलवाना	to cause Y to call X

Set B

The causative marker **-vā** occurs in free variation with **-lā**. The verbal stem undergoes vowel changes, as in

transitive		*transitive (with -**ā**)/causative*	
denā देना	to give	**divānā/dilānā** दिवाना/दिलाना	to cause Y to give X
d^{h}onā धोना	to wash	**d^{h}uvānā/d^{h}ulānā** धुवाना/धुलाना	to cause Y to wash X

Type 4

Some verbs show both consonantal and vowel changes in their corresponding transitive forms. The consonantal alternations are as follows: the intransitive stem-final **k** becomes **c**, and the intransitive stem-final **T** becomes retroflex **R**.

intransitive		*transitive*		*causative*	
biknā	to be sold	**becnā**	to sell X	**bikvānā**	to cause Y to sell X
बिकना		बेचना		बिकवाना	
TūTnā	to be broken	**toRnā**	to break X	**tuRānā/ tuRvānā**	to cause Y to break X
टूटना		तोड़ना		तुड़ाना/तुड़वाना	

Auxiliary/copula verb

Present

The present tense auxiliary/copular verb agrees in number and person with its subject.

honā ***to be***

	singular		*plural*	
first person	**hū̃** हूँ	I am	**hɛ̃** हैं	we are
second person	**hɛ** है	you are	**ho** हो **hɛ̃** हैं	you (familiar) are you (honorific) are
third person	**hɛ** है	he/she/it is	**hɛ̃** हैं	they are

Past

The past tense auxiliary/copular verb agrees in number and gender with its subject.

honā *to be*

	singular		*plural*	
masculine	**tʰā** था	was	**tʰe** थे	were
feminine	**tʰī** थी	was	**tʰī̃** थीं	were

Another conjugation of **honā** is as follows:

	singular			*plural*	
masculine	**huā**	हुआ	happened	**hue**	हुए
feminine	**huī**	हुई		**huī̃**	हुईं

Future

The future tense auxiliary/copular verb agrees in number, gender and person with its subject.

honā *masculine*

	singular		*plural*	
first person	**hū̃gā** हूँगा	I will be	**hõge** होंगे	we will be
second person	**hogā** होगा	you will be	**hoge** होगे	you (familiar) will be
			hõge होंगे	you (honorific) will be
third person	**hogā** होगा	he/she/it will be	**hõge** होंगे	they will be

honā *feminine*

For the feminine forms, replace the word-final vowel of the masculine forms with **ī**.

Subjunctive

For the subjunctive forms of **honā**, simply drop the final syllable (i.e. **gā**, **ge**, **gī**) from the future tense forms.

Main verb

Simple present/imperfective/present habitual

The simple present is formed by adding the following suffixes to the main verbal stem.

	singular		*plural*	
masculine	**-tā**	ता	**-te**	ते
feminine	**-tī**	ती	**-tī**	ती

The main verb is followed by the present auxiliary forms.

Example: verb stem likʰ, *'write'*

Masculine

singular		*plural*	
mɛ̃ likʰtā hū̃ मैं लिखता हूँ	I write	**ham likʰte hɛ̃** हम लिखते हैं	we write
tū likʰtā hɛ तू लिखता है	you write	**tum likʰte ho** तुम लिखते हो	you (familiar) write
		āp likʰte hɛ̃ आप लिखते हैं	you (honorific) write
vo likʰtā hɛ वह लिखता है	he writes	**ve likʰte hɛ̃** वे लिखते हैं	they write

Feminine

Replace **tā** and **te** in the masculine paradigm with **tī**.

Past habitual

The past habitual is derived by substituting the past auxiliary forms for the present auxiliary forms in the simple present tense.

Example: verb stem lik^{h}, *'write'*

Masculine

singular		*plural*	
mɛ̃ lik^{h}tā t^{h}ā मैं लिखता था	I used to write	**ham lik^{h}te t^{h}e** हम लिखते थे	we used to write
tū lik^{h}tā t^{h}ā तू लिखता था	you used to write	**tum lik^{h}te t^{h}e** तुम लिखते थे	you (familiar) used to write
		āp lik^{h}te t^{h}e आप लिखते थे	you (honorific) used to write
vo lik^{h}tā t^{h}ā वह लिखता था	he used to write	**ve lik^{h}te t^{h}e** वे लिखते थे	they used to write

Feminine

Replace **tā** and **te** in the masculine paradigm with **tī**. Also, substitute the auxiliaries **t^{h}ī** and **t^{h}ī̃** for **t^{h}ā** and **t^{h}e**, respectively.

Simple past/perfective

The simple past is formed by adding the following suffixes to the verb stem. No auxiliary verb follows the main verb.

	singular	*plural*
masculine	**-ā**	**-e**
feminine	**-ī**	**-ī̃**

Example: verb stem bɛT^{h}, *'sit'*

Masculine

singular		*plural*	
mɛ̃ bɛT^{h}ā मैं बैठा	I sat	**ham bɛT^{h}e** हम बैठे	we sat
tū bɛT^{h}ā तू बैठा	you sat	**tum bɛT^{h}e** तुम बैठे	you (familiar) sat
		āp bɛT^{h}e आप बैठे	you (honorific) sat

vo bɛT^{h}ā वह बैठा	he sat	**ve bɛT^{h}e** वे बैठे	they sat

Feminine

The verb-final **ā** and **e** are replaced by **ī** and **1**, respectively.

Transitive verb and the agentive postposition ne

The transitive verbs take the agentive postposition **ne** ने with the subject and the verb agreeing with the object instead of the subject. Observe the paradigm of the simple past tense with the transitive verb **lik^{h}**, 'to write'.

Example: verb stem lik^{h}, *'write'*

Masculine

singular		*plural*	
mɛ̃ ne ciTT^{h}ī lik^{h}ī मैं ने चिट्ठी लिखी	I wrote a letter	**ham ne ciTT^{h}ī lik^{h}ī** हम ने चिट्ठी लिखी	we wrote a letter
tū ne ciTT^{h}ī lik^{h}ī तू ने चिट्ठी लिखी	you wrote a letter	**tum ne ciTT^{h}ī lik^{h}ī** तुम ने चिट्ठी लिखी	you (familiar) wrote a letter
		āp ne ciTT^{h}ī lik^{h}ī आप ने चिट्ठी लिखी	you (honorific) wrote a letter
us ne ciTT^{h}ī lik^{h}ī उस ने चिट्ठी लिखी	he wrote a letter	**unhõne ne ciTT^{h}ī lik^{h}ī** उन्होंने चिट्ठी लिखी	they wrote a letter

The verb agrees with **ciTT^{h}ī**, 'letter', which is a feminine singular noun. Therefore the verb stays the same regardless of the change in the subject.

Important transitive verbs that do not take the **ne** postposition are: **milnā**, 'to meet', **lānā**, 'to bring' and **bolnā**, 'to speak'.

The rule of thumb is that the verb does not agree with a constituent that is followed by a postposition. For example, if the object marker **ko** is used with **ciTT^{h}ī**, the verb will agree neither with the subject nor with the object. In such situations, the verb will stay in the masculine singular form.

Present perfect

The present perfect verb forms are formed by adding the present tense auxiliary forms to the simple past tense. Transitive verbs take the **ne** postposition with their subjects.

Example: verb stem bɛT^h, *'sit'*

Masculine

singular		*plural*	
mɛ̃ bɛT^hā hū̃ मैं बैठा हूँ	I have sat [down]	**ham bɛT^he hɛ̃** हम बैठे हैं	we have sat [down]
tū bɛT^hā hɛ तू बैठा है	you have sat [down]	**tum bɛT^he ho** तुम बैठे हो	you (familiar) have sat [down]
		āp bɛT^he hɛ̃ आप बैठे हैं	you (honorific) have sat [down]
vo bɛT^hā hɛ वह बैठा है	He has sat [down]	**ve bɛT^he hɛ̃** वे बैठे हैं	they have sat [down]

Past perfect

The past perfect verb forms are formed by adding the past tense auxiliary forms to the simple past tense. Transitive verbs take the **ne** postposition with their subjects.

Example: verb stem bɛT^h, *'sit'*

Masculine

singular		*plural*	
mɛ̃ bɛT^hā t^hā मैं बैठा था	I had sat [down]	**ham bɛT^he t^he** हम बैठे थे	we had sat [down]
tū bɛT^hā t^hā तू बैठा था	you had sat [down]	**tum bɛT^he t^he** तुम बैठे थे	you (familiar) had sat [down]
		āp bɛT^he t^he आप बैठे थे	you (honorific) had sat [down]
vo bɛT^hā t^hā वह बैठा था	he had sat [down]	**ve bɛT^he t^he** वे बैठे थे	they had sat [down]

Future

The following person–number–gender suffixes with a stem form the future tense:

pronouns	*singular*		*plural*	
	masculine	*feminine*	*masculine*	*feminine*
first person	**-ū̃gā** ऊँगा	**-ū̃gī** ऊँगी	**ẽge** एंगे	**-ẽgī** एंगी
second person	**-egā** एगा	**-egī** एगी	**-oge** ओगे -**ẽge** एंगे	**-ogī** ओगी **-ẽgī** एंगी
third person	**-egā** एगा	**-egī** एगी	**-ẽge** एंगे	**-ẽgī** एंगी

Example: verb stem lik^{h}, ***'write'***

Masculine

singular		*plural*	
mɛ̃ lik^{h}ū̃gā मैं लिखूँगा	I will write	**ham lik^{h}ẽge** हम लिखेंगे	we will write
tū lik^{h}egā तू लिखेगा	you will write	**tum lik^{h}oge** तुम लिखोगे	you (familiar) will write
		āp lik^{h}ẽge आप लिखेंगे	you (honorific) will write
vo lik^{h}egā वह लिखेगा	he will write	**ve lik^{h}ẽge** वे लिखेंगे	they will write

Feminine

Replace the last syllable **gā** and **ge** of the masculine paradigm with **gī**.

Subjunctive/optative

The subjunctive (also called optative and hortative) is used to express suggestion, possibility, doubt, uncertainty, apprehension, wish, desire, encouragement, demand, requirement or potential. Subjunctive formation is outlined below. Subjunctive forms are not coded for gender. Drop the **gā**, **ge** and **gī** endings from the future form, and the remainder will constitute the subjunctive form.

Imperative

The imperative is formed by adding the following endings to the stem:

intimate/ impolite	*familiar*	*polite*	*extra polite*	*future*
no suffix	**-o**	**-iye**	**-iyegā**	**-nā** (=infinitive)

intimate/impolite	**tū jā**	तू जा	Go
familiar	**tum jāo**	तुम जाओ	Go
polite	**āp jāiye**	आप जाइये	Please go
extra polite	**āp jāiyegā**	आप जाइयेगा	Please go
future (non-immediate)	**āp/tum jānā**	आप जाना	(Please) go sometime in future

Negative particles and imperative

nahī̃ नहीं is not used with imperatives

mat मत is usually used with intimate, familiar and future imperatives

na न is usually used with polite, extra polite and future imperatives

Present progressive/continuous

The progressive aspect is expressed by means of the independent word **rah**, which is homophonous with the stem of the verb **rahnā,** 'to live'. The progressive marker agrees with the number and gender of the subject; therefore, it can be realized in one of the following forms:

Progressive marker rah, '*-ing*'

masculine		*feminine*	
singular	*plural*	*singular*	*plural*
rahā	**rahe**	**rahī**	**rahī̃**

Example: verb stem* lik^h*, 'write'

Masculine

singular		*plural*	
mɛ̃ lik^h rahā hū̃	I am writing	**ham lik^h rahe hɛ̃**	we are writing
मैं लिख रहा हूँ		हम लिख रहे हैं	
tū lik^h rahā hɛ	you are writing	**tum lik^h rahe ho**	you (familiar)
तू लिख रहा है		तुम लिख रहे हो	are writing
		āp lik^h rahe hɛ̃	you (honorific)
		आप लिख रहे हैं	are writing
vo lik^h rahā hɛ	he is writing	**ve lik^h rahe hɛ̃**	they are writing
वह लिख रहा है		वे लिख रहे हैं	

Feminine

Replace **rahā** and **rahe** in the masculine paradigm with **rahī**.

Past progressive/continuous

The present auxiliary verb in the present progressive construction is replaced by the past auxiliary verb in the past progressive forms.

Irregular verbs

Here is a list of the Hindi irregular verbs:

jānā	**karnā**	**lenā**	**denā**	**pīnā**
to go	to do	to take	to give	to drink
जाना	करना	लेना	देना	पीना

Simple past

gayā	went	**kiyā**	did	**liyā**	took	**diyā**	gave	**piyā**	drank
गया	(m. sg.)	किया	(m. sg.)	लिया	(m. sg.)	दिया	(m. sg.)	पिया	(m. sg.)
gaye	(m. pl.)	**kiye**	(m. pl.)	**liye**	(m. pl.)	**diye**	(m. pl.)	**piye**	(m. pl.)
गये		किये		लिये		दिये		पिये	

gayī (f. sg.)	**kī** (f. sg.)	**lī** (f. sg.)	**dī** (f. sg.)	**pī** (f. sg.)
गयी	की	ली	दी	पी
gayī̃ (f. pl.)	**kī̃** (f. pl.)	**lī̃** (f. pl.)	**dī̃** (f. pl.)	**pī̃** (f. pl.)
गयीं	की	ली	दी	पी

Imperative

(polite)	**kījiye** कीजिये	**lījiye** लीजिये	**dījiye** दीजिये	**pījiye** पीजिये
(familiar)	–	**lo** लो	**do** दो	**piyo** पियो

Future

lenā to take	**lū̃gā** लूँगा I will take	**loge** लोगे you (तुम) will take	**legā** लेगा will take (m. sg.)	**lẽge** लेंगे will take (m. pl.)
denā to give	**dū̃gā** दूँगा I will give	**doge** दोगे you (तुम) will give	**degā** देगा will give (m. sg.)	**dẽge** देंगे will give (m. pl.)

Participles

Present/imperfective participle

The present participial marker is **-t-** which immediately follows the verbal stem and is, in turn, followed by number and gender markers, as shown below:

masculine		*feminine*	
singular	*plural*	*singular*	*plural*
stem-**t-ā**	stem-**t-e**	stem-**t-ī**	stem-**t-ī**

The present participle may be used as either adjective or adverb. The optional past participial form of the verb **honā**, 'to be', may immediately follow the present participial form. The forms of the optional element are as follows:

masculine		*feminine*	
singular	*plural*	*singular*	*plural*
huā	**hue**	**huī**	**huī̃**

Examples

caltā (huā) laRkā चलता (हुआ) लड़का	walking boy
caltī (huī) laRkī चलती (हुई) लड़की	walking girl

The present participial form and the optional 'to be' form agree in number and gender with the following head noun. The retention of the optional form makes the participial phrase emphatic in nature. The present participle indicates an *ongoing action.*

Past/perfective participle

The past participial form is derived by adding the following suffixes, declined for number and gender, to the verbal stem. Like the present participle, the optional past participial form of the verb **honā**, 'to be', may immediately follow the past participial form.

masculine		*feminine*	
singular	*plural*	*singular*	*plural*
stem-**ā**	stem-**e**	stem-**ī**	stem-**ī̃**

The past participle may be used as either adjective or adverb. The past participial form and the optional 'to be' form agree in number and gender with the following head noun. The retention of the optional form makes the participial phrase emphatic in nature. The past participle indicates a *state.*

Example

bɛT^hā (huā) laRkā बैठा (हुआ) लड़का	a seated boy
bɛT^hī (huī) laRkī बैठी (हुई) लड़की	a seated girl

The irregular past participial is formed the same way as the past tense form.

Absolutive/conjunctive participle

The absolutive/conjunctive participle is formed by adding the invariable **kar** to the verbal stem, as in

stem			*conjunctive participle*		
lik^h	लिख	write	**lik^h kar**	लिख कर	having written
ā	आ	come	**ā kar**	आ कर	having come
pī	पी	drink	**pī kar**	पी कर	having drunk

-te hī **participle, 'as soon as'**

This participle is formed by adding the invariable **-te hī**, 'as soon as', to the verbal stem.

stem			*'as soon as' participle*		
lik^h	लिख	write	**lik^hte hī**	लिखते ही	as soon as [he] wrote
ā	आ	come	**āte hī**	आते ही	as soon as [he] came
pī	पी	drink	**pīte hī**	पीते ही	as soon as [he] drank

Agentive participle

The agentive participle is formed by adding the marker **vālā** to the oblique infinitive form of the verb. **vālā** agrees in number and gender with the following noun.

masculine		*feminine*	
singular	*plural*	*singular*	*plural*
vālā	**vāle**	**vālī**	**vālī**

Examples

stem	*oblique infinitive*	*agentive participle*	
lik^{h} write	**lik^{h}ne**	**lik^{h}ne vālā laRkā** लिखने वाला लड़का	the boy who writes
		lik^{h}ane vāle laRke लिखने वाले लड़के	the boys who write
		lik^{h}ne vālī laRkī लिखने वाली लड़की	the girl who writes
		lik^{h}ne vālī laRkiyā̃ लिखने वाली लड़कियाँ	the girls who write

Key to exercises

Hindi writing system and pronunciation

Exercise 1

1 C 2 A 3 C 4 B 5 B 6 A 7 B 8 B 9 B 10 A

Exercise 2

1 A, D 2 B, D 3 A, B 4 B, C 5 B, D 6 B, D 7 A, D 8 B, D
9 B, D 10 A, B

Exercise 3

(1)	Tāk	टाक	i.e. B
(2)	T^hak	ठक	i.e. B
(3)	Dāg	डाग	i.e. B
(4)	d^hak	धक	i.e. A
(5)	paR	पड़	i.e. B
(6)	sar	सर	i.e. A
(7)	kaR^hī	कढ़ी	i.e. B
(8)	T^hīk	ठीक	i.e. B

Exercise 4

(1)	kāl	काल	i.e. A
(2)	din	दिन	i.e. A
(3)	mil	मिल	i.e. A
(4)	cūk	चूक	i.e. B

(5)	mɛl	मैल	i.e. B
(6)	ser	सेर	i.e. A
(7)	bin	बिन	i.e. A
(8)	bal	बल	i.e. B

Lesson 1

Exercise 1

(a) namaste. (b) Tʰīk hɛ. (c) salām. (d) allāh kā shukra hɛ. (e) (accʰā), namaste. (f) sat srī akāl jī. (g) meharbānī hɛ *or* (allāh kā) shukra hɛ. (h) namaste jī. (i) hukam nahī̃, vintī hɛ.

(a) नमस्ते। (b) ठीक है। (c) सलाम। (d) अल्लाह का शुक्र है। (e) अच्छा। (f) सत् स्री अकाल जी। (g) मेहरबानी है *or* अल्लाह का शुक्र है। (h) नमस्ते जी। (i) हुकम नहीं, विनती है।

Exercise 2

(a) namaste.	namaste.
(b) kyā hāl hɛ?	Tʰīk hɛ.
(c) āp ke mizāj kɛse hɛ̃?	allāh kā shukra hɛ.
(d) xudā hāfiz.	xudā hāfiz.
(e) sab xɛriyat hɛ?	meharbānī hɛ.
(f) salām	salām.

(a) नमस्ते।	नमस्ते।
(b) क्या हाल है?	ठीक है
(c) आप के मिज़ाज कैसे हैं?	अल्लाह का शुक्र है।
(d) खुदा हाफ़िज	खुदा हाफ़िज।
(e) सब ख़ैरियत है?	मेहरबानी है।
(f) सलाम।	सलाम।

Exercise 3

Conversation I

A: salām.
B: salām.

B:	sab xɛriyat hɛ?
A:	meharbānī hɛ, aur āp ke mizāj kɛse hɛ̃?
B:	allāh kā shukra hɛ.

A:	सलाम।
B:	सलाम।
B:	सब ख़ैरियत है?
A:	मेहरबानी है, और आप के मिज़ाज कैसे हैं?
B:	अल्लाह का शुक्र है।

Conversation II

A:	sat srī akāl jī.
B:	sat srī akāl jī.
B:	kyā hāl hɛ?
A:	T^{h}īk hɛ, aur āp?
B:	mɛ̃ b^{h}ī T^{h}īk hũ.
A:	acc^{h}ā, sat srī akāl.
B:	sat srī akāl.

A:	सत् स्री अकाल जी।
B:	सत् स्री अकाल जी।
B:	क्या हाल है?
A:	ठीक है, और आप?
B:	मैं भी ठीक हूँ।
A:	अच्छा, सत् स्री अकाल।
B:	सत् स्री अकाल।

Exercise 4

(a)	Question:	kyā hāl hɛ?
	Answer:	T^{h}īk hɛ.
	Question:	aur āp?
	Answer:	mɛ̃ b^{h}ī T^{h}īk hũ.
(b)	Question:	āp kɛse hɛ̃?
	Answer:	T^{h}īk hũ.

(a)	सवाल:	क्या हाल है?
	जवाब:	ठीक है।

	सवाल:	और आप?
	जवाब:	मैं भी ठीक हूँ।
(b)	सवाल:	आप कैसे हैं?
	जवाब:	ठीक हूँ।

Exercise 5

	long sentences	*short sentences*
(a)	aur āp kɛse hɛ̃?	kɛse hɛ̃?
(b)	mɛ̃ b^{h}ī T^{h}īk hū̃.	T^{h}īk hū̃.
(c)	āp kī meharbānī hɛ.	meharbānī hɛ.
(d)	āp ke mizāj kɛse hɛ̃?	mizāj kɛse hɛ̃?
(a)	और आप कैसे हैं?	कैसे हैं?
(b)	मैं भी ठीक हूँ।	ठीक हूँ।
(c)	आप की मेहरबानी है।	मेहरबानी है।
(d)	आप के मिज़ाज कैसे हैं?	मिज़ाज कैसे हैं?

Exercise 6

Most probably both are Hindus. हिन्दू हैं।

Lesson 2

Exercise 1

mɛ̃ dillī kā hū. mere cār b^{h}āī hɛ̃. merā c^{h}oTā b^{h}āī *Chicago* mẽ kām kartā hɛ. mere do baRe b^{h}āī *England* mẽ rɛhte hɛ̃. merā nām amar hɛ. mɛ̃ *school* jātā hū. merī do bɛhɛnẽ b^{h}ī hɛ̃. mere pitā jī b^{h}ī kām karte hɛ̃. āp kahā̃ rɛhte hɛ̃? āpke kitne b^{h}āī-bɛhɛnẽ hɛ̃. āp kī mātā jī kyā kām kartī hɛ̃.

मैं दिल्ली का हूँ। मेरे चार भाई हैं। मेरा छोटा भाई शिकागो में काम करता है। मेरे दो बड़े भाई इंग्लैंड में रहते हैं। मेरा नाम अमर है। मैं स्कूल जाता हूँ। मेरी दो बहनें भी हैं। मेरे पिताजी भी काम करते हैं। आप कहाँ रहते हैं? आप के कितने भाई-बहनें हैं। आप की माता जी क्या काम करती हैं।

Exercise 2

acc^{h}ā	burā	अच्छा	बुरा
baRā	c^{h}oTā	बड़ा	छोटा
bɛhɛn	b^{h}āī	बहन	भाई
laRkā	laRkī	लड़का	लड़की
ādmī	aurat	आदमी	औरत
hā̃	nahī̃	हाँ	नहीं

Exercise 3

banāras	se	बनारस	से
shɛhɛr	mẽ	शहर	में
das	bɛhɛnẽ	दस	बहनें
cār	b^{h}āī	चार	भाई
do	ādmī	दो	आदमी
kitne	b^{h}āī	कितने	भाई
pīlī	sāRī	पीली	साड़ी

Exercise 4

kahiye	कहिये
xushī	खुशी
baRī xushī huī	बड़ी खुशी हुई
pūrā nām	पूरा नाम
dūsrā	दूसरा
kitne b^{h}āī	कितने भाई
milẽge	मिलेंगे

Exercise 5

a d g a ⓑ a d z x ⓢ ⓤ ⓝ ⓘ ⓨ ⓔ z y x u f g

l l k j @ z x c v b n m a s ⓟ q w e r t y

z x c v Ⓡ a d g a r t y f g h @ s g h j o

r t y f ⓘ b g t ⓧ ⓤ ⓢ ⓗ ⓘ ⓘ z q ⓣ s k x p

c v b n ⓘ w s x e d v r a t g h t @ h z c

q a z w c w s v f r y h n m h u i k @ u c

Voices of two women, Abhilasha Pande and Meenu Bharati
Setting: a crowded shop

ABHILASHA:	(*bumps into Meenu*) māf kījiye.
MEENU:	māfī kī bāt nahī̃. bahut bʰīR hɛ.
ABHILASHA:	sac.
MEENU:	merā nām Meenu Bharati hɛ.
ABHILASHA:	aur merā nām Abhilasha Pande hɛ.
MEENU:	mɛ̃ yahā̃ roz ātī hū̃.
ABHILASHA:	āp dillī kī hɛ̃, na?
MEENU:	jī, hā̃.

ABHILASHA:	(*bumps into Meenu*) माफ़ कीजिये।
MEENU:	माफ़ी की बात नहीं। बहुत भीड़ है।
ABHILASHA:	सच।
MEENU:	मेरा नाम मीनू भारती है।
ABHILASHA:	और मेरा नाम अभिलाषा पाँडे है।
MEENU:	मैं यहाँ रोज़ आती हूँ।
ABHILASHA:	आप दिल्ली की हैं न?
MEENU:	जी हाँ।

Lesson 3

Exercise 1

(a) mujʰ ko jaipur kī TikaT cāhiye/mujʰ ko jaipur ke liye TikaT cāhiye.
(b) kyā āp ko davāī cāhiye?
(c) mujʰ ko do gʰar cāhiye.
(d) mujʰ ko *garage* mẽ *car* cāhiye.
(e) āp ko ye sundar sāRī cāhiye.

(a) मुझ को जयपुर की टिकट चाहिये/मुझ को जयपुर के लिये टिकट चाहिये।
(b) क्या आप को दवाई चाहिये?
(c) मुझ को दो घर चाहिये।
(d) मुझ को गराज में कार चाहिये।
(e) आप को यह सुन्दर साड़ी चाहिये।

Exercise 2

(a) meri̅ ek bɛhɛn hɛ. (b) mere do bʰāi̅ hɛ̃. (c) mere pās ek *computer* hɛ. (d) merā hāl Tʰi̅k hɛ. (e) mujʰ ko sir-dard hɛ. (f) mujʰ ko kām cāhiye. (g) merā laRkā gʰar letā hɛ.

(a) मेरी एक बहन है। (b) मेरे दो भाई हैं। (c) मेरे पास एक कम्प्यूटर है। (d) मेरा हाल ठीक है। (e) मुझ को सिर-दर्द है। (f) मुझ को काम चाहिये। (g) मेरा लड़का घर लेता है।

Exercise 3

mujʰ ko	buxār hɛ.
mere pās	rupiye hɛ̃.
āp ke	gʰar mẽ kitne ādmi̅ hɛ̃?
merā shɛhɛr	bahut sundar hɛ.
ye *flight*	āp ke liye hɛ.
is kā dām	kyā hɛ?

मुझ को	बुख़ार है।
मेरे पास	रुपये हैं।
आप के	घर में कितने आदमी हैं?
मेरा शहर	बहुत सुन्दर है।
यह फ्लाईट	आप के लिये है।
इस का दाम	क्या है?

Exercise 4

WAITER:	namaste.
YOU:	namaste.
WAITER:	āp kɛse hɛ̃?
YOU:	(mɛ̃) Tʰi̅k hũ.
WAITER:	āp ko *menu* cāhiye?
YOU:	nahi̅̃, *lunch* ke liye *special* kyā hɛ?
WAITER:	*lunch-special* shākāhāri̅ (i.e. *vegetarian*) hɛ.
YOU:	shākāhāri̅-*special* Tʰi̅k hɛ. vo kyā hɛ? *or* vegetarian-special Tʰi̅k hɛ. ye kyā hɛ?
WAITER:	dāl, roTi̅, rāytā, sabzi̅ aur cāval.
YOU:	mujʰ ko dāl zarā masāledār cāhiye.
WAITER:	Tʰi̅k hɛ.

WAITER: नमस्ते।
YOU: नमस्ते।
WAITER: आप कैसे हैं?
YOU: (मैं) ठीक हूँ?
WAITER: आप को मैन्यू चाहिये।
YOU: नहीं, *लंच* के लिये स्पैशल क्या है?
WAITER: *लंच-स्पेशल* शाकाहारी (i.e. *vegetarian*) है।
YOU: शाकाहारी-*स्पेशल* ठीक है। वह क्या है? *or*
वैजीटेरियन-स्पेशल ठीक है। यह क्या है?
WAITER: दाल, रोटी, रायता, सब्ज़ी और चावल।
YOU: मुझ को दाल ज़रा मसालेदार चाहिये।
WAITER: ठीक है।

Lesson 4

Exercise 1

mujʰ ko paRʰnā pasand hɛ. mujʰ ko kyā pasand hɛ? mujʰ ko kyā-kyā pasand hɛ̃? mujʰ ko gāne kā shauk hɛ. mujʰ ko tɛrne kā shauk hɛ. mujʰ ko kʰāne kā shauk hɛ.

मुझ को पढ़ना पसन्द है। मुझ को क्या पसन्द है? मुझ को क्या-क्या पसन्द हैं। मुझ को गाने का शौक है। मुझ को तैरने का शौक है। मुझ को खाने का शौक है।

By substituting **āp ko** (आप को) for **mujʰ ko** (मुझ को), you can generate six more sentences.

Exercise 2

(a) gāne ke alāvā John ko nācnā pasand hɛ.
(b) Judy ko kahāniyā̃ aur kavitāẽ likʰne kā shauk hɛ. *or*
Judy ko kahāniyā̃ aur kavitāẽ likʰne ke shauk hɛ̃.
(c) Ramesh ko murgā (or *chicken*) kʰānā nāpasand hɛ.
Ramesh ko *non-vegeterian* (or mā̃sāhārī) kʰānā nāpasand hɛ.
Ramesh ko kavitāẽ nāpasand hɛ̃.
Ramesh ko deshī saŋgīt (or *country music*) nāpasand hɛ.
(d) Ramesh ko samosā kʰānā pasand hɛ.
Ramesh ko shākāhārī (or *vegeterian*) kʰānā pasand hɛ.
Ramesh ko kahāniyā̃ pasand hɛ̃.
Ramesh ko bʰārtīya (or *hindustānī/Indian*) saŋgīt pasand hɛ.

(a) जवाब: गाने के अलावा जॉन को नाचना पसन्द है।
(b) जवाब: जूडी को कहानियाँ और कविताएँ लिखने के शौक हैं।
(c) जवाब: रमेश को मुर्गा (or *चिकन*) खाना नापसन्द है।
रमेश को माँसाहारी खाना नापसन्द है।
रमेश को कविताएँ नापसन्द हैं।
रमेश को देशी-संगीत (or *कन्ट्री* संगीत) नापसन्द है।
(d) जवाब: रमेश को समोसा खाना पसन्द है।
रमेश को शाकाहारी (or *वैजीटेरियन*) खाना पसन्द है।
रमेश को कहानियाँ पसन्द हैं।
रमेश को भारतीय (or हिन्दुस्तानी) संगीत पसन्द है।

Exercise 3

(a) John likes to eat/eating.
John likes food.

(b) John likes to sing/singing.
John likes [the] song.

Exercise 4 (examples)

x karne se manā karnā (to prohibit from doing x); unk*ā* kɛhnā: kamrā sāf karo (their saying: clean your room.)

x करने से मना करना। उन का कहना (कि) कमरा साफ़ करो।

Exercise 5

muj^{h} ko tɛrne kā shauk hɛ. muj^{h} ko tɛrnā pasand hɛ. muj^{h} ko tɛrnā acc^{h}ā lagtā hɛ.

मुझ को तैरने का शौक है। मुझ को तैरना पसन्द है। मुझ को तैरना अच्छा लगता है।

Exercise 6

(a) cats बिल्लियाँ
(b) dogs कुत्ते
(c) spicy foods मसालेदार खाना

(d) cricket (game) क्रिकेट

(e) bʰaratnāTyam भरतनाट्यम्

(f) rock music रॉक संगीत

Lesson 5

Exercise 1

(If you are a female, the final vowel of verb forms given in the italics needs to be replaced by the vowel **ī**.)

merā nām x hɛ.
(number) din *rahū̃gā.*
dillī aur āgrā *jāū̃gā.*
ye dillī (x city) kā patā hɛ:
(*fill out the address*)
(number) dinõ ke bād.
(*or* x (number) tārīx ko).
jī nahī̃.

मेरा नाम x है।
(number) दिन *रहूँगा*।
दिल्ली और आगरा *जाऊँगा*।
यह दिल्ली (x शहर) का पता है।
(fill out the address.)
(number) दिनों के बाद।
(or x (number) तारीख़ को)।
जी नहीं।

Exercise 2

mɛ̃ āp ke liye kyā kar saktā hū̃? ham āgrā jānā cāhte hɛ̃. āgrā kitnī dūr hɛ? bahut dūr nahī̃, lekin āp kab jā rahe hɛ̃? ham kal jāẽge. gāRī subah dillī se caltī hɛ. āp gāRī se jānā cāhte hɛ̃?

मैं आप के लिये क्या कर सकता हूँ? हम आगरा जाना चाहते हैं? आगरा कितनी दूर है? बहुत दूर नहीं, लेकिन आप कब जा रहे हैं? हम कल जाएँगे। गाड़ी सुबह दिल्ली से चलती है। आप गाड़ी से जाना चाहते हैं?

Exercise 3

Priya Rakesh:

tumhārā xat milā. paR^h kar xushī huī. tum kab ā rahe ho? kal mɛ̃ *Chicago* jā rahā hū̃. *Chicago* bahut baRā shɛhɛr hɛ. mɛ̃ *Chicago* hawāī jahāz (*aeroplane*) *se* jāū̃gā. lekin mɛ̃ hawāī jahāz se nahī̃ jānā cāhtā hū. gāRī muj^{h}e hawāī jahāz se zyāda pasand hɛ . bākī sab T^{h}īk hɛ.

tumhāra dost,

Rājīv.

प्रिय राकेश,

तुम्हारा ख़त मिला। पढ़ कर खुशी हुई। तुम कब आ रहे हो? कल मैं शिकागो जा रहा हूँ। शिकागो बहुत बड़ा शहर है। मैं शिकागो हवाई जहाज़ से जाऊँगा। लेकिन मैं हवाई जहाज़ से नहीं जाना चाहता हूँ। गाड़ी मुझे हवाई जहाज़ से ज़्यादा पसन्द है। बाकी सब ठीक है।

तुम्हारा दोस्त,

राजीव।

Exercise 4

āp kahā̃ jā rahī hɛ̃? āp yahā̃ kitne din rahẽgī? āp kis kā kām kar rahī hɛ̃? kyā āp ko cāy bahut pasand hɛ? āp ke kitne b^{h}āī hɛ̃?

आप कहाँ जा रही हैं? आप यहाँ कितने दिन रहेंगी? आप किस का काम कर रही हैं? क्या आप को चाय बहुत पसन्द है? आप के कितने भाई हैं?

Exercise 5 (examples)

agar muj^h ko ek *million dollars* milẽge, to mɛ̃ duniyā kā safar karū̃gā/karū̃gī. rājā/rānī kī tarah rahū̃gā/rahū̃gī. apane liye ek nāv aur Rolls Royce xarīdū̃gā/xarīdū̃gī. apnī patnī/apne pati ke liye hīre xarīdū̃gā/xarīdū̃gī. lekin xushī se pāgal nahī̃ ho jāū̃gā/jāū̃gī, kuc^h der ke bād apnī naukrī karne zarūr jāū̃gā/jāū̃gī.

अगर मुझ को एक मिलियन डॉलर मिलेंगे, तो मैं दुनिया का सफ़र करूँगा/करूँगी। राजा/रानी की तरह रहूँगा/रहूँगी। अपने लिये एक नाव और रोल्स राय्स ख़रीदूँगा/ख़रीदूँगी। अपनी पत्नी/अपने पति के लिये हीरे ख़रीदूँगा/ख़रीदूँगी। लेकिन ख़ुशी से पागल नहीं हो जाऊँगा/जाऊँगी, कुछ देर के बाद अपनी नौकरी करने ज़रूर जाऊँगा/जाऊँगी।

Exercise 6

ham *Robot* hɛ̃. ham *California* se hɛ̃. ham hindī bol sakte hɛ̃. ham hindī samaj^h b^{h}ī sakte hɛ̃. ham hindī gāne gā sakte hɛ̃. hamārī *memory* bahut baRī hɛ. ham har savāl pūc^h sakte hɛ̃ aur har javāb de sakte hɛ̃. yānī har kām kar sakte hɛ̃. ham hameshā kām kar sakte hɛ̃. ham kab^{h}ī nahī̃ t^{h}akte hɛ̃. hamāre pās har savāl kā javāb hɛ. lekin masāledār k^{h}ānā nahī̃ k^{h}ā sakte (hɛ̃).

हम *रोबात* हैं। हम *कैलिफ़ोर्निया* से हैं। हम हिन्दी बोल सकते हैं। हम हिन्दी समझ भी सकते हैं। हम हिन्दी गाने गा सकते हैं। हमारी *मैमोरी* बहुत बड़ी है। हम हर सवाल पूछ सकते हैं और हर जवाब दे सकते हैं। यानी हर काम कर सकते हैं। हम हमेशा काम कर सकते हैं। हम कभी नहीं थकते हैं। हमारे पास हर सवाल का जवाब है। लेकिन मसालेदार खाना नहीं खा सकते (हैं)।

Exercise 7

(a) Shrī Smith *America* agale mahīne jāẽge.
(b) ve *British Airways* se *New York* jāẽge.
(c) jī nahī̃.
(d) kyõ ki ve apne baccõ ko *Disney World* dik^{h}ānā cāhte hɛ̃.
(e) ve *Disney World* sāt din (*or* ek haftā) rahẽge.

(a) श्री स्मिथ अमरीका अगले महीने जाएँगे (जायेंगे)।
(b) वे ब्रिटिश एयरवेज़ से न्यू यॉर्क जाएँगे (जायेंगे)।
(c) जी नहीं।
(d) क्योंकि वे अपने बच्चों को डिज़्नी वर्ड दिखाना चाहते हैं।
(e) वे डिज़्नी वर्ड सात दिन (*or* एक हफ़्ता) रहेंगे।

Lesson 6

Exercise 1

mere dost, ve din kitne acc^{h}e t^{h}e! mɛ̃ ne socā ve din hameshā rahẽge. ve bacpan ke din t^{h}e. mɛ̃ hameshā k^{h}eltā t^{h}ā aur nāctā t^{h}ā. har cīz sundar t^{h}ī. har din nayā t^{h}ā aur har rāt kā andāz t^{h}ā. ab ve din nahī̃ rahe.

मेरे दोस्त, वे दिन कितने अच्छे थे! मैं ने सोचा वे दिन हमेशा रहेंगे। वे दिन बचपन के दिन थे। मैं हमेशा खेलता था और नाचता था। हर चीज़ सुन्दर थी। हर दिन नया था और हर रात का अन्दाज़ था। अब वे दिन नहीं रहे।

Exercise 2

(a) mɛ̃ va^{h}ā̃ gayī. (b) us ne muj^h ko batāyā. (c) ham g^{h}ar āye. (d) tum g^{h}ar der se pahũce. (e) unhõne *police* ko *report* kī. (f) āp ko ye kitāb kab milī.

(a) मैं वहाँ गयी। (b) उस ने मुझ को बताया। (c) हम घर आये। (d) तुम घर देर से पहुँचे। (e) उन्होंने पुलिस को रिर्पोट की। (f) आप को यह किताब कब मिली।

Exercise 3

(a) āp ke mātā-pitā kā janma kahā̃ huā?
(b) āp ke mātā-pitā kā janma kab huā?
(c) kyā un kā parivār amīr t^{h}ā yā garīb t^{h}ā?
(d) un kī shādī kab huī?
(e) un kī umar kitnī t^{h}ī jab un kī shādī huī?
(f) un kī *arranged marriage* huī yā *love marriage*?
(g) kyā āp kī mā̃ āp ke pitā se c^{h}oTī hɛ̃?

(a) आप के माता-पिता का जन्म कहाँ हुआ?
(b) आप के माता-पिता का जन्म कब हुआ?
(c) क्या उन का परविार अमीर था या ग़रीब था?
(d) उन की शादी कब हुई?
(e) उन की उमर कितनी थी जब उन की शादी हुई?
(f) उन की *अरैंज्ड मैरिज* हुई या *लव मैरिज*?
(g) क्या आप की माँ आप के पिता से छोटी हैं?

Exercise 4

(a) kal kis kā janma din t^{h}ā?
(b) kis ke parivār ne ek *party* kī?
(c) vo *party* kab huī?
(d) John ko kis ke bāre mẽ mālūm nahī̃ t^{h}ā?
(e) ye kɛsī *party* t^{h}ī?
(f) John kā janma din kab t^{h}ā?

(a) कल किस का जन्म दिन था?
(b) किस के परिवार ने एक पार्टी की?
(c) वह पार्टी कब हुई?
(d) जान को किस के बारे में मालूम नहीं था?
(e) यह कैसी पार्टी थी?
(f) जॉन का जन्म दिन कब था?

Exercise 5

(a) sac; (b) j^{h}ūT^h; (c) j^{h}ūT^h; (d) j^{h}ūT^h; (e) sac; (f) sac; (g) sac.

(a) purāne zamāne mẽ ādmī g^{h}ar mẽ kām nahī̃ karte t^{h}e.
(b) āj-kal sārā parivār *TV* dek^{h}tā hɛ.
(c) āj-kal ādmī aur auratẽ k^{h}ānā banāte hɛ̃.

(a) सच; (b) झूठ; (c) झूठ; (d) झूठ; (e) सच; (f) सच; (g) सच.

(a) पुराने ज़माने में आदमी घर में काम नहीं करते थे।
(b) आज-कल सारा परिवार टीवी देखता है।
(c) आज-कल आदमी और औरतें खाना बनाते हैं।

Lesson 7

Exercise 1

(a) muj^h ko sitār ātī hɛ. (b) kyā āp tɛr sakte hɛ̃? (c) us ko kahā̃ jānā hɛ? (d) unhõne saŋgīt kab sīk^{h}ā? (e) vo *salesman* hɛ. us ko bāhar jānā paRtā hɛ. (f) John ko bahut kām hɛ. isliye us ko kuc^h fursat nahī̃ hɛ.

(a) मुझ को सितार आती है। (b) क्या आप तैर सकते हैं। (c) उस को कहाँ जाना है? (d) उन्होंने संगीत कब सीखा? (e) वह *सेल्ज़मैन* है। उस को बाहर जाना पड़ता है। (f) जॉन को बहुत काम है। इसलिये उस को कुछ फ़ुरसत नहीं है।

Exercise 2

(a) Bill ko jaldī hɛ kyõki uskī gāRī das minute mẽ jāne vālī hɛ.
(b) *Driver* jaldī karo, mere dost kī *flight* āne vālī hɛ.
(c) sardī kā mausam t^{h}ā, jaldī barf girne vālī t^{h}ī.
(d) *party* ke liye mɛhmān pahũcne vāle hɛ̃.
(e) s^{h}ām kā samay t^{h}ā, and^{h}erā hone vālā t^{h}ā.
(f) āp kab^{h}ī hindustān gaye hɛ̃.

(a) बिल को जल्दी है क्योंकि उसकी गाड़ी दस मिनट में जाने वाली है।
(b) ड्राइवर जल्दी करो, मेरे दोस्त की फ़्लाइट आने वाली है।
(c) सरदी का मौसम था, जल्दी बरफ़ गिरने वाली थी।
(d) पार्टी के लिये मेहमान पहुँचने वाले हैं।
(e) शाम का समय था, अन्धेरा होने वाला था।
(f) आप कभी हिन्दुस्तान गये हैं।

Exercise 3

(a)	ad^{h}yāpak	us ko paR^{h}ānā hɛ.
(b)	*Doctor*	us ko marīz ko dek^{h}nā hɛ.
(c)	gāyak	us ko gānā hɛ.
(d)	*Driver*	us ko *car* calānī hɛ.
(e)	d^{h}obī	us ko kapRe d^{h}one hɛ̃.
(f)	lek^{h}ak	us ko lik^{h}nā hɛ.

(a)	अध्यापक	उस को पढ़ाना है।
(b)	डॉक्टर	उस को मरीज़ को देखना है।
(c)	गायक	उस को गाना है।
(d)	ड्राइवर	उस को कार चलानी है।
(e)	धोबी	उस को कपड़े धोने हैं।
(f)	लेखक	उस को लिखना है।

Exercise 4

(a) kyā āp mere liye *recommendation letter* lik^{h} dẽge?
(b) rāt āyī aur and^{h}erā ho gayā t^{h}ā.
(c) mɛ̃ hindī nahī̃ paR^{h} saktā, āp ye xat paR^{h} dījiye.
(d) vo t^{h}oRā t^{h}oRā tɛr letā hɛ.
(e) us ko bahut acc^{h}ā nācnā ātā hɛ.
(f) mɛ̃ āp kī bāt bilkul b^{h}ūl gayā.

(a) क्या आप मेरे लिये *रिकोमैंडेशन लैटर* लिख देंगे?
(b) रात आयी और अन्धेरा हो गया था।
(c) मैं हिन्दी नहीं पढ़ सकता, आप यह ख़त पढ़ दीजिये।
(d) वह थोड़ा-थोड़ा तैर लेता है।
(e) उस को बहुत अच्छा नाचना आता है।
(f) मैं आप की बात बिल्कुल भूल गया।

Exercise 5 (examples)

bacpan mẽ muj^{h}e dūd^{h} pinā paRtā t^{h}ā. bacpan mẽ muj^{h}e *doctor* ke pās jānā paRtā t^{h}ā. bacpan mẽ muj^{h}e davāī pīnī paRtī t^{h}ī. bacpan mẽ muj^{h}e Tīkā lagvānā paRtā t^{h}ā. bacpan mẽ muj^{h}e mātā pitā ke sāt^{h} cīzẽ xarīdne jānā paRtā t^{h}ā.

बचपन में मुझे दूध पीना पड़ता था। बचपन में मुझे डॉक्टर के पास जाना पड़ता था। बचपन में मुझे दवाई पीनी पड़ती थी। बचपन में मुझे टीका लगवाना पड़ता था। बचपन में मुझे माता-पिता के साथ चीज़ें खरीदने जाना पड़ता था।

Exercise 6

(a) j^{h} ; (b) s; (c) j^{h} ; (d) j^{h} ; (e) s; (f) j^{h}; (g) s

(a) झूठ; (b) सच; (c) झूठ; (d) झूठ; (e) सच; (f) झूठ; (g) सच

Lesson 8

Exercise 1

āiye, tashrīf rak^{h}iye. taklīf kī bāt kyā hɛ? shāyad āp ko daftar mẽ kām zyādā ho. vo āp kā intazār kar rahī t^{h}ī. ādāb arz hɛ.

आइये, तशरीफ़ रखिये। तकलीफ़ की बात क्या है? शायद आप को दफ़्तर में काम ज़्यादा हो। वह आप का इन्तज़ार कर रही थी। आदाब अर्ज़ है।

Exercise 2

(a) māf kī̃jiye, mɛ̃ *cheque* bʰejnā bʰūl gayā.
(b) mɛ̃ ne kʰānā kʰā liyā.
(c) āp kā buxār baRʰ gayā.
(d) āp ne kucʰ javāb nahī̃ diyā.
(e) āp merī salāh mān lījiye.

(a) माफ़ कीजिये, मैं चैक भेजना भूल गया।
(b) मैं ने खाना खा लिया।
(c) आप का बुखार बढ़ गया।
(d) आप ने कुछ जवाब नहीं दिया।
(e) आप मेरी सलाह मान लीजिये।

Exercise 3

(a)	adʰyāpak	cʰātrõ ko paRʰātā hɛ.
(b)	DākTar (*doctor*)	Tīkā lagātā hɛ.
(c)	*cashier*	*cheque cash* kartā hɛ.
(d)	darzī	kapRe banātā hɛ.
(e)	kʰānsāmā	kʰānā banātā hɛ.
(f)	*driver*	*car* calātā hɛ.
(g)	*civil engineer*	imāratẽ banvātā hɛ.

(a)	अध्यापक	छात्रों को पढ़ाता है।
(b)	डॉक्टर	टीका लगाता है।
(c)	*कैशियर*	*चैक कैश* करता है।
(d)	दर्ज़ी	कपड़े बनाता है।
(e)	खानसामा	खाना बनाता है।
(f)	*ड्राइवर*	*कार* चलाता है।
(g)	*सिविल इंजिनियर*	इमारतें बनवाता है।

Exercise 4

(a) shyām ne hilDā se apnī kār calvāyī.
(b) shyām hilDā se apnā xat lik^{h}vāyegā.
(c) shyām hilDā se apnā g^{h}ar banvā rahā hɛ.
(d) shyām hilDā se apnī kahānī sunvā rahā t^{h}ā.
(e) shyām hilDā se apnī laRkī ko paR^{h}vātā hɛ.

(a) श्याम ने हिल्डा से अपनी कार चलवायी।
(b) श्याम हिल्डा से अपना ख़त लिखवायेगा।
(c) श्याम हिल्डा से अपना घर बनवा रहा है।
(d) श्याम हिल्डा से अपनी कहानी सुनवा रहा है।
(e) श्याम हिल्डा से अपनी लड़की को पढ़वाता है।

Exercise 5

(a)	hãsnā:	muj^{h}e vo hãstī laRkī bahut pasand hɛ.
(b)	k^{h}elnā:	k^{h}elte bacce bahut sundar lag rahe t^{h}e.
(c)	gānā:	gātī ciRiyā uR rahī t^{h}ī.
(d)	sitār bajānā:	sitār bajātā ādmī bahut acc^{h}ā hɛ.
(e)	tɛrnā:	tɛrtī mac^{h}aliyõ ko dek^{h}o.
(f)	ronā:	*Doctor* ne rote bacce ko Tīkā lagāyā.
(a)	हँसना:	मुझे वह हँसती लड़की बहुत पसन्द है।
(b)	खेलना:	खेलते बच्चे बहुत सुन्दर लग रहे थे।
(c)	गाना:	गाती चिड़िया उड़ रही थी।
(d)	सितार बजाना:	सितार बजाता आदमी बहुत अच्छा है।
(e)	तैरना:	तैरती मछलियों को देखो।
(f)	रोना:	डॉक्टर ने रोते बच्चे को टीका लगाया।

Exercise 6

mɛ̃ *railway station* apne dost kā intzār kar rahā t^{h}ā. t^{h}oRī der bād gāRī āyī aur merā dost gaRī se utrā. ham bahut xush ho kar mile. is bār pā̃c sāl ke bād hamārī mulākāt huī. t^{h}oRī der bād mɛ̃ ne kahā, 'is bār bahut der ke bād yahā̃ āye ho.' usne javāb diyā, 'acc^{h}ī bāt t^{h}ī ki agar gāRī der se na ātī, to mɛ̃ āj b^{h}ī na ātā'.

मैं रेलवे स्टेशन अपने दोस्त का इन्तज़ार कर रहा था। थोड़ी देर बाद गाड़ी आयी

और मेरा दोस्त गाड़ी से उतरा। हम बहुत खुश हो कर मिले। इस बार पाँच साल के बाद हमारी मुलाकात हुई। थोड़ी देर के बाद मैं ने कहा, 'इस बार बहुत देर के बाद यहाँ आये हो।' उस ने जवाब दिया, 'अच्छी बात थी कि अगर गाड़ी देर से न आती, तो मैं आज भी न आता।'

Lesson 9

Exercise 1

(a) log *laundrymat* kapRe d^{h}one jāte hɛ̃. (b) log *restaurant* k^{h}ānā k^{h}āne jāte hɛ̃. (c) log cinema, *film* dek^{h}ne jāte hɛ̃. (d) log *college* paR^{h}ne jāte hɛ̃. (e) log *swimming pool* tɛrne jāte hɛ̃. (f) log *bar beer* pīne jāte hɛ̃. (g) log *pharmacy* davāī lene jāte hɛ̃.

(a) लोग *लाँड्रीमैट* कपड़े धोने जाते हैं। (b) लोग *रैस्टोरैंट* खाना खाने जाते हैं। (c) लोग *सिनेमा* फिल्म देखने जाते हैं। (d) लोग *कॉलिज* पढ़ने जाते हैं। (e) लोग *स्विमिंग पूल* तैरने जाते हैं। (f) लोग *बार बियर* पीने जाते हैं। (g) लोग *फार्मेसी* दवाई लेने जाते हैं।

Exercise 2

(a) vo bɛT^{h}e hue bolā. (b) John so(y)e hue hā̃s rahā t^{h}ā. (c) ye shɛhɛr soyā sā lagtā hɛ. (d) laRkī royī huī g^{h}ar āyī. (e) aurat ne *swimming pool* par leTe hue kahā.

(a) वह बैठे हुए बोला। (b) जॉन सोये हुए हँस रहा था। (c) यह शहर सोया सा लगता है। (d) लड़की रोयी हुई घर आयी। (e) औरत ने *स्विमिंग पूल* पर लेटे हुए कहा।

Exercise 3

sunī	bāt
lik^{h}ā	xat
hā̃stā	laRkā
caltī	gāRī
b^{h}ūle	log
b^{h}āgtī	billī

सुनी बात
लिखा ख़त
हँसता लड़का
चलती गाड़ी
भूले लोग
भागती बिल्ली

Exercise 4

(a) John se ek kahānī paR^{h}ī gayī.
(b) ham logõ se k^{h}ānā k^{h}āyā jā rahā hɛ.
(c) tum se kyā kiyā jāyegā?
(d) muj^{h} se *chicken curry* banāyī gayī.
(e) Bill se hindustān mẽ paR^{h}ā jāyegā.
(f) kyā āp se gānā gāyā jāyegā?

(a) जॉन से एक कहानी पढ़ी गयी।
(b) हम लोगों से खाना खाया जा रहा है।
(c) तुम से क्या किया जायेगा।
(d) मुझ से *चिकन करी* बनायी गयी।
(e) बिल से हिन्दुस्तान में पढ़ा जायेगा।
(f) क्या आप से गाना गाया जायेगा।

Exercise 5

(a) <u>ham ko</u> vahā̃ jāne kā maukā <u>milā</u>.
(b) John ko hindustān jāne kā maukā aksar miltā hɛ.
(c) ye sunhɛra maukā <u>t^{h}ā</u>.
(d) <u>āp</u> <u>ko</u> kitāb lik^{h}ne kā maukā kab <u>milegā</u>?
(e) is kāgaz mẽ kyā <u>lik^{h}ā</u> hɛ?
(f) billī ko maukā <u>milā</u> aur vo dūd^{h} pī gayī.
(g) ye bahut <u>acc^{h}e</u> <u>mauke</u> kī bāt hɛ.

(a) हम को वहाँ जाने का मौका मिला।
(b) जॉन को हिन्दुस्तान जाने का मौका अक्सर मिलता है।
(c) यह सुनहरा मौका है।
(d) आप को किताब लिखने का मौका कब मिलेगा?
(e) इस कागज़ में क्या लिखा है?

(f) बिल्ली को मौका मिला और वह दूध पी गयी।
(g) यह बहुत अच्छे मौके की बात है।

Lesson 10

Exercise 1

dīvālī	diye jalāye jāte hɛ̃.
	paTāxe calāye jāte hɛ̃.
	rājā rām ke apne rājya lauTne kī xushī mẽ manāyā jātā hɛ.
holī	shatruõ ko b^{h}ī mitra banāyā jātā hɛ.
	gulāl lagāyā jātā hɛ.
	raŋg se k^{h}elā jātā hɛ.
rakshāband^{h}an	d^{h}āgā bā̃d^{h}ā jātā hɛ.

दीवाली	दिये जलाये जाते हैं।
	पटाख़े चलाये जाते हैं।
	राजा राम के अपने राज्य लौटने की ख़ुशी में मनाया जाता है।
होली	शत्रुओं को भी मित्र बनाया जाता है।
	गुलाल लगाया जाता है।
	रंग से खेला जाता है।
रक्षाबन्धन	धागा बाँधा जाता है।

Exercise 2

Enemies are made friends. Lamps are lit. The thread is tied. Fire-crackers are lit. [It] is celebrated in happiness at the return of King Rama to his kingdom. Gulal is used. Colour is played with (lit. [it] is played with colour).

Exercise 3

(a) dīvālī दीवाली; (b) rakshāband^{h}an रक्षाबन्धन; (c) rakshāband^{h}an रक्षाबन्धन; (d) holī होली; (e) dīvālī दीवाली।

Script unit 1

Exercise 1

(a) aman (b) asal (c) jalan (d) kalam (e) kamal (f) garam
(g) jab (h) kab (i) tab (j) sab

Exercise 2

(a) कट (b) गल (c) चल (d) नमक (e) सबक (f) परख (g) सदर
(h) चलन (i) मन (j) पल (k) गरम

Script unit 2

Exercise1

(a) b^{h}ārī (b) baRā (c) kitanā (d) kālā (e) b^{h}ārat (f) gāRī
(g) kinārā (h) gīt (i) gāyab (j) cāval (k) cāhnā (l) ciRiyāg^{h}ar
(m) zarā (n) jīvan (o) jāpān (p) cor (q) mor (r) p^{h}al (s) b^{h}ūt
(t) caut^{h}ā (u) Daul (v) pulis (w) hāt^{h}ī (x) sitār (y) shām

(Note: व is transcribed as v above.)

Exercise 2

जब कि	की	बाज़ार	राजा	रानी
पहचान	नयी	बनारस	कानपुर	माता
पिता	कभी	मिलन	ज़मीन	कार
महीना	साल	दिन	चार	सात
सवेरा	चाय	पानी	पति	भालू

Exercise 3

रुपया	डर
रूखा	नाम
कर	थान
कि	घर
और	डाल

Exercise 1

(a) थाना वहीं है। (b) आप मेरी मदद कर सकते हैं? (c) मैं वहाँ कैसे जाऊँ? (d) यह मेरी गलती नहीं। (e) यहाँ खतरा है। (f) बचाओ! (g) यह बहुत ज़रूरी है। (h) डाक-खाना कहाँ है? (i) किस खिड़की पर जाऊँ? (j) टिकट कितना लगेगा? (k) तार अमरीका भेजना चाहता हूँ।

Script unit 4

Exercise 1

(a) पूछ-ताछ का दफ़्तर (b) मैं रास्ता भूल गयी हूँ। (c) मैं रास्ता भूल गया हूँ। (d) तंग (*or* तङ्ग) मत करो (e) मैं कुंजी (*or* कुञ्जी) ढूंढ़ रहा हूँ। (f) नहीं मिल रही। (g) चिट्ठी हवाई डाक से भेजिये। (h) क्या आप ये सामान सीधे बम्बई (बंबई) भेज सकते हैं? (i) समान के लिये रसीद दीजिये। (j) मेरा सामान नहीं आया।

Exercise 2

(a) ham ek haftā dillī mẽ rahẽgẽ. (b) mɛ̃ yahā̃ c^{h}uTTī par hū̃. (c) ham yahā̃ kām se āye hɛ̃. (d) ye merā pāsporT hɛ. (e) kyā is sāmān par DyūTī lagegī? (f) ye cīzẽ mere apne istemāl ke liye hɛ̃. (g) mere pās DyūTī vālā sāmān nahī̃ hɛ. (h) mere pās kuc^{h} gifTs hɛ̃. (i) is mẽ sirf kapRe aur kitābẽ hɛ̃. (j) is ke alāvā koī aur cīz nahī̃ hɛ.

Script unit 5

Exercise 1

(a) ā i # ye (b) aur # tẽ (c) paR^{h} # tā (d) su # no (e) na # mas # te (f) mi # lẽ # ge (g) sun # kar (h) ād # mī

मूल शब्दावली
English–Hindi glossary

Some basic vocabulary useful for everyday communication is given below. This vocabulary is presented in the following groups:

- body, health and ailments
- colours
- family and relatives
- food and drink
- numbers
- time
- important verbs

The gender of the nouns is specified as masculine (m.) and feminine (f.) Adjectives are given in their base masculine singular form. Since the plural forms of the nouns are predictable from the gender, only the singular forms are listed. Verbs are specified for the agentive (**+/-ne**; in perfective tenses) and experiencer subjects (**+ko**) if they fail to select the regular nominative subjects. Also, if the object of a verb takes a specific postposition instead of the regular **ko** postposition, it is specified in the following way:

wait **X kā intzār karnā**

This shows that the verb **intzār karnā** 'to wait', takes the **kā**, 'of', postposition instead of **ko** or the equivalent of the English 'for'. Verbs are listed in the infinitive form.

Body, health and ailments

Parts of the body and appearance

ankle	**eRī** (f.)	एड़ी

back	**pīTʰ** (f.)	पीठ
bald	**ganjā** (m.)	गंजा
beard	**dāRʰī** (f.)	दाढ़ी
blood	**lahū** (m.), **xūn** (m.)	लहू, खून
body	**sharīr** (m.), **jisma** (m.)	शरीर, जिस्म
chest	**cʰātī** (f.)	छाती
ear	**kān** (m.)	कान
elbow	**kohnī** (f.)	कोहनी
eye	**ā̃kʰ** (f.)	आँख
face	**cehrā** (m.), **mũh** (m.)	चेहरा, मुँह
finger	**uŋglī** (f.)	उंगली
foot	**pɛr** (m.)	पैर
forehead	**mātʰā** (m.)	माथा
hair	**bāl** (m.)	बाल
hand	**hātʰ** (m.)	हाथ
head	**sir** (m.)	सिर
heart	**dil** (m.)	दिल
kidney	**gurdā** (m.)	गुर्दा
knee	**gʰuTnā** (m.)	घुटना
leg	**lāt** (f.)	लात
lip	**hõTʰ** (m.)	होंठ
moustache	**mū̃cʰ** (f.)	मूँछ
mouth	**mũh** (m)	मुँह
neck	**gardan** (f.)	गर्दन
nose	**nāk** (f.)	नाक
shoulder	**kandʰā** (m.)	कंधा
stomach	**peT** (m.)	पेट
throat	**galā** (m.)	गला
thumb	**aŋgūTʰā** (m.)	अंगूठा
toe	**pɛr kī uŋglī** (f.)	पैर की उंगली
tongue	**jībʰ** (f.), **zabān** (f.)	जीभ, ज़बान

Health and ailments

ache, pain	**dard** (m.)	दर्द
ailment	**bīmārī** (f.)	बीमारी
appetite, hunger	**bʰūkʰ** (f.)	भूख
blind	**andʰā** (m.)	अन्धा

blister	**c^{h}ālā** (m.)	छाला
boil	**p^{h}oRā** (m.)	फोड़ा
breath	**sā̃s** (f.)	साँस
burning sensation	**jalan** (f.)	जलन
cholera	**hɛzā** (m.)	हैज़ा
common cold	**zukām** (m.)	ज़ुकाम
cough	**k^{h}ā̃sī** (f.)	खाँसी
deaf	**bɛhrā** (m.)	बहरा
defecation	**TaTTī ānā** (+ko)	टट्टी आना
dumb	**gū̃gā** (m.)	गूँगा
dysentry	**pecish** (f.)	पेचिश
elderly	**būR^{h}ā** (m.)	बूढ़ा
feeling breathless	**sā̃s caR^{h}nā** (+kā)	साँस चढ़ना
feeling giddy	**sir cakrānā** (+kā)	सिर चकराना
health	**svāst^{h}ya** (m.), **sehat** (f.)	स्वास्थ्य, सेहत
healthy	**svast^{h}a, tandrust**	स्वस्थ, तन्दरुस्त
ill	**bīmār** (m.)	बीमार
illness	**bīmārī** (f.)	बीमारी
indigestion	**bad-hazmī** (f.)	बद-हज़मी
injury	**coT** (f.)	चोट
itch	**k^{h}ujlī** (f.)	खुजली
lame	**laŋgRā** (m.)	लंगड़ा
malaria	**maleriyā** (m.)	मलेरिया
rash	**dād** (m.)	दाद
sneeze	**chī̃k** (f.)	छींक
sprain	**moc** (f.)	मोच
swelling	**sūjan** (f.)	सूजन
temperature	**buxār** (m.)	बुखार
thirst	**pyās** (f.)	प्यास
tuberculosis	**tapedik** (m.), **kshaya** (m.)	तपेदिक, क्षय
typhoid	**miyādī buxār** (m.)	मियादी बुख़ार
ulcer	**nāsūr** (m.)	नासूर
unconscious	**behosh**	बेहोश

Colours

black	**kālā**	काला
blue	**nīlā**	नीला

brown	**b^{h}ūrā**	भूरा
colour	**raŋg** (m.)	रंग
green	**harā**	हरा
orange	**santrī**	सन्तरी
pink	**gulābī**	गुलाबी
purple (dark)	**bẽgnī**	बैंगनी
purple (light)	**jāmnī**	जामनी
red	**lāl**	लाल
saffron	**kesarī**	केसरी
sky blue	**āsmānī**	आसमानी
white	**safed**	सफ़ेद
white (skin)	**gorā**	गोरा
yellow	**pīlā**	पीला

Family and relatives

aunt		
father's sister	**buā**	बुआ
father's older brother's wife	**tāī**	ताई
father's younger brother's wife	**cācī**	चाची
mother's brother's wife	**māmī**	मामी
mother's sister	**mausī**	मौसी
	xālā (Muslim)	ख़ाला
brother	**b^{h}āī**	भाई
brother-in law		
husband's older brother	**jeT^h**	जेठ
husband's sister's husband	**nandoī**	नन्दोई
husband's younger brother	**devar**	देवर
wife's brother	**sālā**	साला
wife's sister's husband	**sā̃D^{h}ū**	साँढू
child	**baccā** (m.) **baccī** (f.)	बच्चा, बच्ची
daughter	**beTī**	बेटी
daughter-in-law	**bahū**	बहू
father	**pitā** (Hindu, Sikh)	पिता
	abbā (Muslim)	अब्बा
father-in-law	**sasur**	ससुर
granddaughter		
daughter's daughter	**dohtī**	दोहती
son's daughter	**potī**	पोती

grandfather		
father's father	**dādā**	दादा
mother's father	**nānā**	नाना
grandmother		
father's mother	**dādī**	दादी
mother's mother	**nānī**	नानी
grandson		
daughter's son	**dohtā**	दोहता
son's son	**potā**	पोता
husband	**pati** (Hindu, Sikh)	पति
	xāvind (Muslim)	ख़ाविन्द
mother	**mātā, mā̃** (Hindu, Sikh)	माता, माँ
	ammī (Muslim)	अम्मी
mother-in-law	**sās**	सास
nephew		
brother's son	**b^hatījā**	भतीजा
sister's son	**b^hā̃jā**	भाँजा
niece		
brother's daughter	**b^hatījī**	भतीजी
sister's daughter	**b^hā̃jī**	भाँजी
relative	**rishtedār**	रिश्तेदार
sister	**bɛhɛn**	बहन
sister-in-law		
brother's wife	**b^hāb^hī**	भाभी
husband's sister	**nanad**	ननद
wife's sister	**sālī**	साली
son	**beTā**	बेटा
son-in-law	**javāī**	जवाई
uncle		
father's older brother	**tāū**	ताऊ
father's sister's husband	**p^hūp^hā**	फूफा
father's younger brother	**cācā**	चाचा
mother's brother	**māmā**	मामा
mother's sister's husband	**mausā** (Hindu, Sikh)	मौसा
	xālū (Muslim)	ख़ालू
wife	**patnī** (Hindu, Sikh)	पत्नी
	bībī (Muslim)	बीबी
	g^harvālī	घरवाली

Food and drink

Foodgrains and flours

black beans	**lob^{h}iyā** (m.)	लोभिया
chick-pea flour	**besan** (m.)	बेसन
chick peas	**c^{h}ole** (m. pl.)	छोले
corn	**makaī** (f.)	मकई
flour	**āTā** (m.)	आटा
flour (refined, all purpose)	**mɛdā** (m.)	मैदा
lentils	**dāl** (f.)	दाल
kidney beans	**rājmā̃h** (f.)	राजमाँह
moog beans/lentils	**mū̃g dāl** (f.)	मूँग दाल
rice	**cāval** (m.)	चावल
wheat	**gehū̃** (m.)	गेहूँ

Fruits and nuts

almond	**bādām** (m.)	बादाम
apple	**seb** (m.)	सेब
apricot	**xumānī** (f.)	ख़ुमानी
banana	**kelā** (m.)	केला
cashew nuts	**kājū** (m.)	काजू
fruit	**p^{h}al** (m.)	फल
grapes	**aŋgūr** (m.)	अंगूर
guava	**amrūd** (m.)	अमरूद
lemon	**nīmbū** (m.)	नीम्बू
mango	**ām** (m.)	आम
melon	**k^{h}arbūjā** (m.)	खरबूजा
orange	**santrā** (m.)	सन्तरा
peach	**āRū** (m.)	आड़ू
peanuts	**mū̃gp^{h}alī** (f.)	मूँगफली
pear	**nāshpātī** (f.)	नाशपाती
pistachio	**pistā** (m.)	पिस्ता
plum	**ālūbuxārā** (m.)	आलूबुख़ारा
tangerine	**nāraŋgī** (f.)	नारंगी
walnut	**ak^{h}roT** (m.)	अखरोट
watermelon	**tarbūj** (m.)	तरबूज

Vegetables

beetroot	**cukandar** (m.)	चुकन्दर
bittergourd	**kerelā** (m.)	करेला
cabbage	**bandgob^{h}ī** (f.)	बन्दगोभी
courgette	**torī** (f.)	तोरी
cucumber	**k^{h}īrā** (m.)	खीरा
fenugreek	**met^{h}ī** (f.)	मेथी
garlic	**lɛhsun** (m.)	लहसुन
ginger (fresh)	**adrak** (f.)	अदरक
mustard	**sarsõ** (m.)	सरसों
okra	**b^{h}iNDī** (f.)	भिंडी
onion	**pyāz** (m.)	प्याज़
peas	**maTar** (m.)	मटर
potatoes	**ālū** (m.)	आलू
pumpkin	**kaddū** (m.)	कद्दू
radish	**mūlī** (f.)	मूली
spinach	**pālak** (f.)	पालक
tomato	**TamāTar** (m.)	टमाटर
vegetable	**sabzī** (f.)	सब्ज़ी

Herbs and spices

aniseed	**sãũf** (m.)	सौंफ
asafoetida	**hī̃g** (f.)	हींग
bay leaves	**tez pattā** (m.)	तेज़ पत्ता
black cardamom	**baRī ilāyacī** (f.)	बड़ी इलायची
black pepper	**kālī mirca** (f.)	काली मिर्च
cardamom	**ilāyacī** (f.)	इलायची
chilli	**mirca** (f.)	मिर्च
cinnamon	**dālcīnī** (f.)	दालचीनी
cloves	**lãũg** (m.)	लौंग
coriander	**d^{h}niyā** (m.)	धनिया
cumin	**jīrā** (m.)	जीरा
ginger (dry)	**sãũT^{h}** (f.)	सौंठ
mango powder	**amcūr** (m.)	अमचूर
mint	**paudīnā** (m.)	पौदीना

mixed spices	**garam masālā** (m.)	गरम मसाला
mustard seeds	**rāī** (f.)	राई
nutmeg	**jāyp^hal** (m.)	जायफल
pepper (black)	**kālī mirca** (f.)	काली मिर्च
saffron	**kesar** (m.)	केसर
salt	**namak** (m.)	नमक
tamarind	**imlī** (f.)	इमली
turmeric	**haldī** (f.)	हल्दी

Food items (dishes) etc.

alcoholic drinks	**sharāb** (f.)	शराब
betel leaf	**pān** (m.)	पान
betel nut	**supārī** (f.)	सुपारी
bread (Indian)	**roTī** (f.), **capatī** (f.)	रोटी, चपाती,
	p^hulkā (m.), **nān** (m.)	फुल्का, नान,
	pūrī (f.), **parāT^hā** (m.)	पूरी, पराठा,
	kulcā (m.), **b^haTūrā** (m.)	कुल्चा, भटूरा
bread (Western)	**Dabal roTī** (f.)	डबल रोटी
butter	**makk^han** (m.)	मक्खन
buttermilk	**lassī** (f.)	लस्सी
cheese	**panīr** (m.)	पनीर
coffee	**kāfī** (f.)	काफ़ी
curry (Indian)	**kaR^hī** (f.)	कढ़ी
egg	**aNDā** (m.)	अंडा
food	**k^hānā** (m.)	खाना
non-vegetarian	**mā̃sāhārī**	माँसाहारी
vegetarian	**shākāhārī**	शाकाहारी
juice	**ras** (m.)	रस
lentils	**dāl** (f.)	दाल
meat	**mā̃s** (m.), **goshta** (m.)	माँस, गोश्त
milk	**dūd^h** (m.)	दूध
oil	**tel** (m.)	तेल
purified butter	**g^hī** (f.)	घी
sugar (brown)	**shakkar** (f.)	शक्कर
sugar (white)	**cīnī** (f.)	चीनी
sweets	**miT^hāī** (f.)	मिठाई

tea	**cāy** (f.)	चाय
tobacco	**tambākū** (m.)	तम्बाकू
vinegar	**sirkā** (m.)	सिरका
water	**pānī** (m.), **jal** (m.)	पानी, जल
yoghurt	**dahī** (m./f.)	दही

Cooking processes

baking (oven cooking)	**tandūrī**	तन्दूरी
boiling	**ubālnā** (+ne)	उबालना
cooking	**pakānā** (+ne)	पकाना
cutting	**kāTnā** (+ne)	काटना
frying	**talnā** (+ne)	तलना
grilling	**sẽknā** (+ne)	सेंकना
grinding	**pīsnā** (+ne)	पीसना
kneading	**gū̃dnā** (+ne)	गूँदना
mixing	**milānā** (+ne)	मिलाना
peeling	**c^{h}īlnā** (+ne)	छीलना
roasting	**b^{h}ūnnā** (+ne)	भूनना
rolling	**belnā** (+ne)	बेलना
seasoning	**taRkā lagānā** (+ne)	तड़का लगाना
sieving	**c^{h}ānna** (+ne)	छानना
slicing	**cīrnā** (+ne)	चीरना

Tastes

bitter	**kaRvā**	कड़वा
delicious/tasty	**mazedār**	मज़ेदार
savoury/salty	**namkīn**	नमकीन
sour	**k^{h}aTTā**	खट्टा
spicy	**masāledār, mircavālā,**	मसालेदार, मिर्चवाला
	caTpaTā	चटपटा
sweet	**mīT^{h}ā**	मीठा
taste	**svād**	स्वाद
tasteless	**p^{h}īkā, besvād**	फीका, बेस्वाद

Numbers

Cardinal

1	**ek**	एक
2	**do**	दो
3	**tīn**	तीन
4	**cār**	चार
5	**pā̃c**	पाँच
6	**che**	छह
7	**sāt**	सात
8	**āT^{h}**	आठ
9	**nau**	नौ
10	**das**	दस
11	**gyārah**	ग्यारह
12	**bārah**	बारह
13	**terah**	तेरह
14	**caudah**	चौदह
15	**pandrah**	पन्द्रह
16	**solah**	सोलह
17	**sattrah**	सत्तरह
18	**aThārah**	अठारह
19	**unnīs**	उन्नीस
20	**bīs**	बीस
21	**ikkīs**	इक्कीस
22	**bāīs**	बाईस
23	**teīs**	तेईस
24	**caubīs**	चौबीस
25	**paccīs**	पच्चीस
26	**c^{h}abbīs**	छब्बीस
27	**sattāīs**	सत्ताईस
28	**aT^{h}āīs**	अठाईस
29	**untīs**	उनतीस
30	**tīs**	तीस
31	**ikattīs**	इकत्तीस
32	**battīs**	बत्तीस
33	**tẽtīs**	तैंतीस
34	**cãũtīs**	चौंतीस
35	**pẽtīs**	पैंतीस
36	**c^{h}attīs**	छत्तीस
37	**sẽtīs**	सैंतीस
38	**aRatīs**	अड़तीस
39	**untālīs**	उनतालीस
40	**cālīs**	चालीस
41	**iktālīs**	इकतालीस
42	**byālīs**	ब्यालीस
43	**tẽtālīs**	तैंतालीस
44	**cauvālīs**	चौवालीस
45	**pẽtālīs**	पैंतालीस
46	**c^{h}iyālīs**	छियालीस
47	**sẽtālīs**	सैंतालीस
48	**aRtālīs**	अड़तालीस
49	**uncās**	उनचास
50	**pacās**	पचास
51	**ikyāvan**	इक्यावन
52	**bāvan**	बावन
53	**tirpan**	तिरपन
54	**cauvan**	चौवन
55	**pacpan**	पचपन
56	**c^{h}appan**	छप्पन
57	**sattāvan**	सत्तावन
58	**aTT^{h}āvan**	अट्ठावन
59	**unsaT^{h}**	उनसठ
60	**sāT^{h}**	साठ
61	**iksaT^{h}**	इकसठ
62	**bāsaT^{h}**	बासठ
63	**tiresaT^{h}**	तिरेसठ
64	**cãũsaT^{h}**	चौंसठ
65	**pẽsaT^{h}**	पैंसठ
66	**c^{h}iyāsaT^{h}**	छियासठ
67	**sarsaT^{h}**	सरसठ
68	**aRsaT^{h}**	अड़सठ

69	**unhattar**	उनहत्तर
70	**sattar**	सत्तर
71	**ikhattar**	इकहत्तर
72	**bahattar**	बहत्तर
73	**tihattar**	तिहत्तर
74	**cauhattar**	चौहत्तर
75	**pachattar**	पचहत्तर
76	**c^{h}ihattar**	छिहत्तर
77	**satahattar**	सतहत्तर
78	**aT^{h}hattar**	अठहत्तर
79	**unāsī**	उनासी
80	**assī**	अस्सी
81	**ikāsī**	इकासी
82	**bayāsī**	बयासी
83	**tirāsī**	तिरासी
84	**caurāsī**	चौरासी
85	**paccāsī**	पच्चासी
86	**c^{h}iyāsī**	छियासी
87	**sattāsī**	सत्तासी
88	**aTT^{h}āsī**	अट्ठासी
89	**navāsī**	नवासी
90	**nabbe**	नब्बे
91	**ikyānbe**	इक्यानबे
92	**bānbe**	बानबे
93	**tirānbe**	तिरानबे
94	**caurānbe**	चौरानबे
95	**pañcānbe**	पँचानबे
96	**c^{h}iyānbe**	छियानबे
97	**satānbe**	सतानबे
98	**aTT^{h}ānbe**	अट्ठानबे
99	**ninyānbe**	निन्यानबे
100	**sau**	सौ

0	**shūnya, sifar**	शून्य, सिफ़र
150	**ek sau pacās**	एक सौ पचास
1,000	**hazār**	हज़ार
10,000	**das hazār**	दस हज़ार
100,000 (a hundred thousand)	**ek lāk^{h}**	एक लाख
1,000,000 (a million)	**das lāk^{h}**	दस लाख
10,000,000 (ten million)	**ek karoR**	एक करोड़
100,000,000 (a billion)	**das karoR**	दस करोड़
1,000,000,000 (ten billion)	**arab**	अरब
10,000,000,000 (a hundred billion)	**das arab**	दस अरब
100,000,000,000 (a thousand billion)	**k^{h}arab**	खरब

Ordinal

first	**pɛhlā**	पहला
second	**dūsrā**	दूसरा
third	**tīsrā**	तीसरा
fourth	**caut^{h}ā**	चौथा
fifth	**pā̃cvā̃**	पाँचवाँ

(Afterwards just add the suffix **-vā̃** to the cardinal numbers.)

Fractions

$\frac{1}{4}$	(a quarter)	**(ek) cautʰāī**	(एक) चौथाई
$\frac{1}{2}$	(a half)	**ādʰā**	आधा
$\frac{3}{4}$	(three-quarters)	**paunā**	पौना
$1\frac{1}{4}$	(one-and-a-quarter)	**savā (ek)**	सवा (एक)
$1\frac{1}{2}$	(one-and-a-half)	**DeRʰ**	डेढ़
$1\frac{3}{4}$	(one-and-three-quarters)	**paune do** (i.e. the next number)	पौने दो
$2\frac{1}{4}$		**savā do**	सवा दो
$2\frac{1}{2}$		**Dʰāī** (the numeral two is incorporated in the word)	ढाई
$2\frac{3}{4}$		**paune tīn** (i.e. the next number)	पौने तीन
$3\frac{1}{4}$		**savā tīn**	सवा तीन
$3\frac{1}{2}$		**sāRʰe tīn**	साढ़े तीन
$3\frac{3}{4}$		**paune cār**	पौने चार

Then follow the pattern given below to derive the other fractional numbers:

number + $\frac{1}{4}$	**savā** + number
number + $\frac{1}{2}$	**sāRʰe** + number
number + $\frac{3}{4}$	**paune** + *next* number

Decimal point

decimal	**dashamlav**	दशमलव
(Example: 1.5	**ek dashamlav pā̃c**	एक दशमलव पाँच)

Percentages

percentage	**prati shat**	प्रति शत
(Example: 50 per cent	**pacās prati shat**	पचास प्रति शत)

Time

Hours

o'clock	**baje**	बजे
1:15	**savā (ek)**	सवा (एक)
1:30	**DeR^h**	डेढ़
1:45	**paune do** (i.e. the next number)	पौने दो
2:15	**savā do**	सवा दो
2:30	**D^{h}āī** (the number two is incorporated in the word)	ढाई
2:45	**paune tīn** (i.e. the next number)	पौने तीन
3:15	**savā tīn**	सवा तीन
3:30	**sāR^{h}e tīn**	साढ़े तीन
3:45	**paune cār**	पौने चार

Examples

kitne	**baje**	**hẽ?**	*or*	**vakta**	**kyā**	**hɛ?**
how many	o'clock	are		time	what	is

What time is it?

ek bajā hɛ.	It is 1 o'clock.
deR^h baje hẽ.	It is 1:30.
paune tīn baje hẽ.	It is 2:45.

9:00 a.m.	**savera/subah ke nau**	सवेरे/सुबह के नौ
9:00 p.m.	**rāt ke nau**	रात के नौ
4:20	**cār <u>bajkar</u> bīs minaT**	चार बजकर बीस मिनट
6:50	**sāt bajne mẽ das minaT**	सात बजने में दस मिनट

year	**sāl** (m.)	साल
month	**mahīnā** (m.)	महीना
day	**din** (m.)	दिन
hour	**g^hanTā** (m.)	घन्टा
minute	**minaT** (m.)	मिनट
second	**sɛkinD** (m.) **pal** (m.)	सैकिन्ड, पल

Days of the week

Monday	**somvār** (Hindu, Sikh), **pīr** (Muslim)	सोमवार
Tuesday	**maŋgalvār**	मंगलवार
Wednesday	**bud^{h}vār**	बुधवार
Thursday	**guruvār, brihspativār** (Hindu, Sikh),	गुरुवार, बृहस्पतिवार
	jummerāt (Muslim)	जुम्मेरात
Friday	**shukravār** (Hindu, Sikh),	शुक्रवार
	jummā (Muslim)	जुम्मा
Saturday	**shanivār** (Hindu, Sikh),	शनिवार
	haftā (Muslim)	हफ़्ता
Sunday	**ravivār**	रविवार

Months

The names of the months of the Hindu and Muslim calendar are different from the Christian calendar. However, the Christian calendar is officially used, so the Indian pronunciation of the months is given below:

January	**janvarī**	जनवरी
February	**farvarī**	फरवरी
March	**mārca**	मार्च
April	**aprɛl**	अप्रैल
May	**maī**	मई
June	**jūn**	जून
July	**julāī**	जुलाई
August	**agast**	अगस्त
September	**sitambar**	सितम्बर
October	**aktūbar**	अक्तूबर
November	**navambar**	नवम्बर
December	**disambar**	दिसम्बर

Years

The word 'year' when used as part of a date is translated as **san** सन्. For instance,

1995 (the year) **san unnīs sau pañcānbe** सन् उन्नीस सौ पँचानबे

but one can *not* say: **ek hazār nau sau pañcānbe**.

Important verbs

Hindi verbs are listed in the infinitive form.

Abbreviations

(intr.)	intransitive verb; does not take the **ne** ने postposition in the perfect tenses
(tr.)	transitive verb; takes the **ne** ने postposition in the perfect tenses
(**+ne**)	takes the **ne** ने postposition in the perfect tenses
(**-ne**)	does not take the **ne** ने postposition in the perfect tenses
(**+/-ne**)	may or may not take the **ne** ने postposition in the perfect tenses
(**+ko**)	takes **ko** को with its subject; indicates non-volitional action

accept, agree	**mānnā** (+ne)	मानना
ache	**dard honā** (+ko)	दर्द होना
afraid	**Dar lagnā** (+ko)	डर लगना
agree	**mānnā** (+ne)	मानना
(be) angry	**gussā honā**	गुस्सा होना
	gussā karnā (+ne)	गुस्सा करना
(become) angry	**gussā ānā** (+ko)	गुस्सा आना
appear	**lagnā** (+ko), **nazar ānā** (+ko)	लगना, नज़र आना
be	**honā** (-ne)	होना
be able to	**saknā** (-ne)	सकना
beat	**mārnā** (+ne)	मारना
be born	x **kā janma honā** (-ne)	x का जन्म होना
begin	**shurū honā** (intr.)	शुरू होना
	shurū karnā (tr.)	शुरू करना
break	**toRnā** (+ne)	तोड़ना

bring	**lānā** (-ne)	लाना
burn	**jalnā (intr.), jalānā** (tr.)	जलना, जलाना
buy	**xarīdnā** (+ne)	ख़रीदना
call	**bulānā** (+ne)	बुलाना
catch	**pakaRnā** (+ne)	पकड़ना
celebrate	**manānā** (+ne)	मनाना
change	**badalnā** (+ne)	बदलना
choose	**cunnā** (+ne)	चुनना
climb	**caR^{h}nā** (-ne)	चढ़ना
collide	x **se Takrānā** (+ne)	x से टकराना
come	**ānā** (-ne)	आना
compare	x **kī** y **see tulnā karnā** (+ne)	x की y से तुलना करना
complain	x **se** y **kī shikāyat karnā** (+ne)	x की y से शिकायत करना
complete	**pūrā karnā** (+ne)	पूरा करना
converse	x **se bāt karnā** (+ne)	x से बात करना
cost	x (amount) **lagnā** (-ne)	लगना
count	**ginnā** (+ne)	गिनना
cover	**D^{h}aknā** (+ne)	ढकना
cry	**ronā** (-ne), **cillānā** (-ne)	रोना, चिल्लाना
cut	**kaTnā** (intr.), **kāTnā** (tr.)	कटना, काटना
dance	**nācnā** (+ne)	नाचना
desire	x **kī icc^{h}ā honā** (-ne)	x की इच्छा होना
die	**marnā** (-ne)	मरना
disappear	**gāyab honā** (intr.)	गायब होना
	gāyab karnā (tr.)	गायब करना
dislike	**nāpasand honā** (+ko)	नापसन्द होना
	nāpasand karnā (+ne)	नापसन्द करना
do	**karnā** (+ne)	करना
drink	**pīnā** (+ne)	पीना
drink (alcohol)	**sharāb pīnā** (+ne)	शराब पीना
drive	**kār calānā** (+ne)	कार चलाना
earn	**kamānā** (+ne)	कमाना
enjoy	**mazā honā** (intr.)	मज़ा होना
	mazā karnā (tr.)	मज़ा करना
	mazā lenā (tr.)	मज़ा लेना
eat/dine	**k^{h}ānā k^{h}ānā** (+ne)	खाना खाना

eat breakfast	**nās^{h}tā karnā** (+ne)	नाश्ता करना
enter	**g^{h}usnā** (-ne)	घुसना
fall	**girnā** (-ne)	गिरना
feed	**k^{h}ilānā** (+ne)	खिलाना
feel happy	**xush honā** (-ne)	खुश होना
feel sad	**udās honā** (-ne)	उदास होना
feel sick	**tabīyat xarāb honā** (-ne)	तबीयत ख़राब होना
fight	**laRnā** (-ne)	लड़ना
finish	**xatam honā** (intr.)	खतम होना
	xatam karnā (tr.)	खतम करना
fix, recover, repair	**T^{h}īk honā** (intr.)	ठीक होना
	T^{h}īk karnā (tr.)	ठीक करना
fly	**uRnā** (intr.), **uRānā** (tr.)	उड़ना, उड़ाना
forgive, pardon	**māf karnā** (+ne)	माफ करना
give	**denā** (+ne)	देना
go	**jānā** (-ne)	जाना
go back	**vāpas jānā** (-ne)	वापस जाना
go down/descend	**utarnā** (-ne)	उतरना
grind	**pīsnā** (+ne)	पीसना
hate	x **se nafrat karnā** (+ne)	x से नफ़रत करना
hear	**sunnā** (+ne)	सुनना
	sunāī denā (+ko)	सुनाई देना
hire	**kirāye par lenā** (+ne)	किराये पर लेना
hope	x **kī āshā honā** (-ne)	x की आशा होना
get hot	**garmī paRnā** (-ne)	गरमी पड़ना
(get) hurt	**coT lagnā** (+ko)	चोट लगना
inquire	**pūc^{h}tāc^{h} karnā** (+ne)	पूछताछ करना
invite	x **ke g^{h}ar ānā** (-ne)	x के घर आना
	nyautā denā (+ne)	न्यौता देना
jump	**kūdnā** (-ne)	कूदना
kill	**mārnā** (+ne)	मारना
knock at	**k^{h}aTk^{h}aTānā** (+ne)	खटखटाना
know	**jānnā** (+ne)	जानना
	mālūm honā (+ko)	मालूम होना
	patā honā (+ko)	पता होना
(come to) know	**patā lagnā** (+ko)	पता लगना
laugh	**hãsnā** (-ne)	हँसना
learn	**sīk^{h}nā** (+ne)	सीखना

like	**pasand honā** (+ko)	पसन्द होना
	pasand karnā (+ne)	पसन्द करना
	acc^{h}ā lagnā (+ko)	अच्छा लगना
live	**rɛhnā** (-ne)	रहना
look	**dek^{h}nā** (+ne)	देखना
love	x **se prem honā** (+ko)	x से प्रेम होना
	x **se prem karnā** (+ne)	x से प्रेम करना
make	**banānā** (+ne)	बनाना
meet	**milnā** (-ne)	मिलना
melt	**pig^{h}alnā** (-ne)	पिघलना
mix	**milānā** (+ne)	मिलाना
need, want	**cāhiye** (+ko), **cāhnā** (+ne)	चाहिये, चाहना
	x **kī zrūrat honā** (+ko)	x की ज़रूरत होना
(be) nervous	**g^{h}abrānā (-nū̃)**	घबराना
object	x **par ɛtrāz karnā** (+ne)	x पर ऐतराज़ करना
open	**k^{h}ulnā** (intr.), **k^{h}olnā** (tr.)	खुलना, खोलना
order (someone; but not something)	**āgyā denā (+nū̃)**	आज्ञा देना
	hukam karnā (+ne)	हुक्म करना
peel	**c^{h}īlnā** (+ne)	छीलना
permit	**izāzat denā** (+ne)	इज़ाज़त देना
persuade	**manānā** (+ne)	मनाना
place	**rak^{h}nā** (+ne)	रखना
play	**k^{h}elnā** (+/-ne)	खेलना
play (instrument)	**bajānā** (+ne)	बजाना
pour	**Dālnā** (+ne)	डालना
praise	x **kī tārīf karnā** (+ne)	x की तारीफ़ करना
prepare	**taiyār honā** (intr.)	तैयार होना
	taiyār karnā (tr.)	तैयार कारना
press	**dabānā** (+ne)	दबाना
push	**d^{h}akelnā** (+ne)	धकेलना
put	**rak^{h}nā** (+ne), **Dālnā** (+ne)	रखना, डालना
put off	**Tālnā** (+ne)	टालना
quarrel	x **se laRnā** (-ne)	लड़ना
rain	**bārish honā** (-ne)	बारिश होना
reach	**pahũcnā** (-ne)	पहुँचना
read	**paR^{h}nā** (+ne)	पढ़ना
recognize	**pɛhcānnā** (+ne)	पहचानना

refuse, prohibit	x **se manā karā** (+ne)	x से मना करना
remember	**yād honā** (**intr.** + **ko**)	याद होना
remember, memorize	**yād karnā** (+ne)	याद करना
respect	x **kī izzat karnā** (+ne)	x की इ़ज़्ज़त करना
rest	**ārām karnā** (+ne)	आराम करना
return, come back	**vāpas ānā** (-ne)	वापस आना
	lauTnā (-ne)	लौटना
return (something)	**vāpas karnā** (+ne)	वापस करना
	lauTānā (+ne)	लौटाना
ripe	**paknā** (-ne)	पकना
rise	**uT^{h}nā** (-ne), **caR^{h}nā** (-ne)	उठना, चढ़ना
run	**dauRnā** (-ne), **b^{h}āgnā** (-ne)	दौड़ना, भागना
say	**kεhnā** (+ne)	कहना
seem	**lagnā** (+ko)	लगना
sell	**becnā** (+ne)	बेचना
send	**b^{h}ejnā** (+ne)	भेजना
show	**dik^{h}ānā** (+ne)	दिखाना
(take) shower	**nahānā** (+/-ne)	नहाना
sing	**gānā** (+ne)	गाना
sit	**bεT^{h}nā** (-ne)	बैठना
sleep	**sonā** (-ne)	सोना
slip	**p^{h}ĩsalnā** (-ne)	फिसलना
sneeze	**c^{h}ĩknā** (+/-ne)	छींकना
snow	**barf girnā** (-ne)	बर्फ़ गिरना
speak	**bolnā** (+/-ne)	बोलना
spend (money)	**xarca karnā** (+ne)	खर्च करना
spend (time)	**bitānā** (+ne), **kāTnā** (+ne)	बिताना
spill	**girānā** (+ne)	गिराना
spread	**bic^{h}ānā** (+ne)	बिछाना
stand	**k^{h}aRā honā** (-ne)	खड़ा होना
stay	**rεhnā** (-ne), **T^{h}εhεrnā** (-ne)	रहना, ठहरना
steal	**corī karnā** (+ne)	चोरी करना
stop	**ruknā** (intr.)	रुकना
	roknā (tr.)	रोकना
study	**paR^{h}nā** (+/-ne)	पढ़ना
(be) surprised	**hεrān honā** (-ne)	हैरान होना
swim	**tεrna** (-ne)	तैरना
take care of	**dek^{h}-b^{h}āl karnā** (+ne)	देख-भाल करना

take	**lenā** (+ne)	लेना
taste	**cak^{h}nā** (+ne)	चखना
teach	**paR^{h}ānā** (+ne)	पढ़ाना
telephone	**Tɛlīfon karnā** (+ne)	टैलीफ़ोन करना
tell, mention	**batānā** (+ne)	बताना
think	x **kā xyāl honā** (-ne)	x का ख़्याल होना
	socnā (+ne)	सोचना
throw	**p^{h}ẽknā** (+ne)	फेंकना
tired	**t^{h}aknā** (-ne)	थकना
touch	**c^{h}ūnā** (+ne)	छूना
try	x **kī koshish karnā** (+ne)	की कोशिश करना
turn	**muRnā** (intr.) **moRnā** (tr.)	मुड़ना, मोड़ना
turn over	**palaTnā** (+ne)	पलटना
understand	**samaj^{h}nā** (+/-ne)	समझना
uproot	**uk^{h}āRnā** (+ne)	उखाड़ना
use	x **kā istemāl karnā** (+ne)	x का इस्तेमाल करना
wait	x **kā intzār karnā** (+ne)	x का इंतज़ार करना
wake up	**uT^{h}nā** (-ne)	उठना
walk	**calnā** (-ne)	चलना
want, need	**cāhiye** (+ko), **cāhnā** (+ne)	चाहिये, चाहना
wash	**d^{h}onā** (+ne)	धोना
waste	**gavā̃nā** (+ne)	गवाँना
wear	**pɛhɛnnā** (+ne)	पहनना
weep	**ronā** (-ne)	रोना
win	**jītnā** (+/-ne)	जीतना
worry	x **kī cintā karnā** (+ne)	x की चिन्ता करना
worship	**pūjā karnā** (+ne)	पूजा करना
write	**lik^{h}nā** (+ne)	लिखना

Hindi–English glossary

The Hindi vocabulary items used in the dialogues and reading-practice pieces are presented below in roman alphabetical order. However, it should be pointed out that the vowel symbol **ε** follows **u**, whereas the nasalized vowels (with ~) and short vowels precede their corresponding oral long vowels, respectively.

ab^{h}ī	अभी	right now
ab^{h}ī b^{h}ī	अभी भी	even now
acc^{h}ā	अच्छा	good, okay
acc^{h}āī (f.)	अच्छाई	good (n.), quality, ideal
acc^{h}ā lagnā (+ko)	अच्छा लगना	to like
afsos (m.)	अफ़सोस	sorrow (m.)
aglā	अगला	next
akāl paRnā (-ne)	अकाल पड़ना	famine to occur
akelā	अकेला	alone
aksar	अकसर	often, usually
amīr	अमीर	rich
anāj (m.)	अनाज	grain, corn
andāz (m.)	अन्दाज़	style
and^{h}kāra (m.)	अन्धकार	darkness
angrez (m.)	अंग्रेज़	the English
angrezī (f.)	अंग्रेज़ी	the English language
apnā	अपना	one's own
art^{h}a (m.)	अर्थ	meaning
arz (f.)	अर्ज़	request
asal mẽ	असल में	in fact, in reality
aslī	असली	real, genuine
aTūT	अटूट	unbreakable

aur	और	and, more, other, else
aurat (f.)	औरत	woman
aur b^{h}ī	और भी	even more
ayod^{h}yā (f.)	अयोध्या	Ayodhya (place name)
ā̃k^{h} (f.)	आँख	eye
ādāb (m.)	आदाब	salutation, greetings
ādi	आदि	etc.
ādmī (m.)	आदमी	man
āg (f.)	आग	fire
āj-kal	आज-कल	nowadays
ākramaNa karnā (+ne)	आक्रमण करना	to attack
ām	आम	mango (n.); common (adj.), general
ānā (-ne)	आना	to come
āne vālā	आने वाला	about to come
āp	आप	you (honorific)
āp ke	आप के	your
āp ko	आप को	to you
ārām (m.)	आराम	comfort, rest
ārām karnā (+ne)	आराम करना	to rest
āTā (m.)	आटा	flour
bacānā (+ne)	बचाना	to save
baccā (m.)	बच्चा	child
bacpan (m.)	बचपन	childhood
bahut	बहुत	very
bahut xūb	बहुत खूब	great! splendid!
baje	बजे	o'clock
banānā (+ne)	बनाना	to make
banāras	बनारस	Banaras (one of the oldest cities in India)
banda	बन्द	closed
banda honā (-ne)	बन्द होना	to close
banda karnā (+ne)	बन्द करना	to close
bannā (-ne)	बनना	to be made
banvāsa (m.)	बनवास	exile, residence in forest
baRā	बड़ा	big
baR^{h}nā (-ne)	बढ़ना	to increase, advance

batānā (+ne)	बताना	to tell
bā̃d^{h}nā (+ne)	बाँधना	to tie
bāhar	बाहर	outside, out
bār (f.)	बार	time
bārah	बारह	twelve
bāt (f.)	बात	matter, conversation, topic
becnā (+ne)	बेचना	to sell
bekār	बेकार	useless
beTā (m.)	बेटा	son
beTī (f.)	बेटी	daughter
b^{h}aī	भई	hey, well (excl.)
b^{h}arnā (+ne)	भरना	to fill
b^{h}āgnā (-ne)	भागना	to run
b^{h}āgte (present participle)	भागते	running
b^{h}āī (m.)	भाई	brother/brothers
b^{h}ārat (m.)	भारत	India
b^{h}āratīya	भारतीय	Indian
b^{h}ej denā (+ne)	भेज देना	to send (compound verb)
b^{h}ejnā (+ne)	भेजना	to send
b^{h}ī	भी	also
b^{h}ūlnā (+/-ne)	भूलना	to forget
b^{h}ūt (m.)	भूत	ghost, past
bijlī (f.)	बिजली	electricity, lightning
bimārī (f.)	बिमारी	illness
binā	बिना	without
bindī (f.)	बिन्दी	dot
bībī (f)	बीबी	wife
bīmā (m.)	बीमा	insurance
bolanā (+/-ne)	बोलना	to speak
brindāvan	बृन्दावन	Brindavan (the place where Lord Krishna was brought up)
buj^{h}ānā (+ne)	बुझाना	to extinguish
burā	बुरा	bad
burāī (f.)	बुराई	evil
buxār (m.)	बुखार	fever
bɛhɛn (f.)	बहन	sister
bɛrā (m.)	बैरा	waiter

cak^{h}nā (+ne)	चखना	to taste
calānā (+ne)	चलाना	to drive, to manage (business), to light /play firecrackers
calnā (-ne)	चलना	walk
caudāh	चौदह	fourteen
cā̃d (m.)	चाँद	moon
cā̃ndnī	चाँदनी	moonlit
cāhiye (+ko)	चाहिये	desire, want
cāhnā (+ne)	चाहना	to want
cār	चार	four
cāy (f.)	चाय	tea
c^{h}ātā (m.)	छाता	umbrella
c^{h}īpākar	छिपाकर	secretly
c^{h}oRnā (+ne)	छोड़ना	to leave
c^{h}oTā	छोटा	small
cīn (m.)	चीन	China
cīnī	चीनी	Chinese
cillānā (-ne)	चिल्लाना	to scream
citauRa (m.)	चित्तौड़	Chitaur (a very famous historical place in Rajasthan)
cor (m.)	चोर	thief
corī karnā (+ne)	चोरी करना	to steal
curry (f.)	करी/कढ़ी	curry
cū̃ki	चूँकि	because
daftar (m.)	दफ़्तर	office
dahī (m./f.)	दही	yoghurt
dard (m.)	दर्द	pain, ache
darvāzā (m.)	दरवाज़ा	door
das	दस	ten
dasta (m)	दस्त	diarrhoea
dauRnā (-ne)	दौड़ना	to run
davāī/davā (f.)	दवाई/दवा	medicine
DākTar (m.)	डाक्टर	doctor
Dālnā (+ne)	डालना	to put in, throw, pour
dām (m.)	दाम	price
dek^{h}nā (+ne)	देखना	to see, to look at, to notice

der (f.)	देर	delay, time (period of, slot of)
desha (m.)	देश	country
d^{h}anyavād	धन्यवाद	thanks
d^{h}arma (m.)	धर्म	religion
d^{h}āgā (m.)	धागा	(bracelets of) thread
d^{h}ūm-d^{h}ām se	धूमधाम से	with pomp and show
dik^{h}ānā (+ne)	दिखाना	to show
dillī (f.)	दिल्ली	Delhi (the capital city)
dimāg (m.)	दिमाग़	brain
din (m.)	दिन	day
dīpak/ diyā (m.)	दीपक/दिया	an earthen lamp
dīvālī	दीवाली	Divali, the festival of lights/ lamps
do	दो	two
donõ	दोनों	both
dost (m.)	दोस्त	friend
duniyā (f.)	दुनिया	world
dūr	दूर	far, distant
dūr karnā (+ne)	दूर करना	to dispel, to eliminate
dūsrā (m. adj.)	दूसरा	second, other, another
ek	एक	one
ek-do	एक-दो	one or two
ek dūsre se	एक दूसरे से	with one another, each other
ek-sā	एक-सा	alike
farishtā (m.)	फ़रिश्ता	angel
farka (m.)	फ़र्क	difference
farz (m.)	फर्ज़	duty
fasal (f.)	फसल	crop
furasat (f.)	फ़ुरसत	free time, spare time, leisure
p^{h}ẽknā (+ne)	फेंकना	to throw
galat	ग़लत	wrong
galat-fahamī (f.)	ग़लत-फ़हमी	misconception, misunderstanding
gale lagānā (+ne)	गले लगाना	to embrace
gaye	गये	went

gā̃v (m.)	गाँव	village
gā̃v vālā (m.)	गाँव वाला	villager
gānā (m.); v. (**+ne**)	गाना	song (n.), to sing (v.)
gāRī (f.)	गाड़ी	train, vehicle, cart
g^{h}anTā (m.)	घंटा	hour
g^{h}ar (m.)	घर	house
g^{h}oRā (m.)	घोड़ा	horse
g^{h}oRī (f.)	घोड़ी	mare
ginnā (**+ne**)	गिनना	to count
golī (f.)	गोली	tablet, pill; bullet
gujarāt (m.)	गुजरात	the state of Gujarat
gumnā (**-ne**)	गुमना	to be lost
gussā (m.)	गुस्सा	anger
guT^{h}lī (f.)	गुठली	stone (of a fruit)
gyārah	ग्यारह	eleven
hamāre yahā̃	हमारे यहाँ	at our place (house, country, etc.)
hameshā	हमेशा	always
harānā (**+ne**)	हराना	to defeat
havā (f.)	हवा	air, wind
havāī aDDā (m.)	हवाई अड्डा	airport
hazār	हज़ार	thousand
hā̃	हाँ	yes
hāl (m.)	हाल	condition
hālā̃ ki	हालांकि	although
hāt^h (m.)	हाथ	hand
hindu/hindū	हिन्दु/हिन्दू	a Hindu
hindustān (m.)	हिन्दुस्तान	India
hindustānī	हिन्दुस्तानी	Indian
holī (f.)	होली	Holi, the festival of colours
honā (**-ne**)	होना	to be
hukam (m.)	हुकम	order
hū̃	हूँ	am
hɛ̃	हैं	are
hɛ	है	is
intzār (m./f.)	इंतज़ार	wait

intzār karnā (+ne)	इंतज़ार करना	to wait
isliye	इसलिये	therefore, so, thus, because of this
itnā (m. adj.)	इतना	so much/many, this much/ many
itne mẽ	इतने में	in the meanwhile
īsāī	ईसाई	a Christian
jab (relative pronoun)	जब	when
jab ki	जब कि	while
jahāz (m.)	जहाज़	a ship, vessel, plane
jalānā (+ne)	जलाना	to light, to burn, to kindle
jaldī	जल्दी	quickly, hurry
janma (m.)	जन्म	birth
javāb (m.)	जवाब	answer
javāb denā (+ne)	जवाब देना	to answer, reply
jānā (-ne)	जाना	to go
jāne do (compound verb)	जाने दो	let (someone) go
jāne vāle	जाने वाले	going
jānvar (m.)	जानवर	animal
jeb (f.)	जेब	pocket
jeb kāTnā (+ne)	जेब काटना	to pick [a] pocket
jī	जी	honorific word (optional with greetings)
jīvan (m.)	जीवन	life
jɛsā	जैसा	as
jɛse (ki)	जैसे(कि)	as, as if
jvālāmuk^{h}ī (m.)	ज्वालामुखी	volcano
kab	कब	when
kab^{h}ī	कभी	ever
kab^{h}ī kab^{h}ī	कभी-कभी	sometimes
kab^{h}ī nahī̃	कभी नहीं	never
kahā̃	कहाँ	where
kahānī (f.)	कहानी	story
kaī	कई	several
kal	कल	yesterday, tomorrow
kam	कम	less

kamrā (m.)	कमरा	room
karīb	करीब	about, approximately
karnā (+ne)	करना	to do
kat^{h}ā (f.)	कथा	story
kaTnā (-ne)	कटना	to be cut
kaun sā	कौन सा	which one
kyā!	क्या !	What! I do not believe it!
kā	का	of
kāfī	काफ़ी	enough, sufficient
kāgaz (m.)	कागज़	paper
kām honā (+ko)	काम होना	to have work
kāTnā (+ne)	काटना	to cut
ke alāvā	के अलावा	besides, in addition to
(ke) bād	के बाद	after, later
ke bāre mẽ	के बारे में	about, concerning
(ke) binā	के बिना	without
ke liye	के लिये	for
ke sāt^h	के साथ	with, together
k^{h}alnāyak (m.)	खलनायक	villain
k^{h}ānā (m.; v.) (+ne)	खाना	food (n.), to eat (v.)
k^{h}elnā (+/-ne)	खेलना	to play
k^{h}iRkī (f.)	खिड़की	window
k^{h}olnā (+ne)	खोलना	to open
kis	किस	which
kisī	किसी	someone
kismat (f.)	किस्मत	fortune, fate
kitāb (f.)	किताब	book
kitnā	कितना	how many?
kījie	कीजिए	please do
koī	कोई	some, any, someone, anyone
kuc^h	कुछ	some
kul	कुल	total
kursī (f.)	कुरसी	chair
kɛhnā (+ne)	कहना	to say
kɛhte hɛ̃	कहते हैं	is called
kɛse	कैसे	how
kyā	क्या	what
kyõ	क्यों	why

lagānā (+ne)	लगाना	to attach, to stick, to fix, to apply
lagb^{h}ag	लगभग	about, approximately, almost
lagnā (+ko)	लगना	to seem, to be applied, to appear
lagnā (-ne)	लगना	to take, to cost
lakshmī (f.)	लक्ष्मी	Lakshmi, the goddess of wealth, fortune, prosperity
landan	लन्दन	London
laRāī (f.)	लड़ाई	fight, battle, war
laRkā	लड़का	boy
laRkī	लड़की	girl
lauTanā (-ne)	लौटना	to return, to come back
lāl	लाल	red
lānā (-ne)	लाना	to bring
lekin	लेकिन	but
lenā (+ne)	लेना	to take
lik^{h}nā (+ne)	लिखना	to write
log (m.)	लोग	people
lok (m.)	लोक	people
lok kat^{h}ā (f.)	लोक कथा	folk-tale
mac^{h}lī (f.)	मछली	fish
mahā	महा	great
mahābharat (f.)	महाभारत	one of the two greatest epics from Sanskrit
mahīnā (m.)	महीना	month
man (m.)	मन	mind
man-pasand (f.)	मन पसन्द	favourite
manānā (+ne)	मनाना	to celebrate (festival, holiday), to persuade
mard (m.)	मर्द	man
marīz (m.)	मरीज़	patient
marnā (-ne)	मरना	to die
masālā (m.)	मसाला	spice
masāledār	मसालेदार	spicy
mat	मत	not
matlab (m.)	मतलब	meaning

maukā (m.)	मौका	opportunity
mazā karnā (-ne)	मज़ा करना	to enjoy
mā̃s (m.)	माँस	meat
mālūm honā (+ko)	मालूम होना	to know, to be known
mātā (f.)	माता	mother
mẽ	में	in, during
meharbānī (f.)	मेहरबानी	kindness
milnā (-ne)	मिलना	to meet
milnā	मिलना	to be available
milnā (+ko)	मिलना	to find, to receive
mirca (f.)	मिर्च	chilli peppers
mitra (m.)	मित्र	friend
mizāj (m.)	मिज़ाज	temperament, nature
mugal	मुगल	the Moguls
muj^{h}e, muj^h ko	मुझे = मुझ को	(to) me
mulākāt (f.)	मुलाकात	meeting
mulākāt honā (-ne)	मुलाकात होना	to meet
mushkil	मुश्किल	difficult, difficulty (f.)
mɛ̃	मैं	I
mɛhẽgā	महँगा	expensive
mɛhɛl (m.)	महल	palace
na...na	न...न	neither...nor
na?	न	isn't it?
nahī̃	नहीं	not
nahī̃ to	नहीं तो	otherwise
nakal (f.)	नकल	copy, fake, imitation
namak (m.)	नमक	salt
namaste	नमस्ते	Hindu greetings and replies to greetings; (may be used by other religions too)
nayā	नया	new
nazar (f.)	नज़र	vision
nām (m.)	नाम	name
nāpasand (f.)	नापसन्द	dislike
nāshtā (m.)	नाश्ता	breakfast
ne	ने	agent marker in the perfective tenses.

oh	ओह	exclamation of pain/sorrow
pahũcnā (-ne)	पहुँचना	to reach, to arrive
pakaRnā (+ne)	पकड़ना	to catch
palnā (-ne)	पलना	to be brought up
par	पर	on, at
parājit honā (-ne)	पराजित होना	to be defeated
pareshān	परेशान	troubled
parhez (m.)	परहेज़	abstinence
parhez karnā (+ne)	परहेज़ करना	to abstain, to avoid
paR^{h}nā (-ne)	पढ़ना	to study, to read
parivār (m.)	परिवार	family
paRnā (-ne)	पड़ना	to fall, to lie down
pasand (f.)	पसन्द	choice, liking
pashcim (m.)	पश्चिम	west
pashcimī	पश्चिमी	western
patā (m.)	पता	address
patā lagnā (+ko)	पता लगाना	to come to know
paTāxā (m.)	पटाख़ा	a firecracker
patrā (m.)	पत्रा	astrological chart
pavitratā (f.)	पवित्रता	purification, holiness
paŋkti (f.)	पंक्ति/पंक्ति	line, row
pānā (+ne)	पाना	to find, obtain
pānī (m.)	पानी	water
pās	पास	near
p^{h}al (m.)	फल	fruit
p^{h}ir	फिर	again, then
p^{h}ul-j^{h}aRī (f.)	फुलझड़ी	a kind of firework which emits flower-like sparks
pickārī (f.)	पिचकारी	a syringe-shaped water-gun made of wood or metal
pīlā	पीला	yellow
pīnā (+ne)	पीना	to drink
pracalit honā (-ne)	प्रचलित होना	to be prevalent
prakāsha (m.)	प्रकाश	light
prasanntā (f.)	प्रसन्नता	happiness, joy
prasidd^{h}a	प्रसिद्ध/प्रसिद्ध	famous
pratīka (m.)	प्रतीक	symbol

prācīn	प्राचीन	ancient
prema (m.)	प्रेम	love
pulis vālā (m).	पुलिस वाला	policeman
purānā	पुराना	old (inanimate)
pūc^{h}nā (+ne)	पूछना	to ask
pūjana (n.)	पूजन	worship
pūrā (m.; adj.)	पूरा	full, complete, whole
pūrā karnā (+ne)	पूरा करना	to complete
pɛhlā	पहला	first
pɛhle	पहले	(at) first, ago, previously
pɛsā (m.)	पैसा	money; one hundredth of a rupee
pyār (m.)	प्यार	love
rakshā karnā (+ne)	रक्षा करना	to protect, to defend
rakshāband^{h}an (m.)	रक्षा बन्धन	'the festival of love and protection'
rang-biraŋgā	रंग-बिरंगा	colourful
raŋg (m.)	रंग	colour
raŋgīn	रंगीन	colourful
rājā (m.)	राजा	king, emperor
rājya (m.)	राज्य	kingdom
rākshasa (m.)	राक्षस	demon
rāma (m.)	राम	Lord Rama; (proper name)
rānī (f.)	रानी	queen
rāt (f.)	रात	night
rāvaNa (m.)	रावण	the demon king, Ravana
resham (m.)	रेशम	silk
reshmī	रेशमी	silken
ritu (f.)	ऋतु	season
rivāj (m)	रिवाज	custom
ruknā (-ne)	रुकना	to stop
rupayā (m.)	रुपया	rupees (Indian currency)
rɛhnā (-ne)	रहना	live
sab	सब	all
sabzī (f.)	सब्ज़ी	vegetable
sac (m.)	सच	truth, true

sac!	सच	Truth! It can't be true!
saknā (-ne)	सकना	can, be able to
salāh (f.)	सलाह	advice
salāh lenā (+ne)	सलाह लेना	to seek/take advice
salāh mānnā (+ne)	सलाह मानना	to accept/take advice
salām (m.)	सलाम	Muslim greetings and replies to greetings
samaj^{h}nā (+/-ne)	समझना	to understand
samaya (m.)	समय	time
samrāT (m.)	सम्राट	king, emperor
sandesh (m.)	सन्देश	message
sanskrita (f.)	संस्कृत	Sanskrit
sau	सौ	hundred
savāl (m.)	सवाल	question
saverā (m.)	सवेरा	morning
saŋgīt (m.)	संगीत	music
sāhib (m.)	साहिब	sir
sāl (m.)	साल	year
sāmān (m.)	सामान	baggage, goods, stuff, tools
sāRī (f.)	साड़ी	saree
sāt baje	सात बजे	seven o'clock
se	से	from, with, by, than
sevā (f.)	सेवा	service
shabda (m.)	शब्द	word
sharīr (m.)	शरीर	body
shatābdī (m.)	शताब्दी	century
shatru (m.)	शत्रु	enemy
shatrutā (f.)	शत्रुता	enmity, hostility
shauk (m.)	शौक	hobby, fondness, interest
shādī (f.)	शादी	marriage
shādī-shudā	शदी-शुदा	married
shām (f.)	शाम	evening
shāndār	शानदार	splendid, great
shāyad	शायद	perhaps
shrī krishna	श्रीकृष्ण	Lord Krishna
shub^{h}a	शुभ	auspicious
shukriyā (m.)	शुक्रिया	thanks
shuru karnā (+ne)	शुरू करना	to begin

shɛhɛr (m.)	शहर	city
siŋgār (m.)	सिंगार	make up
sir (m.)	सिर	head
sirf	सिर्फ़	only
sīk^{h}nā (+ne)	सीखना	to learn
socnā (+ne)	सोचना	to think
solvī̃	सोलहवीं	sixteenth
srava-priya	सर्व-प्रिय	loved by all, favourite
subā (f.)	सुबह	morning
sultān (m.)	सुलतान	a sultan, king, emperor
sunharā (m. adj.)	सुनहरा	golden
sunte hī (**sun+te hī** participle)	सुनते ही	as soon as [someone] heard
sūk^{h}ā (m. adj.)	सूखा	dry
sūt (m.)	सूत	cotton
sūtī (adj.)	सूती	cotton
sɛnik (m.)	सैनिक	soldier
tab tak	तब तक	by then
tabīyat (f.)	तबीयत	health, disposition
takiīf denā (+ne)	तकलीफ़ देना	to bother
taklīf (f.)	तकलीफ़	trouble, bother
talāk (m.)	तलाक	divorce
tar	तर	wet
tarī (f.)	तरी	liquid
tashrīf (f.)	तशरीफ़	(a term signifying respect)
tashrīf lānā (-ne)	तशरीफ़ लाना	to grace one's place, welcome, come
tashrīf rak^{h}nā (+ne)	तशरीफ़ रखना	to be seated
tāj (m.)	ताज	crown
tāj mɛhɛl (m.)	ताज महल	the Taj Mahal
tez	तेज़	fast, quick, sharp, strong
t^{h}ā	था	was
T^{h}īk	ठीक	fine; okay
T^{h}īk-T^{h}āk	ठीक-ठाक	fine, hale and hearty
t^{h}oRā	थोड़ा	little, few
Tīkā lagānā (+ne)	टीका लगाना	to give an injection/a shot
to (particle)	तो	then, as regards

tɛrnā (-ne)	तैरना	to swim
tyauhāra (m.)	त्यौहार	festival
umar (f.)	उमर	age
utsāh (m.)	उत्साह	enthusiasm, joy, zeal
uttarād^{h}ikārī (m.)	उत्तराधिकारी	heir
ɛsā	ऐसा	such
vacan (m.)	वचन	promise
vah	वह	that, he, she
vahī (**vah+hī**)	वही	same, that very
varsha (m.)	वर्ष	year
vasanta (m.)	वसन्त	spring
vāh	वाह	ah! excellent! bravo!
vāh! vāh!	वाह ! वाह !	Wow! Wow! bravo!
vāpas	वापस	back
vāpas ānā (-ne)	वापस आना	to come back
vātāvaraNa (m.)	वातावरण	atmosphere, environment
videshī (m.)	विदेशी	foreigner
vijaya (f.)	विजय	victory
vintī (f.)	विनती	request
vo kɛse	वह कैसे	how come?
vɛse	वैसे	otherwise, in addition, like that, similarly
xarāb	ख़राब	bad
xarīdnā (+ne)	ख़रीदना	to buy
xatarnāk	ख़तरनाक	dangerous
xatrā (m.)	ख़तरा	danger
xayāl (m.)	ख़याल	opinion, view
xāskar	ख़ासकर	especially, particularly
xud	खुद	oneself
xudā hāfiz	खुदा हाफ़िज़	goodbye
xush-hālī (f.)	खुश-हाली	prosperity
xushbū (f.)	खुशबू	fragrance (lit. happy smell)
xushī	खुशी	happiness
xɛriyat (f.)	ख़ैरियत	safety, welfare
xyāl (m.)	ख़्याल	opinion, thought

yahā̃	यहाँ	here
yahā̃ tak ki	यहाँ तक कि	to the point, to the extent that
yā	या	or
yād dilānā (+ne)	याद दिलाना	to remind
yānī	यानी	that is, in other words
zarā	ज़रा	little, somewhat
zarūr	ज़रूर	of course, certainly
zarūrat (f.)	ज़रूरत	need, necessity
zarūrī	ज़रूरी	important, urgent, necessary
zor se	ज़ोर से	loudly
zor denā (+ne)	ज़ोर देना	to emphasize
zyādā (invariable)	ज़्यादा	more

Index

N.B. The numbers refer to lesson numbers.